CW00553781

OXFORD POLITICAL THEORY

Series Editors: Will Kymlicka, David Miller, and Alan Ryan

———

NATIONAL RESPONSIBILITY AND GLOBAL JUSTICE

OXFORD POLITICAL THEORY

Oxford Political Theory presents the best new work in contemporary political theory. It is intended to be broad in scope, including original contributions to political philosophy, and also work in applied political theory. The series contains works of outstanding quality with no restriction as to approach or subject matter.

NATIONAL RESPONSIBILITY AND GLOBAL JUSTICE

DAVID MILLER

OXFORD
UNIVERSITY PRESS

OXFORD
UNIVERSITY PRESS

Great Clarendon Street, Oxford ox2 6DP

Oxford University Press is a department of the University of Oxford.
It furthers the University's objective of excellence in research, scholarship,
and education by publishing worldwide in

Oxford New York

Auckland Cape Town Dar es Salaam Hong Kong Karachi
Kuala Lumpur Madrid Melbourne Mexico City Nairobi
New Delhi Shanghai Taipei Toronto

With offices in

Argentina Austria Brazil Chile Czech Republic France Greece
Guatemala Hungary Italy Japan Poland Portugal Singapore
South Korea Switzerland Thailand Turkey Ukraine Vietnam

Oxford is a registered trade mark of Oxford University Press
in the UK and in certain other countries

Published in the United States
by Oxford University Press Inc., New York

© David Miller 2007

The moral rights of the author have been asserted
Database right Oxford University Press (maker)

First published 2007

All rights reserved. No part of this publication may be reproduced,
stored in a retrieval system, or transmitted, in any form or by any means,
without the prior permission in writing of Oxford University Press,
or as expressly permitted by law, or under terms agreed with the appropriate
reprographics rights organization. Enquiries concerning reproduction
outside the scope of the above should be sent to the Rights Department,
Oxford University Press, at the address above

You must not circulate this book in any other binding or cover
and you must impose the same condition on any acquirer

British Library Cataloguing in Publication Data
Data available

Library of Congress Cataloging in Publication Data
Data available

Typeset by SPI Publisher Services, Pondicherry, India
Printed in Great Britain
on acid-free paper by the
MPG Books Group, Bodmin and King's Lynn

ISBN 978-0-19-923505-6

ACKNOWLEDGEMENTS

This book is the result of several years of writing about and debating questions of global justice, world poverty, special obligations to compatriots, and the collective responsibilities of nations for what they do today and have done in the past. These are all very large and contentious issues, and I have learnt a great deal from arguing about them with friends and academic colleagues, many of whom hold views radically different from my own. I have therefore a large debt of gratitude to record. It is owed first to my colleagues in politics, philosophy, and law in Oxford, who have been generous with their time in discussing parts of the text, and especially to the members of the Nuffield political theory workshop, who can always be relied on to give what they read the most thorough scrutiny. Next, audiences at several universities in the UK: Birmingham, Cambridge, Essex, Manchester, the London School of Economics, Queen's Belfast, Reading, St Andrews, Sussex, and University College, London. Then, audiences further afield, at lectures and seminars in the universities of Basel, Chicago, Palermo, Texas (Austin), Texas (A and M), Toronto, Uppsala, and Zurich, and at conferences held in Amsterdam, Leuven, Pasadena, Princeton, and Stockholm. Many individual people have given me valuable comments and suggestions on one or other part of the manuscript. With apologies to those I have missed, they include Veit Bader, Samuel Black, Barbara Bleisch, Gillian Brock, Thom Brooks, Allen Buchanan, Simon Caney, Paula Casal, Clare Chambers, Jerry Cohen, David Copp, Katherine Eddy, Catherine Frost, John Gardner, Matthew Gibney, Chandran Kukathas, Cécile Laborde, Mats Lundstrom, Mara Marin, Andrew Mason, Matt Matravers, David Mepham, Monica Mookherjee, Avia Pasternak, Thomas Pogge, Hans Roth, Samuel Scheffler, Jacob Schiff, Henry Shue, Adam Swift, Kok-Chor Tan, Tiziana Torresi, Isabel Trujillo, Robert van der Veen, Leif Wenar, and Stuart White. There are a few people to whom I owe a greater debt still. I have had an ongoing debate with Hillel Steiner about whether one can devise a metric to estimate the natural resource endowments of different societies, and I am very grateful for his detailed and careful comments on this question. My understanding of human rights, and their connection to needs, owes a great deal to discussions and written exchanges with Barbara Schmitz. Charles Beitz, Daniel Butt, and Cécile Fabre read the entire manuscript in its penultimate version, and offered not only general encouragement, very welcome at that stage, but also a raft of critical comments and constructive ideas to which I have done my best to respond. This applies equally to the lengthy reports submitted by three anonymous readers for Oxford University Press. I am grateful also to Dominic Byatt for his interest in and encouragement of the project, and to Emre Ozcan, for his quick and efficient work in preparing the manuscript for publication.

To help in the writing of this book, I have adapted some passages that originally appeared in the following articles, and I am grateful to the publishers for allowing me to do so:

'Liberalism, Desert and Special Responsibilities', *Philosophical Books*, 44 (2003), 111–17.

'Cosmopolitanism: A Critique', *Critical Review of International Social Philosophy and Policy*, 5 (2003), 80–5.

'Human Rights in a Multicultural World', in D. Amneus and G. Gunner (eds), *Manskliga Rattigheter—Fran Forskningens Frontlinjer* (Uppsala: Iustus Forlag, 2003).

'Holding Nations Responsible', *Ethics*, 114 (2003–4), 240–68.

'Against Global Egalitarianism', *Journal of Ethics*, 9 (2005), 55–79.

'Immigration: The Case for Limits', in A. Cohen and C. Wellman (eds), *Contemporary Debates in Applied Ethics* (Oxford: Blackwell, 2005).

'Reasonable Partiality Towards Compatriots', *Ethical Theory and Moral Practice*, 8 (2005), 63–81.

Authors often complain about the blood and tears it costs them to produce their books. Speaking for myself, I am never happier than when immersed in writing, and the pain is felt entirely by those around me who find that I am incapable of focusing in a useful way on anything else. My final word of thanks, therefore, is to my family, and especially to Sue, for carrying this burden without too much complaint, and for their love and support without which none of this would have been possible.

CONTENTS

CHAPTER 1

Introduction

I switch on the television to watch the evening news. The main stories today are all from what we used to call the Third World, and they all speak of human suffering. The first item contains reports of two massive car bombs that have exploded in Baghdad. One was directed at a line of unemployed Iraqis queuing in the hope of getting a job with the local police; the other was aimed apparently randomly at a market where women and children were shopping. The screen is filled with images first of mutilated bodies, and then of men and women sobbing uncontrollably and crying out for revenge against the bombers, and against the security forces who were supposed to be stopping them. Everywhere the camera points, there is dust, smoke, and destruction.

The second item is about the famine that has struck Niger, the world's second poorest country. Even in more normal times, one child in four dies before reaching the age of 5, and now row upon row of painfully thin bodies makes it all too clear that the death toll is about to rise sharply. The children gaze vacantly into space while flies crawl over their faces, and their mothers plead for a doctor to come quickly: but health care in Niger has been privatized and few can afford it. The reporter's voice tells us that this famine was predictable; indeed, she herself had been warning about what was to come in dispatches sent a couple of months earlier. But the response of the international aid donors has been far too slow, and the food that has now arrived in the far south of the country cannot be distributed because the government has failed to keep the roads in usable condition. Now facing the camera, the reporter says that the world cares nothing for this forgotten country until its conscience is pricked—too late—by the images that have just been broadcast.

The third item brings me closer to home, to the very edge of the gulf that divides the developed from the undeveloped world. It is about Melilla, a tiny Spanish enclave on the North African coast that borders on Morocco. Melilla has become a major target for immigrants trying to get out of Africa and get into Europe, so the Spanish authorities have erected a fearsome fence topped with razor wire along the border. During the night, however, several hundred desperate migrants have rushed the fence, using makeshift ladders. A few were shot dead; many more displayed broken limbs and deep gashes on their hands where the wire has cut them. They have been rounded up and are now being sent back to Morocco to be dumped somewhere out in the Sahara. Interviewed by the reporter, they reveal that they have travelled thousands of miles—from Cameroon, Senegal, Mali, and other countries in West and Central Africa—and will keep on trying to enter Europe—'the promised land'—even if they die in the attempt.

As I watch these stories, I experience a complex bundle of thoughts and emotions, a bundle too that is quite different in each case. The first emotion is of course one of sympathy with the people who are appearing in the reports. These are not just poor people: they are people who fall below some absolute line that we all recognize; they are wounded, suffering, starving, or dying. And the harm that has come to them has not come from the hand of nature, but directly or indirectly from other human beings, so alongside sympathy comes another feeling, anger at the people who have done this, or who have let it happen. But there is also a kind of bewilderment: *why* is this happening? What is going on to produce this misery, and what should we be doing about it?

As I watch the Iraqis trying to find their relatives among the carnage that the car bombs have caused, I think that these are the people who have already suffered so much, under Saddam's brutal dictatorship, in the war to depose him, and now in what is supposed to be a new era of peace but is turning into a nightmare. Their hopes and fears are the normal ones of people everywhere and are easy to understand. But then when I start to think about the suicide bombers, understanding is replaced by incomprehension. What on earth can they be trying to achieve by killing and injuring hundreds of their own people at random? If their aim is to force the Americans out of the country, why aren't they targeting the troops? If they think that by destroying civil authority in Iraq they will create the space in which a new Islamic caliphate can be established, still, why blow up innocent civilians? Since the bombers are almost certainly Sunni Muslims, the minority group in Iraq, and their victims are mostly Shi'ites, if they are hoping to foment a civil war, won't their own community be the one that finally gets massacred? I am angry at the bombers, but I do not know how to direct my anger because I cannot make sense of what they are doing.

The Nigérien famine looks easier to understand. We have seen the same story played out on our screens depressingly many times before. Here are the famine victims, lying helplessly, hoping some-how that relief will arrive. There are the Western aid workers and the medics, angry at the slow pace at which the help is getting through, critical of Western governments for their inaction, and the Nigérien government for being obstructive. But I am still not sure why this famine has occurred. Was it simply crop failure caused by drought, or had it more to do with the decisions of the Nigérien government, who had been told by the International Monetary Fund (IMF) to abandon stockpiling of emergency supplies that might otherwise have kept people going until the next harvest? But then I hear some-thing strange and disturbing: in the villages where the women and children are starving, there may be food locked away in grain stores by the men, who have gone off to look for work elsewhere, across the border in Nigeria for instance. It is part of the local culture that women should support themselves from what they can produce on their own tiny plots, while the men control what is grown on the large family fields where the women also work. Could it be this that explains why the famine is so severe?

When the Melilla story reaches the screen, I find my sympathy for the young African men who are trying to cross the fence tempered by a kind of indignation. Surely, they must understand that this is not the way to get into Europe. What clearer indication could there be of the proposition that illegal immigrants are not welcome than a double fence up to six metres tall with rolls of razor wire along the top? Do they think they have some kind of natural right to enter Spain in defiance of the laws that apply to everyone else who might like to move there? And why are they so sure that all their troubles will be over if they can only slip through the net? Although I can understand their plight, which must indeed be desperate if they are willing to try, time and again, to risk life and limb to get across the border; I also think they are deluded and are responsible for their delusion. But is my reaction partly a selfish one, inspired by a fear that the comfortable life I enjoy with my fellow-Europeans is going to be rudely disrupted if millions of the world's poor are allowed to come in?

How typical are my responses to these three news stories? It is hard to be sure. There may be people, better people than me perhaps, whose sympathy for the victims obliterates all other emotions. Watching those young men in Morocco being herded back on to transport planes, they can see only the desperation and the wounds, and would never think of asking whether the migrants have not brought their troubles on themselves. There is also another cast of mind that, when stories about the developing world are aired, can see only the gap between them and us, and our responsibility for maintaining that gap by the impact we make on those countries. If there are suicide bombers in Baghdad, this is because of what we in the West have done to Iraq; similarly if there are women and children starving in Niger and men climbing over razor wire in Melilla. All responsibility and blame for what is happening should land straight back on our own doorstep. Both of these are simplifying responses, one focusing just on the people who are suffering, the other looking only at the people and governments of the affluent West who, being rich and powerful, could remove the causes of the suffering if they chose, and are therefore culpable if they do not. But I think most people will react in ways that are more complex than either of these, even if not in exactly the ways I have reported for myself. Their sympathy will be mixed with questions about responsibility, and they will be confused about why these tragedies have occurred, who is to blame, and what is now to be done to prevent them recurring.

At any rate, these are the people to whom this book is addressed, people who share my view that the answer to the question 'what do we owe to the world's poor?' is complex rather than simple. My aim is to develop a way of thinking about this problem, and the larger problem within which it is embedded, the problem of global justice, that will guide us when faced with situations such as those I have just described. Such a framework would not provide immediate solutions to the problems of Iraq, Niger, or Melilla, but it will at least tell us where to look for the answers. This book is primarily a work of political philosophy rather than public policy or developmental economics, so my intention is not to offer policy proposals to the IMF or the World Bank or to national governments, but rather to explore some fundamental questions, such as these: should global justice be understood as requiring some kind of equality between people everywhere, or is there a better way of understanding it? Should we think instead in terms of a global minimum level of rights and resources below which no one should be allowed to fall, and if so how should we decide where to set this threshold? What role does responsibility has to play when we make these judgements, and can we attribute collective responsibility to nations for how they fare as well as to individuals? When confronted with cases of severe deprivation like the Nigérien famine victims, how do we decide whose responsibility it is to come to their aid?

In this opening chapter, I want to set out in brief some under-lying themes that run throughout this book in preparation for the more detailed discussions that follow later. The first theme is one that emerges directly from thinking about the three cases reported earlier. When we respond to the people caught up in events like the Baghdad suicide bombings, the Nigérien famine and the Melilla border conflict, we find ourselves pulled in two different directions. On one side, we are inclined to see them simply as victims, people in other words to whom things have happened that they are pow-erless to resist. Our concern is with what has been done to them, with the deprivation and suffering that they have to bear. On the other side, we are also inclined to see them as agents, as people who make choices that have implications either for themselves or for others. From this perspective we begin to ask questions about responsibility, about whether the deprivation and suffering are self-inflicted, inflicted by others, or caused in some other way. If we think now about what justice means in such cases, both perspectives seem important. On the one hand, human beings are needy and vulnerable creatures who cannot live decent, let alone flourishing, lives unless they are given at least a minimum bundle of freedoms, opportunities, and resources. They must have freedom to think and act, the opportunity to learn and work, and the resources to feed and clothe themselves. Where people lack these conditions, it seems that those who are better endowed have obligations of justice to help provide them. On the other hand, human beings are choosing agents who must take responsibility for their own lives. This means that they should be allowed to enjoy the benefits of success, but it also means that they must bear the burdens of failure. And where their actions impose costs on others, they should be held liable for those costs, which entails in some cases making redress to the people whose interests they have damaged.

Trying to keep these two perspectives in balance sometimes leads us into practical dilemmas. What if somebody, or some group of people, had opportunities that, used properly, could have provided them with a decent standard of living, but as a result of their past actions they have become destitute in a way that leaves them with no means of escape? What does justice require now, of those able to come to their assistance? Or suppose a person behaves in a way that is damaging to others, but also damaging to himself, so that now he cannot compensate the people he has harmed without reducing himself to destitution. Can we demand that he should nevertheless make redress? There are no easy answers to these questions. Nonetheless, if we are not attentive to both perspectives on the human condition—if we do not try always to see human beings both as needy and vulnerable creatures and as responsible agents— we cannot properly understand what justice means, and especially perhaps what global justice means.

When we ignore the first perspective, we can fall victim to a kind of individualism that says, roughly, that anyone anywhere can make a decent life for themselves if only they make an effort and behave sensibly. There is also a collective analogue to this, which says that poor countries can always bootstrap themselves out of poverty by following policies that have already proved their success—the favourite examples being those of Southeast Asian countries like South Korea that over a couple of generations have lifted themselves from a position below the poverty line to one that is comparable to many European states. There are many reasons why this view is false. People may be subjected to forms of coercion that prevent them from improving their position significantly, as the example of the women farmers in Niger suggests. Or they may be in the thrall of cultural traditions that have the same effect: we have to tread carefully here, because to suppose that people can never see beyond their inherited cultures would mean denying their responsible agency altogether. Nevertheless, we cannot assume that people from different cultural backgrounds will reason about economic matters in the same way as, say, New York bankers, and therefore hold them liable when they do not act in ways that the bankers might regard as economically prudent. And they may also simply not have access to resources of land or capital that would allow then to get started. When we respond to the plight of the famine victims in Niger, we should do so overwhelmingly in terms of the first perspective, as needy and vulnerable people who have no chance of living a decent life, in the short to medium term anyway, unless others come to their aid.

Not to respond to the needs of the famine victims would be a moral failure, a failure of respect. But it is also a failure of respect if we ignore the second perspective, and treat people simply as passive recipients of our aid, and not as agents who are potentially able to take charge of their own lives and improve their situation by their own efforts. For instance, sometimes we may have to decide between a policy that simply hands people food and other con-sumption goods, and one that provides opportunities for them to produce these goods themselves. Quite apart from considerations of efficiency that may tell in favour of the second policy, it also shows greater respect for the people whose claims we are recognizing. Our relationship becomes a more equal one to the extent that we consider not only their needs but also their capacities for choice and responsibility.

Adopting the agency perspective may seem more problematic when we are considering not individual people but communities of people. Given the extent of global inequality, a person's life chances—how much freedom they enjoy, what economic opportu-nities they have, what level of health care they can expect, and so forth—depend much more on which society they belong to than on their individual choices, efforts, and talents. So can we extend the idea of responsibility so that it encompasses political communities—nations, for example, as well as individuals? Might people legiti-mately become better or worse off not just by virtue of their own agency but also by virtue of their membership in these larger units? Many of those who are willing to accept the agency perspective, and its implications for justice, in the case of individuals are reluctant to accept its collective analogue. One of my tasks here will be to try to overcome this reluctance, by defending the idea of national responsibility, and arguing that global inequalities between societies can be justified when they can be shown to result from practices, policies, and decisions for which the members of those societies can be held collectively responsible. This is not of course the same as saying that *existing* inequalities at global level are fair. National responsibility has its conditions and limits, and so to make judgements about wealth and poverty in the world as we find it, we must discover what these conditions and limits are and then apply the relevant criteria. And of course we must not abandon the first perspective in making these judgements. When people find themselves in desperate straits, the question we should be asking is not whether they are responsible for their own condition, individually or collectively, but who should now be held responsible for coming to their aid—a different sense of responsibility, which we will need in due course to distinguish carefully from the first.

The observation that people's life chances are to a large extent determined by the society they belong to introduces my second theme, which is how far we should regard the problem of global justice as a problem of personal ethics and how far as an institutional question. Let me explain this contrast. I used the examples of Iraq, Niger, and Melilla as a way of raising the general question 'what do we owe to the world's poor?', and in the course of doing so I focused on my own responses to these human disasters and how far I felt a sense of responsibility and obligation towards the victims. I think this is how many people first approach the question of global justice, and it has spawned a rich philosophical literature which begins, for example, with cases that involve passers-by pulling drowning children out of ponds, asks why things should be any different when the people whose lives are endangered live far away, and examines how much of the burden of saving lives any one person can reasonably be expected to take upon her own shoulders.[1] This approach sees global justice as a matter of personal ethics: what am I, as an individual, bound to do for people in other political communities, particularly for people whose lives are very bad? Governments and other institutions come into the picture only in a secondary way, where it can be shown that acting through these institutions is the most effective

---

[1] The *locus classicus* here is P. Singer, 'Famine, Affluence and Morality', *Philosophy and Public Affairs*, 1 (1972), 229–43. I discuss Singer's way of thinking about global poverty in Chapter 9.

way to discharge duties that belong primarily to individuals. But one might come to think that this approach was completely wrong. We should instead see institutions, in a broad sense, as the primary subject of global justice, since it is institutions that primarily determine people's life chances at global level. Our attention should be focused on national governments and the policies they pursue, but also on the global market and how it operates, international institutions like the World Bank and the IMF, the international aid organizations, and so forth. The question of global justice is a question about which set of institutional arrangements will bring about a globally fair allocation of rights, opportunities, resources, and so forth. This, after all, is how the question of *social* justice is usually posed. On this view, our responsibility as individuals is simply to press for the adoption of a just institutional regime, once we have determined what that is.[2]

Neither of these approaches seems to me to be wholly adequate. To begin with the personal ethics approach: the problem with this is that it treats the behaviour of everyone else as parametric. The question it asks, typically, is about the extent of the obligation that I, as a comparatively affluent member of a rich society, have towards distant strangers whose lives are poor. But the same question might be asked of everyone else whose position is broadly similar to mine, and indeed of many other people, for example better-off members of poor societies who have the power to change the pattern of distribution in those societies. Granting that the condition of the world's poor is morally unacceptable—they fall below a threshold that virtually everyone would recognize as constituting a minimally decent standard of life—the responsibility to remedy that condition seems to fall potentially on a huge number of individuals and institutions, all able to provide relief. How can I possibly decide what my own share of that responsibility should be? If other people are already contributing something to the relief of global poverty, say through charitable donations, does that give me more or less reason to contribute myself? It might seem to give me less reason because the most urgent cases are already being taken care of by the charity, by means of others' donations; but equally it might

---

[2] For a strong defence of the institutional approach to global justice, see, e.g., T. Pogge, 'Cosmopolitanism and Sovereignty', in T. Pogge (ed.), *World Poverty and Human Rights* (Cambridge: Polity Press, 2002), 169–77.

seem to give me more reason, because if I fail to contribute to a cause whose value I recognize while others do in fact contribute, I am behaving unfairly—freeriding on their charitable behaviour. Or should I think more about what has caused the poverty in the first place, and whether I can apply sanctions to the institutions responsible, which might in some cases be multinational corporations or government agencies? The harder we look at the problem, the less it resembles walking past a pond in which a child is drowning. World poverty is a macro-problem that requires a systemic solution, and so thinking about it in terms of individual moral obligations seems an irrelevance.

So we might conclude that global justice is an institutional question—a matter of reforming a wide range of institutions so that together they can deliver a set of outcomes that are fair for individuals everywhere. If we assume for the moment that a world state is not a real possibility, these institutions would include not only existing political institutions, national and international, but the entire set of rules and practices by which the global economy operates, for instance patterns of capital investment and trade, the ownership of natural resources, environmental policies, flows of development aid, and so forth. These institutions together constitute a system that influences significantly whether people in any one place become relatively well-off or relatively badly-off, and although no one has designed the system to be the way that it is, it is clearly susceptible to being reformed by concerted political action, and therefore a fit subject for assessment by principles of justice. Without jumping ahead and laying down what those principles should be, at global level, it seems safe to say, looking at patterns of exploitation, inequality and poverty in today's world, that global justice would demand far-reaching institutional changes.

If we had to choose, the institutional approach to global justice seems to me preferable to the personal ethics approach: but it may be better still to draw on both approaches. The reason for this is that there are questions that the institutional approach, taken by itself, cannot answer. If global outcomes could always and straightforwardly be explained in terms of the impact of institutions, there would be no problem. But sometimes we encounter situations that cannot be explained in these terms, and where the relevant question may be: what institutions, if any, ought we to create? Natural disasters, such as the tsunami that engulfed large coastal areas of South Asia at the end of 2004, are one example. Disaster relief in this case involved both individuals and governments contributing massive amounts of aid, and no doubt if questioned most people would say that they had a duty to contribute. Some people, perhaps, might have regarded this as a humanitarian gesture rather than a duty of justice; nevertheless, it is now widely recognized that where natural events—earthquakes, floods, droughts, and so forth—leave people in a desperate plight, there is a global responsibility to respond to this, which justifies the setting up of institutions to stockpile essential goods, coordinate relief efforts, and so forth. The point I want to make is that if we do indeed see this responsibility as a matter of justice, as I think we should, then justice comes before the institutions that will discharge it. We set the institutions up because global justice demands that we should do so. Clearly, then, justice must have at least some pre-institutional components. We must owe something to the victims of natural disasters simply by virtue of the fact that they are in a desperate situation, and we have the means that could be used to help them. This is an obligation of justice that exists between individual people in advance of setting up institutions through which that obligation can most effectively be discharged. So to understand global justice, we must also understand the nature and extent of that obligation: what can people require of each other independently of their institutional relationships?

There is a second reason why we cannot entirely set aside the personal ethics approach. When thinking about the justice of institutions, we tend to regard them as free-standing structures with distributive and other consequences. But of course they are also made up of individuals whose choices and decisions affect what the institution does, though not always in ways that the individuals involved can predict or control. One question that arises immediately, therefore, is how far individuals can be held responsible for the effects of the institutions they are involved in. Suppose that these effects are harmful to outsiders: suppose that a multinational company employs workers in a developing country using a technology that seriously damages their health. Do the shareholders in the company have an obligation to pay compensation to the sick employees? Or the government of a democratic country tries to bring about a regime change in another society, but inadvertently provokes a civil war. What responsibilities fall on the citizens of that democracy to make recompense? Can they legitimately be taxed to rebuild the society their government has damaged? The problem in these cases is that the injustice perpetrated by the institutions is easy to see, but it may be less easy to see whether and how the injustice can be put right without investigating the responsibilities and obligations of the individual people involved in them. Unless we can show that their personal responsibility extends to include making the various compensatory transfers, we may find ourselves in a kind of deadlock in which we know that the victims of institutional action have suffered unjustly, but we also know that it would be unjust to take resources from the individual people who have participated in those institutions. Still greater problems arise when those particular individuals have left the scene to be replaced by others, as we see in Chapter 6.

My aim, therefore, will be to develop a theory of global justice that combines both approaches. I shall focus mainly on principles of justice that apply to institutions—principles of equality, for instance—but I shall be guided in developing these principles by a view about the nature and limits of personal obligation in the absence of institutions, a view that is expounded particularly in Chapter 2. And this introduces my third theme, the general shape that we should expect a theory of global justice to take.

Global justice is a relatively new idea; justice itself is a very old one. In between the two, we find the idea of *social* justice, an idea that made its first appearance in the later part of the nineteenth century and rose to prominence in the twentieth century. Social justice is sometimes regarded as simply another term for distributive justice, but in fact it means something more specific than that. Questions of distributive justice arise when there is some divisible good to be allocated among a number of claimants, which means that it is relevant within groups of all sizes, from families upwards. Social justice, by contrast, refers to the distribution of rights, opportunities, and resources among the members of large societies, and the idea emerged only when it became possible to see that distribution as arising from the workings of social institutions—laws of property and contract, the organization of work, the tax system, the provision of public services, and so forth—and therefore as alterable by political action, and especially by the state.[3] In other words, the idea of social justice presupposed the growth of the social sciences on the one hand, and political institutions capable of delivering policies for the regulation of industry, education, health care, pensions, and the like on the other—once these conditions exist, it becomes a relevant practical question whether the prevailing distribution of rights, opportunities, and resources treats all citizens fairly.

Global justice asks the same question, but now about all human beings rather than about the citizens of a particular state. The idea has emerged as we have begun to understand better why people's life chances differ so widely between societies, and as institutions have emerged that can make some impact on global inequalities, through political change, capital investment, trade policies, and so forth. So it is natural to assume that ideas and theories first developed to explain what social justice means within state boundaries can be stretched to apply at global level: if, for example, social justice requires a certain form of equality among citizens, global justice will require that same form of equality, but now among human beings everywhere. Of course, promoting such equality at global level may turn out to be a harder task, and the institutions that can achieve it may be different from those used at national level, but these are problems of implementation rather than questions about what justice *means* when it becomes global in scope.

This natural assumption is, however, one that I want to reject. We should not take it for granted that global justice is simply social justice with a wider scope. Instead, we need to develop a theory of justice that fits the international context, which in several important ways is different from the national context. In saying this, I am assuming something about justice in general, namely that the principles that tell us what counts as a just distribution of some good are specific to the context in which the distribution is taking place. There is no one master principle (or connected set of principles) that defines justice in all times and all places. Instead, the relevant principle will depend on what is being distributed, by whom, and among

---

[3] I have expanded on this claim about how the idea of social justice first emerged, and what conditions are required for it to remain meaningful, in *Principles of Social Justice* (Cambridge, MA: Harvard University Press, 1999), chs. 1 and 12.

whom: especially on the kind of relationship that exists between the people among whom the distribution is occurring.[4]

At one level, the idea that justice is contextually determined should be perfectly familiar. In our daily lives, we know what fairness demands of us as we move from, say, family to school to workplace to social club to political office and so forth. Even if the resource we are distributing is the same in each case—money, for instance—the principles that we apply to govern the distribution may differ in each context. Family resources might be allocated according to need, workplace proceeds according to desert or merit, and tax revenues on the basis of equality (at least among groups such as children or pensioners). Theories of justice, however, tend to search for some overriding principle that can accommodate and explain this diversity. They claim, for example, that justice is fundamentally a matter of treating people as equals and then try to show that to achieve this we should apply different criteria of distribution in different circumstances. In my view, this way of understanding justice is mistaken. One can of course give a purely formal definition of justice, such as that embodied in the famous claim that justice is a matter of giving each person his or her due. But then on the contextual view that I favour, we decide what is due to a person by looking at the context in which a particular distribution is taking place. What is due may be an equal share of some good, or a share that is determined by a person's needs, or their deserts, or in some other way.

I shall not try to defend this contextual understanding of justice here.[5] But it forms the essential background to the theory of global justice that I develop in this book. I do not start with the assumption that valid principles of global justice must be the same as valid principles of social justice, but with a wider scope. Instead, we need to ask whether the institutions and modes of human association that we find within nation-states, and which form the context within which ideas of social justice are developed and applied, are also to be found at international level, and if not how we should understand human

[4] I have put forward a theory of justice that takes this form in *Principles of Social Justice*, ch. 2.

[5] I have done so in 'Two Ways to Think about Justice', *Politics, Philosophy and Economics*, 1 (2002), 5–28, where I argue among other things that contextualism should not be understood as a form of relativism about justice.

relationships across national borders. Only then can we begin to ask what global justice should mean.

Those who advocate the view that global justice is social justice writ large have defended their position in several different ways. One involves denying that national borders any longer have the importance they once had in marking off separate spheres of human interaction. The intensification of investment and trade across these borders, the physical movement of people on either a temporary or a permanent basis, the growth in communications media with a global scope (television and the Internet, in particular), and the emergence of transnational political institutions such as the EU, all mean that we can now speak meaningfully of international society or even of a world community. My relationship with physically distant strangers, mediated as it is by links of these several different types, is no longer different in any kind from my relationship with my compatriots. So even on a contextual view of justice, there is no reason to separate principles of global justice from principles of social justice.

There are several ways of responding to this argument, but here I shall focus on one particularly salient difference between the national and global contexts of justice. Social justice is justice practised among people who are citizens of the same political community. Justice for them is, at least in part, a matter of establishing the conditions under which they can continue to act as free and equal citizens: it includes, for instance, a range of rights such as freedom of expression and the right to vote that define the status of citizen, as well as rights to material resources (such as a minimum income) that enable people to function effectively as citizens in the political sense. There is no equivalent to this at global level. On the contrary, if we consider how people relate to one another at that level, one very important mode is as citizens of independent national communities, where each citizen body has a collective interest in determining the future of its own community. Of course, what the members of one nation-state decide typically has an impact on what happens to people elsewhere, and a theory of global justice must take this into account. But 'having an impact' is very different from having a citizenship relationship with fellow-members of your political community. Now we should not assume that this state of affairs will last for ever: we can imagine a course of political change that leads eventually to a world state within which human beings everywhere would indeed relate to one another as equal citizens, as well as other less attractive futures. I shall shortly be asking about how far, in general, our thinking about justice should be conditioned by existing empirical realities. But the question I am addressing here is whether we have already reached the point where there is no significant difference, from the point of view of justice, between the modes of human association we find within and across national borders. My claim is that there is still at least one very significant difference, sufficient to drive a wedge between social and global justice.[6]

A different way of trying to dislodge the wedge proceeds as follows. Suppose I am confronted with a fellow-citizen who lacks the resources to lead a minimally decent life—he has no access to housing, for instance. Assuming that he is not himself responsible for this condition, that person's need imposes a duty of justice on me. I must try to ensure, either directly or through political action, that his need is met. But now consider a person living in another country whose predicament is the same—she also has no access to housing. Since it was need that imposed a duty of justice in the first case, how can need fail to impose an equally compelling duty in the second? Surely, the fact that one person is a fellow-citizen while the other is not is morally irrelevant?[7] For practical reasons, it may be better for national governments to implement housing policies or indeed for charities for the homeless to operate on a national basis, but the underlying duty of justice, based as it is on unmet need, is universal in scope.

Many people find this chain of reasoning, and its implication that there is no fundamental difference between social and global justice, compelling. But where it falls down is in assuming that when a principle of justice embodies a criterion such as need to determine people's claims, no further question arises about the *scope* of the principle—where the scope of a principle means the set of people to whom the principle applies. But this is far from obvious. We are quite familiar with principles with limited scope. For instance, the criterion for getting a first-class degree from the University of

---

[6] See also here T. Nagel, 'The Problem of Global Justice', *Philosophy and Public Affairs*, 33 (2005), 113–47. I discuss Nagel's position at greater length in Chapter 10.

[7] Or in another formulation, a person's nationality is a morally arbitrary feature. I discuss this version of the argument in Chapter 2.

Oxford is producing academic work of a particular standard: it is plainly unfair if Jane, whose work is of the same standard as John's, gets a second-class degree while John gets a first. But this applies only to students who are already members of the university. Jessica's work may also be as good as John's, but if she is a student at Harvard, say, she does not deserve a first from Oxford. Here the criterion embodied in the principle—academic merit—and the scope of the principle are clearly distinct. Furthermore, there seems to be nothing objectionable about this. So if we want to say that in the case of the two people in need, we are equally obliged to help both of them, there has to be an independent argument as to why the scope of the need principle should be universal. What has to be shown, in short, is that someone's being a fellow-citizen is a morally irrelevant consideration when we are deciding what the scope of that principle should be. But this requires a substantive argument. It cannot be deduced merely from the fact that the second person shares the characteristic of the first that in his case brings a duty of justice into play.

None of this means that we owe nothing to the homeless person who is not a fellow-citizen. We may indeed owe something to her, as a matter of justice, and in the course of this book I shall be trying to explain what this is. But this does not obliterate the distinction between social and global justice: what it shows is that need may have a role to play in our theory of global justice, but not necessarily the same role that it plays when we think about social justice.

There is a final challenge to my approach to global justice that I want to consider. I have proposed that our thinking about global justice should primarily be focused on institutions: we should be looking at the institutions at global level that primarily determine people's life chances, and asking which principles of justice apply to them. In arguing for the separation of social and global justice, I have drawn attention particularly to citizenship in nation-states as a key factor that differentiates people's relationships within political communities from their relationships at global level. But it might seem that these premises give the resulting theory a conservative bias. In particular, they take for granted an institutional arrangement that might itself be regarded as unjust: the existence of separate states each delivering a separate bundle of rights, opportunities, and resources to its own members, but not to outsiders. Should not a theory of global justice start with a blank sheet, so to speak, and having established its basic principles go on to ask whether the existence of independent states is consistent with these principles, or whether some supranational system of political authority is not in fact required by justice?

This challenge raises a fundamental question about the idea of justice itself, and how we should understand it. To what extent should our principles of justice be tailored to fit either the facts of human life in general or the facts of life given human relationships of a particular kind? David Hume famously answered this question by delineating features of human existence in whose absence, he thought, the 'cautious, jealous virtue of justice would never once have been dreamed of'.[8] Following John Rawls, we can call these 'the circumstances of justice'.[9] According to Hume, the very idea of justice presupposes certain contingent features of the human condition, namely that resources are scarce relative to human desires, human benevolence is limited, and external goods can be readily transferred from person to person. In the absence of these features, there would be no need to have principles of justice to regulate the distribution of resources: 'if men were supplied with every thing in the same abundance, or if *every one* had the same affection and tender regard for *every one* as for himself; justice and injustice would be equally unknown among mankind'.[10]

Not everyone will accept Hume's particular account of the circumstances of justice. Nevertheless, the underlying idea that justice is a virtue whose purpose is to regulate human behaviour and human institutions, and which must therefore reflect certain facts about that behaviour and those institutions, seems sound. The problem is to know which of these facts to treat as parameters that our theory of justice must recognize, and which to regard as contingencies that the theory may seek to alter. If the theory abstracts too far from prevailing circumstances, it is liable to become a merely speculative exercise, of no practical use in guiding either our public policy or

[8] D. Hume, 'An Enquiry Concerning the Principles of Morals', in *Enquiries Concerning Human Understanding and Concerning the Principles of Morals*, ed. L. A. Selby-Bigge, rev. P. H. Nidditch (Oxford: Clarendon Press, 1975), 184.
[9] J. Rawls, *A Theory of Justice* (Cambridge, MA: Harvard University Press, 1971), section 22.
[10] D. Hume, *A Treatise of Human Nature*, ed. L. A. Selby-Bigge, rev. P. H. Nidditch (Oxford: Clarendon Press, 1978), 495.

the individual decisions we make as citizens. If the theory assumes too much by way of empirical constraints, on the other hand, it may become excessively conservative, in the sense of being too closely tied to contingent aspects of a particular society or group of societies, and therefore no longer able to function as a critical tool for social change.[11] Rawls, in his later work, describes his theory of international justice as a 'realistic utopia', and what he means by this seemingly oxymoronic phrase is that the theory aims to push towards the limits of practical possibility—in other words to lay down principles for a world that is better than ours, but is still feasible given what we know about the human condition and the laws that govern it. The problem then is to know what the limits of practical possibility really are. As Rawls puts it:

I recognize that there are questions about how the limits of the practically possible are discerned and what the conditions of our social world in fact are. The problem here is that the limits of the possible are not given by the actual, for we can to a greater or lesser extent change political and social institutions and much else. Hence we have to rely on conjecture and speculation, arguing as best we can that the social world we envision is feasible and might actually exist, if not now then at some future time under happier circumstances.[12]

The particular question we are examining is whether the circumstances of global justice should be taken to include the existence of separate states whose members belong to different national cultures, and who therefore value their capacity to be politically self-determining. In a world like this, the idea of global justice must be composed of principles that, along with other institutions, such states could comply with. Such principles might entail, for instance, a requirement that states should cooperate to regulate trade or provide development aid, but not a requirement that could only be fulfilled by states giving up their autonomy entirely in favour of some supranational body. But are we right to impose such a condition? Why not

---

[11] I have explored the general issue raised here more fully in 'Political Philosophy for Earthlings', in D. Leopold and M. Stears (eds), *Political Theory: Methods and Approaches* (Oxford: Oxford University Press, forthcoming). See also the discussion in Michael Blake, 'Distributive Justice, State Coercion and Autonomy', *Philosophy and Public Affairs*, 30 (2001), 257–96, esp. section 1.

[12] J. Rawls, *The Law of Peoples* (Cambridge, MA: Harvard University Press, 1999), 12.

say instead that if global justice requires some form of world government, then so much the worse for national self-determination?

To answer these questions we have, as Rawls says, to rely to some extent on 'conjecture and speculation', about, for instance, the depth of people's attachment to their national communities, or the likely form of a global government (How democratic would it be?).[13] We may be able to ground our conjectures and speculations in evidence from the past and the present—evidence, for instance, about how far transnational federations such as the EU have been able to go in subjecting their member-states to a uniform system of authority without provoking resistance from below. But there is bound to be an element of indeterminacy about this: we are living at a time when it is harder than it has ever been to predict the direction and pace of change across the globe, and so it is better in the end to be modest and say that the theory of global justice presented here is one made to fit the world in roughly its present condition—a world made up of separate states, each enjoying some degree of autonomy, though markedly unequal in power; a world in which economic interactions between peoples are largely market-driven, and in which income and wealth inequalities between peoples are huge; a world, therefore, in which there is no free movement across national borders but in which rich states in particular tend to impose strict entry controls; a world in which environmental and natural resource problems spill across those borders and require international solutions. Our principles of global justice should be ones that, if followed by governments, international organizations and individual people, would change this world considerably, but not change it out of all recognition. Those who believe that nothing short of a total revolution in our global relationships will bring about real justice will doubtless find it unheroic. Others, believing that international relations can never transcend the pursuit of national interests, will find it idealistic, or utopian in the bad sense.

To put this in more conventional academic terms, the conception of global justice that I present here corresponds (as does Rawls's *The Law of Peoples*) to what Charles Beitz has called 'social liberalism' as contrasted with 'cosmopolitan liberalism' on the one hand and

---

[13] I say a little more about this in Chapter 2.

'laissez-faire liberalism' on the other.[14] As Beitz explains, what is distinctive about social liberalism is the idea that the pursuit of justice involves a division of labour between domestic and international spheres, with states having the primary responsibility for promoting social justice among their citizens, while the chief task of the international community is to create the conditions under which that responsibility can be discharged. This will in some cases involve intervention where states are unable or unwilling to provide minimum levels of rights and resources to their citizens. But there is no fundamental challenge to the idea of state autonomy, and no attempt to achieve global uniformity, in the sense of people everywhere enjoying the same bundle of rights, resources, and opportunities. Global justice, on the view I am defending, is justice for a world of difference, not merely because ironing out differences between nations would be unfeasible or involve high levels of coercion, but because people greatly value living under their own rules and according to their own cultural beliefs.

I began this chapter by reflecting on some human tragedies that we have become only too accustomed to facing, thanks to the medium that brings them into our living rooms on a daily basis. I assumed that I was not alone in wondering how to respond, either individually or politically as a citizen of a democratic state. At one level, they are indeed simply tragedies—they involve human beings who are suffering or dying, and who urgently need help. But at another level they represent the outcome of long and complex chains of causation in which many other human beings are implicated, and where questions about responsibility inevitably arise. In trying to think about cases such as these, I have proposed three general guidelines. First, always to see human beings as both patients and agents: needy and vulnerable creatures who cannot survive without the help of others, but at the same time people who can make choices and take responsibility for their lives. Second, to understand the demands of justice as applying to us *both* as individuals—the personal ethics approach—*and* as participants in large scale human associations, including states—the institutional approach. Third, to understand *global* justice in a way that takes account of the large differences

---

[14] See C. Beitz, 'International Liberalism and Distributive Justice: A Survey of Recent Thought', *World Politics*, 51 (1999), 269–96.

between domestic and international contexts, and does not, therefore, merely involve giving a wider scope to familiar principles of *social* justice. This contrast between social and global justice is the main theme of Chapters 2 and 3, where I explore the arguments of those who would deny the relevance of such a distinction. Such arguments are usually launched from a position that following Beitz we may call 'cosmopolitan liberalism', so I begin by examining what it means to be a cosmopolitan.

CHAPTER 2

—

Cosmopolitanism

I

'Cosmopolitan' is probably now the preferred self-description of most political philosophers who write about global justice. It is not hard to see the attraction of such a label. In popular speech, to be cosmopolitan is to be open-minded, sophisticated, forward-looking, etc.; conversely, the antonyms of 'cosmopolitan' would include 'insular', 'parochial', 'narrow-minded', 'hidebound', and so forth. The editors of the popular fashion magazine *Cosmopolitan* knew what they were doing when they chose that title. However cosmopolitanism as a perspective on global justice must refer to something more specific than this. But what exactly? Our first task must be to try to pin down the meaning or meanings of 'cosmopolitanism' more precisely, before going on to evaluate it.[1]

The term derives originally from the Greek *kosmopolites*, a citizen of the world, and it was popularized by the Stoic philosophers of antiquity.[2] Their claim was that human beings everywhere formed a single community, governed by a law that was discovered through the use of reason—though in some versions of Stoicism cosmopolitan citizenship was reserved for the wise and the good. In what

---

[1] I shall not try to examine all of the different senses of cosmopolitanism. In particular, I shall have nothing to say here about *cultural* cosmopolitanism. For discussions that range more widely, see S. Scheffler, 'Conceptions of Cosmopolitanism', in S. Scheffler, *Boundaries and Allegiances: Problems of Justice and Responsibility in Liberal Thought* (Oxford: Oxford University Press, 2001); K. C. Tan, *Justice without Borders: Cosmopolitanism, Nationalism and Patriotism* (Cambridge: Cambridge University Press, 2004), ch. 1; K. A. Appiah, *Cosmopolitanism: Ethics in a World of Strangers* (London: Allen Lane, 2006).

[2] For my reading of Stoicism I have drawn upon M. Schofield, *The Stoic Idea of the City* (Cambridge: Cambridge University Press, 1991).

sense was this community political? The Stoics did not imagine that the *kosmopolis* either did or should have human rulers, although some envisaged it as being under divine kingship. So we should not interpret Stoic cosmopolitanism as involving a demand for world government in the conventional sense. Nonetheless, Stoic philosophy played an influential part in the ideology of the Roman Empire, and it is easy to see why: if what really matters is one's membership in the cosmic city and not the territorially bounded human city, then imperial conquest—at least by the wise and the good—does no wrong, and may do some good. Does cosmopolitanism, then, have implications for worldly politics, and might it be said always to lend support to (benign) forms of imperialism?

Before we leap to any such conclusion, we need to draw a distinction between moral and political versions of cosmopolitanism. Moral cosmopolitanism, in its most general formulation, says simply that human beings are all subject to the same set of moral laws: we must treat others in accordance with those laws no matter where in the universe they live; they likewise must treat us in the same way. Political cosmopolitanism says that this can be achieved only if everyone is ultimately subject to the same authority with the power to enforce those laws. The first of these positions does not entail the second, and indeed many would deny that moral cosmopolitanism has any specific political implications. Charles Beitz, for example, writes:

Cosmopolitanism need not make any assumptions at all about the best political structure for international affairs; whether there should be an overarching, global political organization, and if so, how authority should be divided between the global organization and its subordinate political elements, is properly understood as a problem for normative political science rather than for political philosophy itself. Indeed, cosmopolitanism is consistent with a conception of the world in which states constitute the principal forms of human social and political organization. . . .[3]

Political cosmopolitanism is less popular today than moral cosmopolitanism, and I shall discuss it only briefly, but before doing that I want to draw attention to the way in which the ambiguity inherent in the term may be helpful to the moral version.

---

[3] C. Beitz, 'International Relations, Philosophy of', in E. Craig (ed.), *Routledge Encyclopaedia of Philosophy* (London: Routledge, 1998), IV, 831.

Cosmopolitanism invites us to see ourselves as citizens of the world. But if we are not to take that in a political sense—we do not aspire to a share in political authority at global level—what does it mean? The idea of citizenship gets its moral force from the experience of people living together in cities, people who identify with one another, face common enemies, and so forth. The cosmopolitan version takes that idea and stretches it so as to embrace the whole of humanity, regardless of what relationships, if any, may exist between people across the globe. It assumes that the moral force of citizenship can survive such stretching. But this, to say the least, is something that needs to be argued for.[4] The problem can be traced right back to the original Stoic idea of cosmopolitanism. As Schofield puts it:

…the doctrine of the cosmic city attempts to retain community and citizenship while removing all contingency—such as physical proximity or mutual acquaintance—from the notion of citizenship. What citizenship now consists in is nothing but obedience by a plurality of persons to the injunctions of right reason on the just treatment of other persons: i.e. to law as nature formulates it. Such a conception of the citizen is manifestly unstable.[5]

Most advocates of political cosmopolitanism do not in fact advocate world government in its most literal sense—a government at global level enjoying the powers to make and enforce law and policy that national governments typically have today—but something far more modest, for instance a system of international law backed up by coercive sanctions, or a world federation in which powers are divided in such a way that the centre only enjoys limited authority. It is not hard to see why world government proper appeals only to those with a strongly technocratic cast of mind.[6] It seems

[4] For a fuller discussion of the way in which ideas of cosmopolitan citizenship are parasitic on an ethos of citizenship that (up to now at least) has only been achievable within bounded political communities, see my essay 'Bounded Citizenship', in K. Hutchings and R. Dannreuther (eds), *Cosmopolitan Citizenship* (London: Macmillan, 1999) and in D. Miller, *Citizenship and National Identity* (Cambridge: Polity Press, 2000).

[5] Schofield, *The Stoic Idea of the City*, 103.

[6] And also perhaps to those with a deep fear of war between states. It appears that the high point of enthusiasm for world government occurred in the years immediately after 1945. See L. Cabrera, *Political Theory of Global Justice: A Cosmopolitan Case for the World State* (London: Routledge, 2004), ch. 5.

to run contrary to the sheer diversity of human cultures, and to the wish of people everywhere to belong to communities that are able to determine their own future paths. For liberals, the greatest appeal of world government has lain in the promise of an end to armed conflict, but even Kant ended his essay on perpetual peace by describing world government as 'a universal despotism which saps all man's energies and ends in the graveyard of freedom', a view echoed more recently by Isaiah Berlin for whom a cosmopolitan world 'would lead to a tremendous desiccation of everything that is human'.[7]

The objections to world government, then, are twofold. If we assume that the cultural differences between societies that we find in today's world are not only well-entrenched, but are positively valuable as providing the settings within which different forms of human excellence can evolve, then the idea that a single authority should legislate for all societies despite these differences must seem far-fetched. It has proved difficult enough to create multinational states in which all the constituent communities feel equally at home, and equally represented in the public sphere, and even the European Union, sometimes held up as the forerunner of a world state to come, has achieved such legitimacy as it presently enjoys by drawing upon the common political heritage of a group of liberal states. Furthermore, it is hard to see how a world state could be subject to effective democratic control. Current nation-states are only able to practise democracy in an attenuated form — periodic elections and some government responsiveness to public opinion — and achieving even this level of democracy requires a democratic public who speak the same language (or at a minimum, participate in official bilingualism) are exposed to the same mass media, form parties and other political associations, and so forth. Again, it is the comparative absence of such a democratic public at European level that makes it difficult to speak of the European Union as itself democratic, as opposed to being a federation or confederation whose component parts are

---

[7] I. Kant, 'Perpetual Peace: A Philosophical Sketch', in H. Reiss (ed.), *Kant's Political Writings* (Cambridge: Cambridge University Press, 1971), 114; N. Gardels, 'Two Concepts of Nationalism: An Interview with Isaiah Berlin', *New York Review of Books*, 21 November 1991, 22. For more on Berlin's hostility to cosmopolitanism, see my 'Crooked Timber or Bent Twig? Isaiah Berlin's Nationalism', *Political Studies*, 53 (2005), 100–23.

democracies.[8] These problems would be many times worse if we try to envisage a form of government that is both genuinely global and genuinely democratic.

II

There is much more that could be said about political cosmopolitanism, but my main interest in this chapter is in moral cosmopolitanism and its implications for global justice. So what does cosmopolitanism mean as an ethical doctrine with no direct institutional implications? Here we must tread very carefully, because it is easy to slip unnoticed between weaker and stronger versions of moral cosmopolitanism, and in doing so to derive ethical principles that are quite controversial from a premise that is almost platitudinous. This weak cosmopolitan premise can be formulated in a number of slightly different ways: one formulation states that every human being has equal moral worth; another that every human being is equally an object of moral concern; yet another that we owe every human being impartial consideration of their claims upon us.[9] What these formulations have in common is the idea that we owe all human beings moral consideration of some kind—their claims must count with us when we decide how to act or what institutions to establish—and also that *in some sense* that consideration must involve treating their claims equally. Exactly what kind of equal consideration is entailed by the weak cosmopolitan premise is the question we have to answer in this chapter and Chapter 3. But we can perhaps get a better sense of what the premise means by seeing what kinds of behaviour it rules out. Suppose my government decides to dispose of its nuclear waste by dumping it in some foreign land,

[8] See, e.g., D. Grimm, 'Does Europe Need a Constitution?', *European Law Journal*, 1 (1995), 282–302; J. Weiler, *The Constitution of Europe* (Cambridge: Cambridge University Press, 1999), Part II.

[9] Versions of this cosmopolitan premise can be found *inter alia* in Beitz, 'International Relations, Philosophy of', 830–1; C. Beitz, 'Cosmopolitanism and Global Justice', in G. Brock and D. Moellendorf (eds), *Current Debates in Global Justice* (Dordrecht: Springer, 2005), 17; B. Barry, 'Statism and Nationalism: A Cosmopolitan Critique', in I. Shapiro and L. Brilmayer (eds), *Nomos 49: Global Justice* (New York: New York University Press, 1999), 35–6; T. Pogge, 'Cosmopolitanism and Sovereignty', in T. Pogge (ed.), *World Poverty and Human Rights* (Cambridge: Polity Press, 2002), 169–70; Tan, *Justice without Borders*, 1 and 94.

and when it is pointed out that this may prove hazardous to the people who live there, simply declares that that is of no concern to us. This amounts to failing to give any consideration at all to the needs, interests, or other claims of the people involved, which would be a clear violation of the cosmopolitan premise. Another way of violating the premise would be to treat different groups of people in different ways without giving any grounds for the unequal treatment—adopting, say, a policy whereby light-skinned people get better access to medical care than dark-skinned people, without trying to justify this in any way at all, or in any way that might conceivably serve as a relevant moral ground (just repeating 'because they are light-skinned' does not qualify).

An equal consideration principle that would rule out the kinds of behaviour described in the last paragraph would be accepted by almost everyone (with the exception perhaps of a few extreme racists), so if that were all moral cosmopolitanism meant, we could safely say that we are all cosmopolitans now. But those who self-consciously describe themselves as cosmopolitans want to get something stronger out of this premise, a requirement of equal treatment that goes beyond saying that all human beings must be considered in some way when we are deciding how to act. For example, they may want to argue that our institutions and practices must be based on the principle of giving equal weight to the interests of all those affected by them. Or they may claim that we are bound to apply one or other strong, substantive principle of equality at global level, for example a principle of equal access to resources or a principle of equal opportunity. Whether such principles can be defended in their own terms, it is important to see that they cannot be derived from the weak cosmopolitan premise.

The gulf that divides weak from strong cosmopolitanism can perhaps best be explained in the following way. Weak cosmopolitanism is in the first place a claim about moral value. It says that the various good and bad things that can happen to people should be valued in the same way no matter who those people are and where in the world they live. A world in which there is a starving peasant in Ethiopia is to that extent as bad as a world in which there is a starving peasant in Poland, all else being equal. The fate of both these people makes a claim on us. But this does not by itself settle whether, as moral agents, we have an equal responsibility to respond to both claims.

The fact that both cases of starvation are equally bad does not tell me whether I have more reason or less to go to the aid of the Ethiopian than to go to the aid of the Pole. On the contrary, as an agent I may well have an obligation grounded in moral reasons to act to help one of these people before the other—to take a straightforward case, I may have entered an undertaking to support food aid to Ethiopia. This obligation cannot be defeated merely by pointing out that the condition of both people is equally a matter of moral concern.

A simple example may help to bring out this gap between our moral assessments of states of affairs, and the reasons we have for acting in relation to those states of affairs. Suppose a child goes missing and there are fears for her safety. This is equally bad no matter whose child it is, and there are some agents, for instance the police, who should devote equal resources to finding the child in all cases. But there are other agents whose reasons for action will depend on their relationship to the child. If the child is mine, then I have a strong reason, indeed an overwhelming reason, to devote all my time and energy to finding her—a *moral* reason, to be clear, not merely a strong desire, by virtue of our special relationship. If the child comes from my village, then I have a stronger reason to contribute to the search than I would have in the case of a child from another community.[10] Of course if I have information that might help find that distant child, then I should give it to the police at once. It is not that I lack any responsibilities to the distant child. But nearly everyone thinks that I have a much greater responsibility to my own child, or to one I am connected to in some other way. The important point is that this is perfectly consistent with the view that it is equally bad, equally a matter of moral concern, when any child goes missing.[11]

---

[10] Several readers have found this claim implausible. What if I am visiting a friend in another village and a child from that village goes missing? Ought I not to join in the search for that child? The answer, of course, is that I should, so long as I can contribute positively to the rescue attempt, and if I have some special talent that makes my contribution indispensable, I may have a moral *obligation* to join in. But all of this is consistent with saying that I have a *stronger* reason when the child is one from my own village, as shown, for example, by the costs in time and effort I can reasonably be expected to bear in the course of the search.

[11] There is ambiguity here about what it means to show people 'equal moral concern'. As I am using the

It might be said in reply here that if claims about the equal value of human beings have no implications for how we should act, they become redundant. All moral claims must in some way or other guide our behaviour. But this is acknowledged in the example just given. The value of the distant child is registered in my obligation to supply relevant information to the police. In a similar way, the cosmopolitan premise means that we cannot be wholly indifferent to the fate of human beings with whom we have no special relationship of any kind. There is something that we owe them—but weak cosmopolitanism by itself does not tell us what that something is, and certainly does not tell us that we owe them equal treatment in a substantive sense. So cosmopolitans who go on to argue that their cosmopolitan convictions are best expressed through practical doctrines such as the doctrine of human rights, or global equality of opportunity, need to add a further premise about what we owe to other human beings as such—a premise that, to repeat, is not contained in the idea of cosmopolitanism as such. Some independent reason has to be given why cosmopolitan concern should be expressed by implementing the particular conception of global justice favoured by any individual author.

When presented with examples such as that of the missing child, many cosmopolitans will concede that the weak form of egalitarianism contained in the cosmopolitan premise does not exclude special responsibilities and special obligations such as those that obtain between parents and their children. They do not object to the idea of special duties as such, but they are critical of the idea that *nations*, in particular, can serve as the source of such duties. Their cosmopolitanism, in other words, is developed in opposition to a form of nationalism that holds that we owe more to our fellow-nationals

term, it simply expresses the weak cosmopolitan premise that requires us to count as equally bad a harm or a welfare loss, no matter who bears it, and therefore as having to give reasons when we act on behalf of one person or one group rather than another. 'Concern', however, may also be used to signal the special reasons that motivate us to act on behalf of particular groups: Richard Miller, for instance, contrasts 'cosmopolitan respect' which is owed to everyone equally with 'patriotic concern' which justifies our support for schemes that provide benefits exclusively to compatriots. 'Concern' is a sufficiently loose term that both of these uses are legitimate: the important thing is to be clear which is being employed. See R. Miller, 'Cosmopolitan Respect and Patriotic Concern', *Philosophy and Public Affairs*, 27 (1998), 202–4.

than we owe to human beings in general merely by virtue of the fact that we share with them the various cultural and other features that make up a national identity. So is it possible to move from the weak cosmopolitan premise to a stronger form of cosmopolitanism that excludes special obligations to compatriots, except in cases where it can be shown that recognizing and acting upon such obligations actually helps to serve cosmopolitan aims?[12]

III

One popular way of making such a move proceeds as follows. We start with the premise that principles of justice are principles of equal treatment—they are principles that require us not to discriminate on morally irrelevant grounds such as (in most instances) a person's race or sex. What equal treatment means more concretely does not matter here—there are different 'currencies of justice' that might be used—but for the sake of concrete illustration let me assume that the relevant principle is equality of opportunity, a principle of justice that is widely recognized within nation-states as an aim that governments ought to pursue.[13] The cosmopolitan move then involves arguing that a person's nationality is an irrelevant feature when we are considering what opportunities they should have, so the principle should be given a global application. As the argument is often put, nationality is a 'morally arbitrary' feature of persons in the same way as their hair colour or the social class of their parents.

[12] I add this rider because strong cosmopolitans can of course recognize and endorse special obligations to compatriots where it can be shown that acting on these is the most effective means of bringing about global justice. For arguments of this kind, see, for instance, R. E. Goodin, 'What Is So Special about Our Fellow Countrymen?', *Ethics*, 98 (1987–8), 663–86; M. Nussbaum, 'Patriotism and Cosmopolitanism' and 'Reply', in J. Cohen (ed.), *For Love of Country: Debating the Limits of Patriotism* (Boston, MA: Beacon Press, 1996); P. Singer, *One World: The Ethics of Globalization* (New Haven, CT and London: Yale University Press, 2002), ch. 5. How convincing such arguments are is another matter: see my critical discussion in *On Nationality* (Oxford: Clarendon Press, 1995), ch. 3.

[13] I shall be looking specifically at equality of opportunity as a purported principle of global justice in Chapter 3. Nothing I say here depends on which currency of justice—opportunities, resources, welfare, etc.—one chooses to fill out the equality principle. Moreover the principle in question could be any comparative principle of justice, where what a person is owed depends on what others will also receive—so various desert principles, for instance, would also be included.

So they are owed equal treatment as a matter of justice no matter which society they belong to.

If, however, we look carefully at the way this argument moves from premise to conclusion, we find that it relies on a crucial equivocation about what it means for some feature of a person to be morally arbitrary. In one sense, a person's nationality might be described as morally arbitrary because in the great majority of cases the person in question will not be morally responsible for her national membership—people are simply born into a nation and acquire the advantages and disadvantages of membership as they grow up regardless of their choice. In this spirit, Simon Caney writes that 'people should not be penalized because of the vagaries of happenstance, and their fortunes should not be set by factors like nationality and citizenship'.[14] Here 'nationality and citizenship' are assimilated to other features for which people cannot be held morally responsible—Caney mentions 'class or social status or ethnicity'—and the implicit assumption is that if someone is not morally responsible for possessing a certain feature, then unequal treatment on the basis of that feature cannot be justified.

But 'morally arbitrary' may also be used to signal the conclusion of the argument as opposed to its premise. Here a morally arbitrary feature of persons is a feature that should not be allowed to affect the way they are treated—it is a morally irrelevant characteristic, something we are bound to ignore when deciding how to act towards them. Obviously, if nationality is a morally arbitrary feature in this second sense, then inequalities of treatment based on national belonging are unjustified; this follows by definition. What needs to be shown is why we should regard nationality as morally arbitrary in this second sense.

---

[14] S. Caney, 'Cosmopolitan Justice and Equalizing Opportunities', in T. Pogge (ed.), *Global Justice* (Oxford: Blackwell, 2001), 125. c.f. T. Pogge: 'Nationality is just one further deep contingency (like genetic endowment, race, gender, and social class), one more potential basis of institutional inequalities that are inescapable and present from birth.' (T. Pogge, *Realizing Rawls* [Ithaca, NY: Cornell University Press, 1989], 247.) Other formulations of the arbitrariness claim can be found in Tan, *Justice without Borders*, 27–8 and 159–60, and in D. Moellendorf, *Cosmopolitan Justice* (Boulder, CO: Westview Press, 2002), 55–6 and 79. Thomas Nagel, who does not embrace cosmopolitanism, nevertheless sees the claim as having considerable force: see T. Nagel, 'The Problem of Global Justice', *Philosophy and Public Affairs*, 33 (2005), 126.

In order to link the two senses of moral arbitrariness—the argument's premise and its conclusion—we need a substantive principle. Here is a likely candidate: if two people are differentiated only by features for which they are not morally responsible (arbitrariness in sense 1), then it is wrong that they should be treated differently (arbitrariness in sense 2). This principle would certainly do the job, but unfortunately it is quite implausible. We can see this by thinking about people who have different *needs*, where these needs are not the results of actions for which their bearers are morally responsible (think for instance of people who have been handicapped from birth). Need differences are morally arbitrary in sense 1, but they are not morally arbitrary in sense 2. Virtually everyone thinks that people with greater needs should be given additional resources, whatever precise characterization of the moral duty involved they prefer to give.

So we have yet to be given a reason why it is wrong if people are better or worse off on account of their national membership. Why regard nationality as a morally irrelevant characteristic like hair colour rather than a morally relevant characteristic like differential need? The fact that in some sense it is 'happenstance' that I belong to this nation rather to any other does not settle the question, for the reason just given. It is equally 'happenstance' that somebody should be born with a physical handicap. There has to be a *substantive* argument for the irrelevance of nationality, not merely a formal argument that trades on the ambiguity of 'arbitrariness'.

An argument of the right kind would be one that showed that nationality is not the kind of human relationship that can support special obligations among members. The assumption here is that it is indeed morally permissible to recognize special obligations to members of certain groups—the family being the most obvious example—but this does not extend to just any group of which someone might happen to be a member. Indeed, it may seem obvious that there are groups that cannot possibly support such obligations—racist groups, for instance, whose existence is premised on a belief in the superiority of the favoured race. So the cosmopolitan critic of national duties can deploy a pincer strategy, arguing on the one hand that nations are not, in relevant respects, similar to groups such as the family within which almost everyone would allow special duties to obtain,[15] while on the other hand arguing that the reasons offered to support duties to compatriots would also apply to racists or to members of criminal conspiracies, who could justifiably claim that they owed special duties to other members of their race or gang.[16] To escape this critique, we need to show what differentiates nations and other groups that can legitimately support special duties from these other attachments which have no such ethical significance.

What follows, therefore, is an attempt to defeat strong versions of cosmopolitanism by showing that nations are indeed communities of the kind that can support special obligations. It does not address those who think that there can be no local duties, duties not owed to humanity at large, not even within family groups. As I have indicated, most cosmopolitans are willing to accept such duties when presented with cases such as the missing child, but many are convinced that national obligations cannot be defended in the same way. This task having been achieved, I will conclude by asking what weak cosmopolitanism *does* imply with respect to principles of global justice.

IV

The question we must ask, then, is when do attachments legitimately ground special duties of the kind that nationhood is thought to impose? To get this question into proper focus, we need to begin by distinguishing between relationships that are merely instrumentally valuable and those that are also intrinsically valuable.[17] Both types of relationship can support special duties, but there is a difference

[15] These critics include H. Brighouse, 'Against Nationalism', in J. Couture, K. Nielsen and M. Seymour (eds), *Rethinking Nationalism* (Calgary, Canada: University of Calgary Press, 1998) and C. Wellman, 'Friends, Compatriots, and Special Political Obligations', *Political Theory*, 29 (2001), 217–36. For discussion of the nation/family analogy, see J. McMahan, 'The Limits of National Partiality' and T. Hurka, 'The Justification of National Partiality', both in R. McKim and J. McMahan (eds), *The Morality of Nationalism* (New York: Oxford University Press, 1997).

[16] Simon Caney calls this the 'obnoxious identity' objection to nationalism. See S. Caney, 'Individuals, Nations and Obligations', in S. Caney, D. George, and P. Jones (eds), *National Rights, International Obligations* (Boulder, CO: Westview Press, 1996).

[17] The significance of this distinction is discussed at greater length in S. Scheffler, 'Relationships and Responsibilities', in Scheffler, *Boundaries and Allegiances*.

in the *kind* of special duties supported that can best be brought out through an example. Compare a group of friends with a group of people who associate for a specific purpose, say a group of work colleagues who decide to form a syndicate to own a racehorse. In the case of the friends, although there are certainly instrumental benefits to friendship—friends can call on each other for help when they get into difficulties, for example—there is also the intrinsic value of the friendship itself. People's lives go better just by virtue of being involved in this kind of relationship; when friendships dissolve for one reason or another, this is a loss. The syndicate, by contrast, only exists because the members need to join to bear the cost of owning a horse. If any of them could do it single-handed, that would be better still for the lucky ones, and it does not matter if the syndicate collapses and a new consortium is formed. So the only duties that arise in the case of the syndicate are those inherent in the cooperative practice itself. These might be contractual—each member might have agreed to pay so much per month for the stabling costs of the horse when he joined—or they might be duties of fairness—each might take it in turns to drive the horse to race meetings even if there was no antecedent agreement to do this. But there is no duty to keep the syndicate in existence, and no duties to the other members over and above those that their particular relationship entails. Friendship on the other hand creates open-ended duties to support and help one's friends, to keep the relationship alive by staying in touch, and so forth, and the grounds for these are that a valuable form of relationship would be lost if these duties were not acknowledged and acted upon.

Ground-level special duties,[18] therefore, arise only from relationships that are intrinsically valuable. Furthermore the duties in question must be integral to the relationship in the sense that the relationship could not exist in the form that it does unless the duties were generally acknowledged. In other words, the duties are not merely an ethical superstructure erected on top of an attachment whose real basis is something else—emotion, say, or self-interest—but they are central to the way that the relationship is understood by the participants. You cannot be somebody's friend unless you

---

[18] I use this phrase to refer to special duties that arise directly from membership of a group or a relationship of some other kind, as opposed to duties that arise from promises, contracts, cooperative practices, etc.

understand that this entails giving them certain kinds of priority in your life—being ready to drop what you are doing and go to them when they need you. I do not mean that when we think about friends and friendship, it is the duties that occupy centre stage; we are much more likely to take them for granted, only giving them conscious consideration when we find ourselves in a situation of moral conflict. The point is that we cannot treat friendship just as an emotional attachment—say as a relationship entered into simply because of the fun we get out of being with our friends—without changing its essential character, and losing part of what gives it value.[19]

A final condition for the existence of ground-level special duties is that the attachments that ground them should not inherently involve injustice; they should not be relationships whose very existence is premised on the unjust treatment of others. The injustice that undercuts the value of relationships can be of different kinds: it might involve the exploitative treatment of outsiders, or the unjust exclusion of would-be members. So, for example, a gang of boys, part of whose *raison d'être* is the bullying of weaker classmates, is not the kind of group to which one can have special duties; nor is the Mafia; nor is a racist group that excludes members of the disfavoured races. Once again, it is possible for attachments like these to give rise to duties of certain kinds: there can be honour among thieves, and I suppose one has some moral and not merely prudential reason to keep one's agreements with fellow mafiosi and so forth.[20] But one does not have special duties to the members of these groupings as such. The pervasive injustice that they generate deprives them of such intrinsic value as they might otherwise have had, so they are not the kind of attachments that can legitimately support ground-level special duties.

The last condition may be difficult to apply because any group has the potential to act in unjust ways, and so it may be hard to decide whether the injustice is inherent in the group or incidental

---

[19] For development of this claim about friendship, see J. Raz, 'Liberating Duties', in J. Raz (ed.), *Ethics in the Public Domain* (Oxford: Clarendon Press, 1994).

[20] This should be further qualified: one can have moral obligations to co-participants in unjust groups, but not to perform unjust acts. Someone who has agreed to go may have an obligation to attend a Mafia member's wedding, but the same argument does not apply to carrying out an execution, say.

to it. Every gang is liable to humiliate those who do not belong; even groups of friends can act unfairly towards people who would like to join the circle but are not permitted to. Families may create social injustice by virtue of the undeserved advantages that they give to their offspring. This issue becomes critical when we come to the case of nations, because critics are inclined to see nations as exclusive clubs whose very existence is premised on the exclusion of outsiders both from membership and from the resources that the nation controls. I shall return to this shortly. What needs stressing at this point is the distinction between groups founded on injustice, so to speak, and groups that contingently may act in unjust ways, but without the injustice becoming an essential part of the group's distinctive character. Only groups of the first kind lack the value that can ground special duties.

So now let us ask whether nations can meet the three conditions I have identified.[21] First, are the relationships that exist among compatriots intrinsically valuable?[22] It is sometimes argued that, in so far as national identity and national solidarity have any value at all, it is purely instrumental—it makes it possible for states with a national basis to achieve certain political goals, such as stable democracy. It is certainly true that such instrumental values feature more prominently in ethical defences of nationality than they do, for instance, in accounts of the family[23]: we think it cheapens the value of family life when the family is characterized merely as an effective tool for

[21] '*Can* meet' needs to be emphasized here. Veit Bader has drawn attention to several respects in which existing nation-states diverge from the communitarian model that is used to justify special obligations to compatriots: see V. Bader, 'Reasonable Impartiality and Priority for Compatriots: A Criticism of Liberal Nationalism's Main Flaws', *Ethical Theory and Moral Practice*, 8 (2005), 83–103. These points are well-taken, so long as we recognize that such divergences are a matter of degree. We have obligations to our compatriots *to the extent* that our nation meets the conditions described in the text. A similar point might be made about families and other forms of attachment.

[22] The question whether nations are intrinsically valuable communities is discussed at greater length in M. Moore, *The Ethics of Nationalism* (Oxford: Oxford University Press, 2001), ch. 2.

[23] One reason for this, I believe, is that ethical defences of nationality are aimed at those who are either doubtful that national allegiances have intrinsic value, or who think that such value as they have is outweighed by their harmful consequences. To people in this frame of mind, it makes most sense to highlight the instrumental arguments—nationality as a resource for democracy, social justice, individual autonomy, and so forth.

socializing children, or a form of mutual insurance against hardship for the members, even though it does undoubtedly serve these ends. However the point to make about the instrumental value of nationality is that it is parasitic on its intrinsic value in the following sense: compatriots must first believe that their association is valuable for its own sake, and be committed to preserving it over time, in order to be able to reap the other benefits that national solidarity brings with it. Whatever value we as outsiders may attach to other people's sense of national belonging, a political association that was entered into and supported purely for instrumental reasons could not work in the way that a national community does. And in fact the way that most people think about their nationality reveals that its value for them is indeed intrinsic. They would, for instance, profoundly regret the loss of their distinct national identity, even if they were guaranteed the other goods that nationality makes possible, stable democracy, social justice, and so forth.

There is of course a logical gap between nationality being intrinsically *valued* and its being intrinsically *valuable*, but, echoing John Stuart Mill's famous remark that 'the sole evidence it is possible to produce that anything is desirable, is that people do actually desire it',[24] the onus surely falls on those who want to deny the value of national attachments to show why people's actual valuations are misguided. One reason that is sometimes given is that whereas family or friendship relationships, say, are 'real'—the bonds that link me to friends and relations are based on direct knowledge and interaction—in the case of nations the bonds are 'artificial' or 'imaginary', since I can have no direct experience of 99.9 per cent of my compatriots. But this critique would apply to many other attachments besides national ones, for instance to churches, or professional associations, or football supporters' clubs. In all these cases what links the members is a set of shared understandings about what it is that they are members of, and what distinguishes them from

---

[24] J. S. Mill, *Utilitarianism* in H. B. Acton (ed.), *Utilitarianism; On Liberty; Considerations on Representative Government* (London: Dent, 1972), 32. Since generations of undergraduates have been taught to observe, quite correctly, that there can be no entailment from 'desired' to 'desirable', it is worth underlining that Mill's argument is only about the *evidence* that can be brought in support of a desirability claim.

outsiders, and this is a strong enough link to create a relationship that can have genuine value.

Note also here that the value of nationality cannot be dissipated by observing that some people who would normally be counted as members of a nation claim to attach no value at all to their membership—they claim to have a cosmopolitan sense of selfhood, for instance. For the same is true of families, which often contain members who claim to be indifferent to family ties, and may indeed show their indifference in the way that they behave. We say that these members have got it wrong—that they are failing to recognize the value of something that does indeed have value, and we hope we can show that their lives are impoverished by turning their backs on their family ties.[25] In the case of nations, people who deny the significance of their national identity in circumstances where such an identity is accessible to them[26] are missing out on the opportunity to place their individual lives in the context of a collective project that has been handed down from generation to generation, involving among other things the shaping of the physical environment in which they live, and whose future they could help to determine, by political participation and in other ways. The issue here is not whether this is the highest human good—for most people it is unlikely to be—but whether it is *one* of the human goods that have intrinsic value, alongside family life, creative work, and so forth. Cosmopolitans who deny the intrinsic value of nationality may be motivated by the worry that if they recognize special duties to compatriots, these will obliterate duties to humanity at large. If so,

[25] At any rate impoverished in that respect: there may be cases in which the breaking of family ties is necessary to achieve a good of some other kind, for instance the case of Gauguin who (Bernard Williams famously suggested) might have been justified in abandoning his family in order to fulfil himself as an artist in Tahiti: see B. Williams, 'Moral Luck', in B. Williams (ed.), *Moral Luck: Philosophical Papers 1973–80* (Cambridge: Cambridge University Press, 1981). Here the intrinsic value of family membership is trumped, but not eliminated, by the value of artistic creativity.

[26] This clause is needed to cover cases in which national identity develops in such a way as to exclude certain groups in the population who had previously shared it, but now find it has become irreconcilable with other aspects of their identity that are not reasonably revisable—the position of Jews in Nazi Germany is an extreme example of this. Valuing national identities does not entail believing that they must trump other identities whenever there is conflict—see my discussion in Miller, *On Nationality*, ch. 2.

their worries are groundless: the question at this point is not what weight we should attach to national duties, but whether national membership has intrinsic value of the kind that can justify special duties in the first place, independently of the question whether these duties can override cosmopolitan, or for that matter familial, etc., duties. Is the cosmopolitan self really one that is indifferent to national membership,[27] or simply one that recognizes competing attachments of many other different kinds?

The next question is whether special duties to compatriots are integral to the idea of nationhood. The counterclaim is that it is possible to value national identity in the sense of taking pleasure in the various cultural features and cultural activities that one shares with one's fellow countrymen, while thinking that this has no ethical significance and that one's moral duties are all global in scope. Now it is certainly possible to envisage cultural attachments that take this form—people might have a collective identity somewhat like the identity of a group of music fans for whom going along to concerts of blues music, say, is an important part of their lives, who enjoy mingling with other fans, and so forth, but would not say they had any special responsibilities either towards the other participants or to keep their particular brand of music alive. But such an identity would be very different from national identities as we currently experience them, and it could not function in the way that national identity now does: it could not underpin political values like social justice or deliberative democracy, nor could it locate people within an intergenerational project of the sort described in the previous paragraph. These functions presuppose that nations are ethical communities whose members have special responsibilities both to support one another and to preserve their community. Belonging to them constitutes a good that is different in kind from the good that the music fans enjoy.

Those who favour a purely cultural understanding of nationhood might reply that even if something is lost when compatriots cease to

---

[27] As the poet asks, rhetorically:

> 'Breathes there the man with soul so dead,
> Who never to himself has said,
> This is my own, my native land!'

(W. Scott, 'The Lay of the Last Minstrel', in J. MacQueen and T. Scott (eds), *The Oxford Book of Scottish Verse* (Oxford: Oxford University Press, 1989), 429.

recognize special duties to one another, this is more than compensated for by the potential gain in justice overall. So this brings us to the question whether injustice is integral to national attachments in the way that it is, for instance, to membership in a racist group. Why might we think that national attachments, in their present form, are inherently unjust? In recognizing such attachments, we draw a distinction between insiders and outsiders, and regard ourselves as having more extensive and weightier obligations to our compatriots. But it may appear that this inevitably works to the disadvantage of all those who are left outside the circle, whose claims on us are now reduced. By granting ethical weight to national attachments, we unavoidably help to perpetrate global injustice.

Samuel Scheffler has called this 'the distributive objection' to special responsibilities.[28] The objection holds that such responsibilities can be justified only when they are consistent with general responsibilities that show an equal regard for all human beings. To illustrate the point, he asks us to imagine three persons Alice, Beth, and Carla who initially have equal responsibilities to each other. Alice and Beth, however, join an In Group while Carla does not, and as a result acquire special responsibilities to one another that exclude Carla. This disadvantages Carla in so far as Alice and Beth, by virtue of their special relationship, can now legitimately give priority to each other's demands and needs, which means that Carla has a lesser claim on their resources. Alice and Beth have become better off than Carla by virtue of joining the In Group; but, the distributive objection concludes, this just shows that In Groups (such as nations) that entail special responsibilities are inconsistent with recognizing the equal moral claims of all persons.

Scheffler considers a number of responses to this objection; in particular he points out that the objection might be circumvented if we bring into the picture a fourth person, Denise, and consider how the creation of the Alice–Beth In Group changes her responsibilities to Carla. He suggests that because Alice and Beth are now looking out for each other, Carla and Denise can legitimately give one another greater priority even without forming a group of their own, and this restores Carla's position. The distributive objection derives its main force, Scheffler suggests, from cases where the In Group are

---

[28] See S. Scheffler, 'Families, Nations and Strangers' and 'The Conflict between Justice and Responsibility', in Scheffler, *Boundaries and Allegiances*.

also a privileged group in relation to the outsiders: if Americans are allowed to give special weight to the interests of their compatriots at the expense of the Third World, it will not be much comfort to the inhabitants of Chad or Bangladesh to be told that 'they may rely all the more heavily on one another or ... they may pursue their own projects unburdened by excessive concern for the welfare of affluent Westerners'.[29]

Although Scheffler's diagnosis here is carefully executed, I think that his initial formulation of the problem is ambiguous in one crucial respect. When introducing the distinction between general and special responsibilities, he does not say whether such responsibilities are to be understood as requiring some form of *equal* treatment, or whether as requiring, for instance, the provision of a certain fixed level of resources. On the latter view, one might think of the general responsibilities of human beings to one another in terms of a set of human rights that must be fulfilled and protected for people everywhere. This would not be inconsistent with a special responsibility to provide a higher level of resources to some human beings but not others. How would this play out in the Alice–Beth–Carla case? Each has a responsibility to secure the human rights of the others, and this responsibility does not alter when the In Group is formed; Alice and Beth simply have to do things for each other over and above this minimum. It may be true, as Scheffler points out, that because of these extra commitments, they are less inclined to do supererogatory things for Carla. But why would this amount to any kind of injustice to her? More seriously, what if Alice cannot protect the rights of both Beth and Carla—she hasn't enough resources to secure the subsistence rights of both? With the formation of the In Group, she will acquire a special responsibility to help Beth, but again can Carla complain of injustice if the choice is simply between Alice helping Beth and Alice helping Carla? So long as the general responsibilities of Alice and Beth to Carla continue to take priority over their special responsibilities to each other, it does not seem that Carla's position is worsened in a relevant way when the In Group is formed, even under circumstances of inequality.

The force of the distributive objection to special responsibilities among compatriots therefore depends entirely on how we specify

---

[29] Scheffler, 'The Conflict between Justice and Responsibility', in Scheffler, *Boundaries and Allegiances*, 89.

the general responsibilities that obtain beforehand. If we say that we have an obligation to treat people everywhere equally in some strong and substantive sense—provide them with equal opportunities or equal levels of welfare, for instance—then it immediately follows that by recognizing local duties we will almost certainly causing injustice to the Carlas of the world. But this of course means that the distributive objection cannot be used to *ground* this view of global responsibilities. If our global responsibilities are to be understood in some other, non-comparative, way—for instance, as I suggested above, as an obligation to ensure that people everywhere have access to a minimum set of resources—then there is no inherent injustice involved in recognizing greater responsibilities to compatriots. Both sets of responsibilities can in principle be discharged at once.[30] Recall that I am not here attempting to reply to those who, following the lead of William Godwin, believe that special responsibilities are never justified—that we must always decide how to act after giving equal weight to the interests of everyone who might be affected by our action[31]—but to those who believe that such responsibilities can be justified within relationships of certain kinds—families, especially—but not within nations. What I have sought to show here is that there is no good reason to exclude nations as a source of special duties. They can meet the conditions specified earlier, namely that the relationships in question should be intrinsically valuable, the duties in question should be integral to those relationships, and maintaining the relationships does not intrinsically involve injustice to outsiders.

V

Let me take stock of where we have got to in our discussion of (moral) cosmopolitanism. The key distinction has been between weak and strong versions of cosmopolitanism, where weak cosmopolitanism requires us to show equal *moral concern* for human beings everywhere, while strong cosmopolitanism goes beyond this

---

[30] There may of course be conflicts *in practice* between the two sets of responsibilities. I discuss how these might be resolved in the next section of this chapter.

[31] The original source is W. Godwin, *Enquiry Concerning Political Justice*, I. Kramnick (ed.) (Harmondsworth, UK: Penguin, 1976), Book II, ch. 2.

to demand that we should afford them equal *treatment*, in a substantive sense. I have tried to expose the flaws in various arguments that attempt to link these two positions in such a way that strong cosmopolitanism follows directly from weak cosmopolitanism. And I have tried to show that weak cosmopolitanism is consistent with the recognition that we have special responsibilities to compatriots in addition to the general responsibilities that we have to humanity at large.

But I have not yet tried to specify what such a split-level ethical position might look like, beyond pointing out that there is no inherent contradiction in recognizing both special and general duties—a contradiction arises only if we say that the general duties are duties of equal treatment, which in this context is a question-begging move.[32] But what if, in practice, we have to choose between fulfilling the two types of responsibilities, say because there are not sufficient resources to meet both? What if our duty to promote social justice at home collides with our duty to promote global justice abroad? How should we resolve this kind of practical dilemma without abandoning weak cosmopolitanism?

We might propose giving one set of duties strict priority over the other. So, for instance, whenever local and global duties conflict, local duties should be discharged first, and then, depending on what resources are available, our global duties next. But this proposal, though logically coherent, is very implausible. It would mean, for instance, that there was no limit to the harm that we should be willing to inflict on outsiders if this proved to be necessary in the course of carrying out our local duties, say duties to provide fellow-nationals with a certain level of security. But most of us would recoil from this position. Although we may acknowledge a duty to provide our compatriots with adequate health care, for instance, this would not extend to killing foreigners in order to secure a supply of kidneys or other body parts for transplanting. In this case, our global duty to respect human rights takes precedence over an obligation of distributive justice that we owe to our compatriots. Within each category there are duties of different weight, and it is simply implausible to

---

[32] For further reflection on the shape of an ethical position that includes both general and special duties, see S. Scheffler, 'Families, Nations and Strangers', in Scheffler, *Boundaries and Allegiances*.

think that *any* duty owed to a fellow-national must be given priority over *any* duty that is global in scope.

Nor, on the other hand, does it seem plausible to give strict priority to global duties, particularly if we assume that these duties include a requirement that human beings everywhere should receive equal treatment—treatment, that is, that varies only according to personal characteristics like special need and never according to their nationality.[33] Suppose that a flu pandemic breaks out and the government only has sufficient vaccine to inoculate a limited number of vulnerable people against the disease. It does not seem wrong in this case to give priority to treating compatriots, that is to supply the vaccine to all those fellow-citizens identified by age or other relevant criteria as belonging to the vulnerable group, before sending any surplus abroad, even though it is reasonable to assume that some foreigners will be *more* vulnerable to the flu than some compatriots selected for vaccination.[34] And this remains true even if we know that those more vulnerable foreigners will not receive the vaccine from their own health services.

If neither of these strict priority proposals is acceptable, we might next consider *weighting* duties according to whether they are local or global in scope, with local duties being given a greater weight. Under this proposal, then, the final weight of a duty would be the product of two factors—the seriousness of the duty as determined by its content, and the closeness of our attachment to the people to whom the duty is owed. But this proposal, although it might succeed in modelling our considered ethical judgements in some cases, does not seem appropriate in all of them. For instance, if we consider the duty to give aid in cases where people need our help but are not in desperate, life-threatening circumstances, something like the weighting model might apply. We owe a stronger duty to those we are attached to in some way, but if we have to choose between helping a few associates and a very much larger number of strangers,

[33] A strict priority proposal of this kind is defended in Tan, *Justice without Borders*, ch. 7.

[34] I am appealing here to the reader's ethical intuitions. It is important not to be distracted by the thought that the vaccine will be distributed more quickly and efficiently to compatriots than to outsiders, so imagine that the delivery mechanism would work equally well if the vaccine were randomly assigned as between insiders and outsiders. I claim that our special responsibility to compatriots in this case justifies the policy of giving them priority in the distribution.

then we may think that we should help the strangers—the weight of numbers tipping the scales against the weight of association. But in other cases the weighting model looks wrong. If we return to the case of killing a stranger in order to obtain body parts, it does not seem that this can be defended by ratcheting up the closeness of our association with those who will be saved in this way. We do not think it is more justified to kill a stranger to obtain body parts for family members than it is to kill a stranger to obtain body parts for compatriots. In both cases we recognize an absolute prohibition on killing someone for this reason, and the weighting model does not allow for unconditional duties of this kind.

So a plausible split-level ethics that makes room both for global responsibilities and for special responsibilities to compatriots and others is going to have a more complex structure than either the strict priority proposal or the weighting proposal. I shall not put forward an alternative proposal in any detail here, but by way of illustration consider the responsibility to protect human rights, which I suggested above might be central to the ethics of weak cosmopolitanism. What is involved in the protection of human rights? Later in this book, I shall develop an account of human rights which sees them as providing the conditions for human beings everywhere to lead minimally decent lives. Without spelling this out in advance, it is fairly easy to see that these conditions can be roughly divided into those that involve the *absence* of certain factors that prevent people leading minimally decent lives and the *presence* of other factors; correspondingly the duty to respect human rights divides into a set of negative and a set of positive duties. On the one hand, we have a duty not to assault or injure others, not to restrict their freedom of movement or expression without good cause, not to abuse them in ways that destroy their self-respect, and so forth. These are duties to *refrain* from acting in harmful ways. On the other hand, we have duties to ensure that people everywhere have access to resources such as food, drinkable water, medical aid, and so forth. These are duties to *act* in beneficial ways when it is necessary to do so—to provide the food or the medical aid in cases where people currently lack them.

The point of drawing this distinction is not to suggest that from the recipients' point of view duties of the first kind are more important than duties of the second; in general there is no reason to think that. The distinction becomes important, however, when we take up the perspective of the agent whose duty is to protect rights, for here it seems that (other things being equal) there is a more stringent duty to refrain from violating rights by causing harm than to fulfil rights positively by acting beneficially, corresponding to the familiar (though much debated) distinction in moral philosophy between acts and omissions. Furthermore, whereas negative duties clearly fall on all agents, whether individual or collective, in the case of positive duties there is a substantive question about *whose* responsibility it is to provide the resources needed to secure basic rights, whenever there are many agents each of whom could potentially discharge the duty in question.[35] In international contexts, it may be clear enough that action is urgently needed to protect the rights of a vulnerable group of people, but much less clear which of many possible nations is the one on whom the responsibility falls.

Indeed when we think about the protection of basic rights in a world in which there are many agents whose activities may impinge upon such rights, the picture becomes more complex still. The duty to respect basic rights fragments into at least the following four sub-duties:

1. The negative duty to refrain from infringing basic rights by our own actions—for example killing or injuring innocent people.
2. The positive duty to secure the basic rights of the people we are responsible for protecting—for example supplying food to people who cannot provide it for themselves, where we have been identified as the responsible agent.
3. The positive duty to prevent rights violations by other parties—for example intervening to prevent a genocide or some lesser abuse of human rights.
4. The positive duty to secure the basic rights of people when others have failed in their responsibility—for example supplying food to people who are themselves responsible for their own hunger, or towards whom third parties have failed in their duty of aid.

These duties are not equally stringent. Their relative stringency depends on two factors: whether the duty is negative or positive in

[35] I will look at this question in much greater detail in Chapter 4.

character, that is whether failing to comply with it involves an active violation of rights or merely a failure to fulfil them, and whether the agent in question is the *primary* bearer of the duty, in either case. I assume, as before, that negative duties weigh more heavily than positive ones, other things being equal, and also that it is more urgent not to violate duties oneself than to prevent others from violating theirs. On these assumptions, duty 1 is clearly considerably more stringent than duty 4, with duties 2 and 3 falling somewhere in between, though their relative weight is difficult to determine—is it more urgent to supply food aid in a famine, or to prevent someone else's genocide, if the number of victims would be the same in both cases? This variability of strength is important when we turn to consider how these duties might relate to the local duties we have to compatriots, duties either to protect *their* human rights, or duties of justice more generally. We begin to see why neither a simple priority rule nor a system of weights that makes local duties count for more gives the right answer in all cases. It will depend which of the sub-duties is at issue.

If, for instance, we take the first sub-duty, the duty to refrain from infringing basic rights, then I think that this excludes giving any greater weight to the claims of compatriots. I have already suggested that one could not justify infringing the basic rights of outsiders even where this was necessary to provide the resources to protect the basic rights of compatriots: to vary the example, the government of a nation whose members are starving would not be justified in seizing resources from another nation if this meant that some of *that* nation's members would fall below the threshold for adequate nutrition. I am also doubtful that one would be justified in infringing a stranger's rights in order to avoid infringing a compatriot's. If we think about cases modelled on the trolley problem made famous by Judith Thomson,[36] I do not think it would be justifiable to switch the trolley from a track on which it was hurtling towards a compatriot

---

[36] J. J. Thomson, 'The Trolley Problem', in J. J. Thomson, *Rights, Restitution and Risk: Essays in Moral Theory* (Cambridge, MA: Harvard University Press, 1986). Its first appearance was in P. Foot, 'The Problem of Abortion and the Doctrine of Double Effect', *Oxford Review*, 5 (1967), 5–15, reprinted in P. Foot, *Virtues and Vices and Other Essays in Moral Philosophy* (Oxford: Clarendon Press, 2002).

on to a track on which it would hurtle towards a foreigner.[37] Nor do I think, if one takes the view that when the difference between the numbers on the two tracks becomes large enough, one ought to switch the trolley, that there should be any additional weighting in favour of compatriots.[38] If one should switch the trolley to kill one in order to save ten, then the identity of the ten and the one is irrelevant. At this level, morality appears to me to require strict equality of treatment at least as far as nationality is concerned.[39]

Turning to the second sub-duty, however—the duty to provide resources of various kinds—the picture changes quite radically. Considering first cases in which the claims we are responding to are qualitatively similar, a strong form of priority for compatriots seems to apply: if because of material shortages we have to choose between securing the subsistence rights of compatriots and the equivalent rights of others, we should favour our compatriots. But priority in this strict form does not extend to all positive duties in category 2. Even basic rights can be more or less urgent, and once it is established that we have a particular responsibility to starving people in a foreign country, this duty may take precedence over our duty to supply elementary education, say, to fellow-nationals (that governments do not act on this principle may be explained by the fact that we currently lack adequate mechanisms for assigning positive duties, so no country believes it has a special responsibility to render aid in such a case). So here perhaps we should apply a weighting model, and think of partiality towards compatriots as a matter of giving their rights-claims greater (though not absolute) weight when deciding how to use scarce resources.

If we consider cases in which our duties to foreigners take the form of sub-duties 3 and 4, then these are likely to be trumped by duties to compatriots of types 1 and 2. In particular, where the sub-duty is

[37] Thus if a meteorite is on course to devastate an area of the USA, the American government would not be justified in despatching Bruce Willis to deflect the path of the meteorite so that it hits an area of Canada with the same population.

[38] See also here the discussion in T. Pogge, 'The Bounds of Nationalism', in J. Couture, K. Nielsen, and M. Seymour (eds), *Rethinking Nationalism* (Calgary, Canada: University of Calgary Press, 1998), and in T. Pogge, *World Poverty and Human Rights* (Cambridge: Polity Press, 2002).

[39] It does not, however, require impartiality in cases involving family and friends. One should switch the trolley so that it kills a stranger rather than one's spouse or child. What makes the difference here needs further exploration.

of type 4, a reasonable view would be that all obligations of social justice towards fellow-nationals should take precedence over international obligations that arise from failures of responsibility by third parties—this despite the fact that the *condition* we are responding to may be much worse in the case of outsiders. How can this view be defended? It relies on the idea that the strength of a duty depends not only on the urgency of the demand it responds to but also on the role played by the agent in question in bringing that situation about: I have a much greater responsibility to rescue a child I have carelessly pushed into the river than to rescue a child somebody else has pushed in, particularly if that somebody else could now perform the rescue with relative ease.[40] We need of course to show that similar considerations about agency and responsibility apply to collectives, especially to nations, as they do to individuals, and that will be one of the main tasks of the present book. But for present purposes I hope I have said enough to indicate how weak cosmopolitanism may be compatible with a split-level view of agents' responsibilities. No human being's claims are ever discounted entirely, but the strength of the duties they impose on us, as particular agents standing in relationships to other agents, is quite variable, and the resulting picture of global ethics is a complex one.

I have shown that strong cosmopolitanism is not entailed by weak cosmopolitanism; but I have not yet tried to show what exactly is wrong with strong cosmopolitanism, other than that it conflicts with an intuitively plausible picture of agents' responsibilities. So it would still be possible for someone to present an independent argument to the effect that justice requires a strong form of equality at global level, and that our understanding of special responsibilities therefore needs to be reshaped to become consistent with such a requirement. In Chapter 3, accordingly, I examine global egalitarianism as a free-standing conception of global justice and provide some reasons for rejecting it.

---

[40] Again it is important to stress that I *should* rescue the drowning child if the person who pushed him refuses to do so, so long as the rescue does not expose me to significant levels of risk. But the fact that I am not responsible for the child's plight makes a difference to the level of risk I can be asked to bear as well as to other morally relevant aspects of the situation—for instance I may use reasonable force to make the pusher carry out the rescue himself, may demand compensation from him if my clothes are damaged in the course of the rescue, and so forth.

CHAPTER 3

Global Egalitarianism

I

Anyone surveying the current state of the world's peoples cannot help but be struck by the vast disparity in living standards and life prospects between the global rich and the global poor. Some of the most revealing figures are those contained in the Human Development Index (HDI) published annually by the UN, which ranks countries using three basic criteria: life expectancy, level of education (adult literacy plus school enrolment), and per capita gross domestic product (GDP), adjusted to take account of purchasing power differences (which gives a reasonable estimate of average income).[1] At the top of the scale we find a cluster of European and other developed societies where life expectancy is around 80 years, educational ratings are close to 1, and per capita GDP stands somewhere in the region of $30,000. At the bottom there is a group of countries in sub-Saharan Africa, in which life expectancy at around 40 years is only half that in the developed world, educational ratings run between about 0.2 and 0.6 (corresponding to adult literacy figures that range between 13% at the bottom to 70% at the top) and per capita GDP averages around $1,000, with many countries falling well below that figure. It is hard to grasp the significance of differences like this in human terms. Moreover, over the last few decades the gap between rich and poor countries has tended to widen rather than close, and there is little sign of an upward trend overall among the countries

---

[1] I have used figures from the United Nations Development Programme, *Human Development Report 2005*, available at http://hdr.undp.org/reports/global/ 2005.

that score the lowest (the position has improved slightly in some, but got worse in others).

Global egalitarianism is fuelled by evidence such as this about the extent of global inequality. How can we be living in a just world when people living in one region have average incomes some thirty times larger than those living in another (because the figures are averages, they seemingly cannot reflect individual features like how talented people are or how hard they work), and can also expect to live for twice as long? And how much would those from the richer societies have to give up in order to raise the position of those living on a dollar or so a day to give them something we would consider a decent life? These are good questions, and our theory of global justice must provide answers. But it is important to see that we do not have to leap to the conclusion that what justice requires is some form of global equality. The reasons we have for thinking that the existing distribution of life expectancy, education, and income is unjust might not be *egalitarian* reasons.

To canvass some alternatives: we might think that global distribution is unjust simply because of the low absolute position of those living in the poorest countries. We might in other words think that every human being should expect to live for something close to 80 years, should expect to have at least secondary education, and should be able to earn an income sufficient to buy a range of necessities such as food that provides adequate nutrition. This would set a threshold that everyone as a matter of justice must reach, but inequalities above the threshold would not be unjust merely by virtue of being inequalities.[2] Or we might think that global inequalities are unjust by virtue of the way they have arisen—because the wealth of the richer countries is in some way responsible for the poverty of the poorer countries. We may think that the developed West has exploited the rest of the world historically, and that current inequalities are largely a result of that fact. Had the same inequalities arisen in a different way, not involving exploitation, they would not be unjust.

These are not the only reasons we might have for condemning the huge disparities we see in the world today. The problem they are meant to illustrate is that our reactions to global inequalities may be

---

[2] Can such a threshold be defined in a non-arbitrary way? I discuss this issue in some detail in Chapter 7.

overdetermined, and this is a problem if we are going to use those reactions to help build a theory of global justice. My aim in this chapter is to show that global egalitarianism is not the right theory: what global justice requires is not that people everywhere should be made equal in certain material respects (resources and opportunities are the two 'currencies' I shall consider). But that by no means entails that existing inequalities are unproblematic from the point of view of justice; on the contrary, it is clear to me that a just world would also be a world in which disparities between rich and poor countries would be far smaller than those that now exist. Why this is so will emerge in due course. For now, the task is to break the hold that global egalitarianism has had on our thinking about global justice.

Many people have been drawn to this view because they assume that what justice requires is always and everywhere a certain kind of equality: since justice requires equality *within* societies, it must also require equality *between* them (or between people who live in different societies). But this assumption is mistaken. The only kind of equality that justice always requires is formal equality: equality between people who are in all relevant respects the same. If there is nothing of any significance to distinguish between two people, then they should be treated in the same way as a matter of justice. Everything then turns on what should count as a relevant difference. I shall suggest that substantive rather than formal equality—people actually receiving the same bundle of rights, or resources, or whatever it is whose distribution is at issue—is only required by justice in certain quite specific circumstances. In other circumstances, a fair distribution may be one in which what people get depends on their deserts, choices, or needs; it may be one that simply guarantees everyone a certain minimum level of resources; it may be one that comes about through fair procedures—for instance a lottery that people have voluntarily chosen to enter. It is fruitless, as I suggested in Chapter 1, to try to specify what justice requires without considering the context in which the distribution is taking place—who is distributing what to whom and under what circumstances. So when should we say that what justice requires is substantive equality?[3]

---

[3] For a fuller statement of the position set out in the following paragraphs, see my *Principles of Social Justice* (Cambridge, MA: Harvard University Press, 1999), ch. 11.

One circumstance is where there really are no relevant differences between the people among whom the distribution is being made, or, more likely perhaps, where it is impossible to obtain reliable evidence about differences that might be relevant if they were revealed. Imagine having to allocate a supply of food between ten people about whom you are given no information at all. There are various reasons that would tell in favour of sharing the food equally. Some of them might be malnourished, and by giving each an equal share you would minimize the risk of leaving anyone still hungry. Even if they are all adequately nourished, an unequal distribution is likely to benefit the winners less than it harms the losers. Moreover, given that food is an all-round benefit to human beings, and given the absence of any information about the ten, perhaps each has a claim to the benefit that only an equal distribution can meet. How robust this claim is can be disputed: might it be enough to distribute the food using a fair procedure such as a lottery which gave each person an equal chance? Would that be a strong enough form of equality to satisfy justice, leaving aside the other grounds favouring an equal distribution? Let us just say that the absence of known relevant differences can sometimes be sufficient to ground a substantive and not merely procedural claim for equal treatment. Some have thought that this argument can be applied to the earth's natural resources, and have used this to justify a form of global egalitarianism. I shall consider this position shortly. But before that I want to consider a second set of circumstances in which justice may require substantive equality.

These are cases in which the claim for equal treatment stems from membership of groups of various kinds. These are groups constituted on the basis of equality—people who are admitted to them are admitted as equal members, people with the same status as other members. To preserve this equality, basic rights within the group must be equally assigned, and members who are denied equal rights can legitimately complain of unjust treatment. It is not necessary that all benefits that the group creates or provides should be allocated in this way; the claim for equal treatment applies only to those rights and opportunities that are fundamental in the sense that they serve to define a person's position in the group. The most familiar example of this phenomenon in the contemporary world is the form of membership provided by citizenship in nation-states.

Although citizenship has not always been understood as requiring all citizens to be treated as equals—earlier conceptions sometimes made room for two or more classes of citizen—this understanding has now become definitive of the very idea. It then follows that to introduce inequalities in basic rights—for instance to opt for a form of plural voting of the kind once advocated by John Stuart Mill, or to create a two-tier system of welfare provision—would be to act unjustly towards those with lesser rights, who would justifiably regard such policies as denying their equal status as full members of the community in question.

Principles of equality based on membership are important components of distributive justice, but their obvious limitation is that their scope is restricted to those who are already members of the group or community in question. There is no injustice in the fact that a French citizen enjoys rights that I as a British citizen do not have and vice versa. To prove that such an inequality was unjust, it would be necessary to show that we are both members of some larger community and that our status as equal members was being undermined by the different sets of rights we enjoyed. This might in due course come to pass (say as cultural and political integration within the EU increases), so it is important to say that the scope of egalitarian justice based on membership is not fixed for all time. On the other hand, it does not seem that a membership-based case can plausibly be made for global egalitarianism. The idea that we are all members of a world community and that our status as equal members is being damaged by the unequal rights that we enjoy seems far-fetched as things now stand. I commented in Chapter 2 on the implausibility of presenting 'cosmopolitan citizenship' as simply an enlarged version of national forms of citizenship, given that the latter rely on cultural and political ties among citizens that stem from their common national identity. So it seems that any defence of global egalitarianism cannot rely on arguments that make sense only when applied to those who belong to groups of a certain kind.

We must therefore conclude that global principles of equality can only be defended in the first way, by showing that there are no relevant differences between people belonging to different societies when it comes to the distribution of resources (understood in a broad sense). People have equal claims, because there is nothing that serves to distinguish between them. But equal claims to what? I shall consider two candidate principles of global equality that have found defenders among theorists of global justice, equality of natural resources, and equality of opportunity. Each principle, I believe, is subjected to the same two basic objections. The first I shall call the *metric* problem: the problem of establishing a global measure of resources or opportunities that would allow us to determine whether two people do in fact have equal resources or opportunities. The second I shall call the *dynamic* problem: the problem posed for global equality by the fact that people belong to independent political communities which make decisions that influence the future availability of resources and opportunities. The next three sections of this chapter develop these objections.

II

It is easy to see why an equal entitlement to natural resources has proved popular as a principle of global equality. On the one hand, having access to natural resources of greater or lesser value—fertile land, mineral wealth, and the harvests of the sea—is one important factor that determines the overall wealth or poverty of the people who enjoy it. On the other hand, such access is very unequally distributed between nations. It is not as though nations have bid for the territories they inhabit through some kind of global auction in which each person is given a chip of equal value. Territories have been acquired historically by more or less dubious means, and often without foreknowledge of the future value of the assets they contained. That a nation's territory should turn out to contain oilfields, or to be particularly suitable for growing a grape favoured for wine-making, is therefore a piece of good fortune that may nonetheless have significant consequences for the living standards of the people in question. Being born into a country with a relatively high level of per capita natural resource values seems like a morally irrelevant form of advantage that is ripe for correction by egalitarian redistribution.

One might of course challenge the empirical assumption being made here that having access to valuable natural resources always or usually contributes positively to the wealth and welfare of nations. Later in this book I shall present some evidence that supports this challenge. But for the moment I shall continue to accept the assumption that having natural resources is normally a source of relative advantage. Should we conclude that global justice requires a redistributive scheme whereby, for example, resource-rich countries are taxed to support the resource-poor?

It is important here to distinguish between two different motivations that we might have for introducing such a scheme. We might on the one hand be looking for a way of raising funds that can be used to support a global minimum for people everywhere: we think that all human beings are entitled as a matter of justice to resources that will enable them to lead minimally decent lives, and that those who have a surplus of resources are obliged to contribute to this goal. A scheme that targets the ownership of natural resources is attractive partly because their presence is relatively easy to identify, and partly because their distribution seems morally arbitrary for the reasons just given. Thus proposals such as the Global Resources Tax favoured by Thomas Pogge, which would tax *extracted* natural resources at a fixed rate, may seem a plausible way of helping the world's poor, as well as slowing the rate at which natural resources are used up.[4] Such proposals are not, however, egalitarian in inspiration: they do not seek to *equalize* access to natural resources. So although they still require some answer to the question I shall be raising in a moment, namely how are we to attach a value to natural resources of different kinds, that question is less troublesome precisely because the aim is not to achieve equality in any form. Some rough and ready way of valuing extracted resources might be sufficient for the purposes of the Global Resources Tax.

A proposal that is genuinely egalitarian, by contrast, is Hillel Steiner's Global Fund.[5] Starting from the premise that each person is entitled to an equal share of the world's unimproved natural resources, Steiner proposes that a nation's natural resource holdings should be computed by aggregating the property values of all the

[4] See T. Pogge, 'An Egalitarian Law of Peoples', *Philosophy and Public Affairs*, 23 (1994), 195–224.

[5] See H. Steiner, *An Essay on Rights* (Oxford: Blackwell, 1994), ch. 8; H. Steiner, 'Territorial Justice', in S. Caney, D. George, and P. Jones (eds), *National Rights, International Obligations* (Boulder, CO: Westview Press, 1996); H. Steiner, 'Just Taxation and International Redistribution', in I. Shapiro and L. Brilmayer (eds), *Nomos XLI: Global Justice* (New York: New York University Press, 1999).

sites that fall within its domain: nations whose holdings per capita are above the global average would pay into the fund, and nations whose holdings fall below the average would draw out of it. In other words, resource-rich nations would be taxed according to the per capita value of their landholdings; resource-poor nations would draw from the fund according to the size of their per capita shortfall.

The question we must ask is how these property values are going to be calculated, bearing in mind that Steiner wants to distinguish 'raw' natural resources from the improvements that have been wrought by human labour: if a site has a skyscraper built upon it, what counts is the value of the site without the skyscraper, not its current value. These values cannot be determined simply by looking at the physical characteristics of a particular parcel of land. For one thing, location clearly matters, as Steiner concedes himself:

Evidently the ownership of an acre in the Sahara Desert is of a different value, and consequently attracts a different payment liability, from the ownership of an acre in downtown Manhattan or the heart of Tokyo. Similar things can be said about real estate in the Saudi oil fields, the Amazon rain forests, the Arctic Tundra, the Iowa corn belt, the Bangladeshi coast and the City of London.[6]

Steiner's examples might lead the unwary reader to think that what matters in determining these property values is primarily the physical features of a site such as the presence of oil underground or the fertility of the soil. But though these features certainly do matter in some cases, equally or more important is location itself: an acre of ground in central London or Tokyo might have physical features not all that different from an acre in the Iowa corn belt, but a vastly different economic value, as indicated by the selling price of the site or the rent that could be charged for occupying it (Steiner's own suggested indicators). So how are these values determined?

Physical features aside, three types of factors seem important. The first is the set of rules and conditions under which the site is to be held. Is it to be held as private property or under some form of communal ownership? If as private property, how restrictive are the conditions on what may be done with the site, for instance the kinds of building that can be erected there, or the productive uses to which

---

[6] Steiner, 'Territorial Justice', 146.

the site may be put? What tax regime will be applied locally? And so forth. Answers to these questions can make a big difference to the value of unimproved property. What if a piece of land could be used for growing grapes to make fine wine, but local law prohibits wine production? Or what if there is an oilfield directly under the city of Mecca, but the Saudi government has declared that to be a sacred site for all time? How are site values to be decided in these cases? It is tempting to resolve this problem by declaring a site's value to be the value it would realize under some privileged set of rules and conditions—for instance under a libertarian property regime that gave full and unconditional rights to the owners of sites. But two problems immediately arise: why choose this particular regime, and why regard it as fair to tax nations on the basis of the aggregate value their property *would* have had if they had chosen to adopt a libertarian regime? The proposed resolution is not neutral as a way of defining equality of resources in a world where people hold different sets of cultural and political values and apply these values when determining the rights of ownership attaching to sites within their domains.

The second set of factors influencing property values are the abilities and the preferences of the people who might use the property and consume what is produced there. The example of land from which fine wine could be produced again makes this point. For a site to become a valuable vineyard requires someone with expertise in the planting and care of vines, and customers who are willing to pay for the product. But what if there are no skilled viniculturalists available, or no consumers willing to drink alcohol? It might be said in reply here that the relevant constituencies are global rather than national: viniculturalists can be flown in, and there is an international wine market on which the produce can be sold. But this is entirely a contingent matter. Whether there are people willing to work on a particular site, whether the products of the site are such that they have potentially a global as well as a local sale, are matters quite unconnected to the site itself, though potentially important in determining its value. The aspect I want to highlight is the contribution that local cultures make to site values, by determining the available set of skills (through the education system, etc.), and by shaping the preferences of both producers and consumers. This contribution stands over and above the formal set of rules and conditions: wine-growing may be legally permitted, but it will not occur if the local population has strong religious convictions that prohibit the production and consumption of alcohol.

Third, we need to consider what we can call neighbourhood effects on site values. What a particular site is worth may be heavily dependent on what is already being done on sites close by. Why, after all, is a site in central London or Tokyo worth so much more than a site twenty or thirty miles away on the edge of the city? Not primarily because of different legal rules, or the differential availability of willing producers and consumers. City centre sites are worth a lot simply because they stand next to others on which various business activities, producing or consuming, are being engaged in, and from which therefore people can easily move to the site in question. Imagine for a moment that it became widely believed that a particular city centre was polluted with a chemical that was dangerous to human health, as a result of which very few people were willing to shop or work there. Clearly, the value of all sites in that district would plummet as economic activities sharply declined. Putting it the other way round, the value of an acre in downtown Manhattan is primarily determined by the ongoing practice of very large numbers of human beings who see it as being in their interest to go there to produce and consume, and who thereby generate a level of activity which means that a firm deciding where to conduct its business has a large incentive to locate to Manhattan.

The upshot of all this is that natural resource values—the values of unimproved sites—are not set by nature itself, but almost entirely by human decision and behaviour. If we are looking at the wealth of nations, then, aggregate property values depend on political decisions about the rules and conditions for holding sites, cultural values that affect skills and preferences, and forms of human behaviour that determine the character of particular neighbourhoods. It would be wrong to say that the physical availability of resources makes no difference at all, but the point is that even a resource such as an oilfield only becomes valuable when located within a human environment that allows the oil to be extracted and sold.

Steiner's proposal to tax nations according to the aggregated property values of the sites they contain therefore appears arbitrary. The rationale for the tax is that it serves to correct the unequal per capita distribution of natural resources between nations. But we can now see that property values, even of unimproved sites, are to a large extent an artefact of human choice and human decision. Nations contribute to the creation of their own aggregate property values in at least the three ways we have just traced. So if they are taxed on that basis, they are to a considerable extent being taxed according to the values they adhere to collectively and the choices they have made, which is certainly not what Steiner intends. Indeed, the line that he draws between the 'raw' natural resource values of sites and the improvements made by human agency now looks untenable. If a building is erected on a site that increases the value of that site, the tax basis is still supposed to be the prior unimproved value; but if buildings are erected on five *neighbouring* sites, and this also increases the value of the original site, it is the enhanced value that is used for tax purposes.

More generally, the idea of global equality of resources remains indeterminate in the absence of a non-arbitrary way of determining resource values. When Ronald Dworkin famously proposed using the device of a hypothetical auction as a way of identifying an equal distribution of heterogeneous resources among a set of persons with equally heterogeneous tastes, he made it clear that prior to the auction decisions have to be made about the principles according to which lots are going to be divided up and about the publicly enforceable rules that will govern the use of items acquired through the auction.[7] Until these things are decided, no one is in a position to judge how valuable a particular resource might be to him or her. Starting from a liberal ideal of freedom of choice, and arguing that the auctioneer must provide bidders with the greatest possible opportunity to use the resources they acquire in the way that they wish, Dworkin defends principles that are likewise liberal—thus he advocates rules governing the use of items that would broadly support a free market.[8] So Dworkin's model does give us a metric that can define equality of resources, but only if we presuppose this liberal background, according to which, for example, enforceable

[7] See R. Dworkin, 'What is Equality? Part 2: Equality of Resources', *Philosophy and Public Affairs*, 10 (1981), 283–345 and R. Dworkin, 'What is Equality? Part 3: The Place of Liberty', *Iowa Law Review*, 73 (1987–8), 1–54, both now reprinted as R. Dworkin, *Sovereign Virtue: The Theory and Practice of Equality* (Cambridge, MA: Harvard University Press, 2000), chs. 2 and 3.

[8] Dworkin, 'The Place of Liberty', sections III–IV.

religious restrictions on the use of resources are excluded as illegitimate: anyone planning to bid for a potential vineyard knows that he will be permitted to make and sell wine if he chooses. But this makes it inappropriate as a way of defining equality of resources at global level in circumstances where not all cultures embrace these liberal ideals. So even if we were convinced that global justice is best understood in terms of a principle of equality (*pace* the arguments in the first section of this chapter), and that equality of resources would be the right way to cash this out, we are left with no way of determining when, in fact, a distribution of resources qualifies as an equal distribution—and therefore no way of implementing egalitarian proposals such as Steiner's Global Fund.

III

One might in any case come to think that equality of (unimproved natural) resources is too narrow a conception of egalitarian justice, regardless of whether its scope is national or global. How well a person's life goes is determined by many factors besides his or her entitlement to natural resources. In domestic contexts, the relevant conception is often taken to be *equality of opportunity*. An influential statement of this principle is by John Rawls, who defines 'fair equality of opportunity' as follows:

> ...those who are at the same level of talent and ability, and have the same willingness to use them, should have the same prospects of success regardless of their initial place in the social system, that is, irrespective of the income class into which they are born. In all sectors of society there should be roughly equal prospects of culture and achievement for everyone similarly motivated and endowed.[9]

Several authors have proposed that global justice should be understood in similar terms, as requiring that people of similar talent and similar motivation should have the same life chances (in particular access to educational and job opportunities and the rewards they bring) no matter which society they were born into.[10] This is clearly

---

[9] J. Rawls, *A Theory of Justice* (Cambridge, MA: Harvard University Press, 1971), 73.

[10] See, for instance, S. Caney, 'Cosmopolitan Justice and Equalizing Opportunities', in T. Pogge (ed.), *Global Justice* (Oxford: Blackwell, 2001); S. Caney, 'Global

a demanding principle, but so too is its domestic analogue, which has nevertheless proved important as a guiding beacon for public policy. So is global equality of opportunity the best interpretation of global justice?

We must begin by asking what it means, more precisely, for opportunities to be equal at global level. Does it require, for instance, that people with the same talent and motivation should have *identical* opportunity sets no matter which society they are born into? This seems to be the implication of Moellendorf's claim that 'if equality of opportunity were realized, a child growing up in rural Mozambique would be statistically as likely as the child of a senior executive at a Swiss bank to reach the position of the latter's parent.'[11] But surely such a requirement would be too strong. It would, for instance, require unlimited rights of migration coupled with unrestricted admission to citizenship, given that some positions, such as chief executive of *Credit Suisse*, or president of the USA, presuppose membership of particular societies. Moreover even leaving aside the difficulty of being able to apply formally for certain positions, the child from rural Mozambique would be less fluent in German, French, or Italian than his Swiss counterpart, and on that ground alone less likely to succeed in the competition to become a Swiss banker.[12] So unless advocates of global equality of opportunity envisage a borderless world in which everyone speaks Esperanto, it is more plausible to interpret the principle as requiring *equivalent* opportunity sets. It would be satisfied provided the child from rural Mozambique had the same chance to attain an executive post in

Equality of Opportunity and the Sovereignty of States', in A. Coates (ed.), *International Justice* (Aldershot, UK: Ashgate, 2000); D. Moellendorf, *Cosmopolitan Justice* (Boulder, CO: Westview Press, 2002), ch. 4.

[11] Moellendorf, *Cosmopolitan Justice*, 49.

[12] This issue is raised by Bernard Boxhill in 'Global Equality of Opportunity and National Integrity', *Social Philosophy and Policy*, 5 (1987), 143–68. Boxhill discusses the implications of cultural diversity for global equality of opportunity without distinguishing as sharply as I would wish between culture's role in defining 'success' and culture's role in motivating people to strive for success, however defined. In the present discussion, I am bracketing the issue of motivation by defining equal opportunity as opportunity for people of similar talent and motivation. It may well be the case that children in rural Mozambique are not taught to aspire to be bank executives, but for purposes of argument I am assuming that we have a child with the appropriate motivation, and asking under what circumstances such a child could be judged to have equal opportunities with his Swiss counterpart.

a bank somewhere, perhaps in Mozambique itself, with the same salary and other benefits as the position aimed at by the (equally talented and motivated) child of a Swiss banker.

By taking this specific case, we can understand what it would mean for two opportunity sets to be equivalent but not identical. But now consider more fully how we might apply this idea. In order to decide whether two opportunity sets are equivalent, we have to apply some kind of metric, and the metric we use can either be finer-grained or broader-grained. In the case just discussed, we found that the broader-grained metric 'opportunity to become chief executive of a national bank' was preferable to the finer-grained 'opportunity to become chief executive of a Swiss bank': we do not think that the Mozambiquean child is disadvantaged in any significant way by having a lesser opportunity to head a Swiss bank so long as he has a greater opportunity than the Swiss child to head a similar bank in Mozambique. So let us now consider, more generally, how fine-grained or broad-grained our metric of equality should be. If we make it too fine-grained, then we will get lots of meaningless results like the one just mentioned—equalities and inequalities that just do not matter because they are too specific to engage our ethical attention. But if we try to make it as broad-grained as possible, then we run into controversy about how, if at all, different components of our metric should be evaluated relative to one another.[13]

Let me attempt to make this clearer through an example. Suppose we have two relatively isolated villages, broadly similar in size and general composition. Suppose that village A has a football pitch but no tennis court, and village B has a tennis court but no football

---

[13] Replying to Boxhill's concern about cultural diversity, Simon Caney suggests the following: 'Global equality of opportunity requires that persons (of equal ability and motivation) have equal opportunities to attain an equal number of positions of a commensurate standard of living.' ('Cosmopolitan Justice and Equalizing Opportunities', 130). This, however, is simultaneously too narrow and too vague. It is too narrow in focusing exclusively on opportunities to attain jobs; and it is too vague when it uses the metric 'a commensurate standard of living' to compare them. What does this mean? Does it refer simply to salary, perhaps adjusted to take account of differences in purchasing power? Or does it mean 'standard of living' in a much wider sense, in which case we would need to know how the different components that make up someone's life are to be weighed against each other? For a penetrating critique of Caney's view, see G. Brock, 'Egalitarianism, Ideals, and Cosmopolitan Justice', *Philosophical Forum*, 36 (2005), 1–30.

pitch. Do members of the two communities have equal opportunities
or not? In the morally relevant sense I think that they do: football
pitches and tennis courts seem to fall naturally into the broader category of 'sporting facilities', and measured in terms of this metric the
two communities are more or less equally endowed. It would seem
morally perverse for members of B to complain of injustice by using
'access to football pitches' as the relevant metric. But now suppose
also that village A possesses a school but no church, and village B
possesses a church but no school. Can we still say that people in
these two villages enjoy equal opportunities? I think almost all of us
would say that they do not. We think that the opportunities provided
by a school and a church are just different, that if someone were
to suggest a metric such as 'access to enlightenment' in terms of
which the two villages should be judged as equally endowed, this
would just be a piece of sophistry. It is also worth noticing that
while most of us would judge that the villagers in A were better off
by virtue of having a village school, those who thought that having
a church was more important would *also* resist the idea that there
was some overarching metric in terms of which the two villages
could be judged. They would not think that the religious deprivation
suffered by people in A could somehow be compensated for by their
educational advantages.

Now the question is: how are we able to judge that in the football
pitch/tennis court case there is no significant inequality between
A and B, whereas in the school/church case there is significant
inequality? The answer must be that we have cultural understandings that tell us that football pitches and tennis courts are naturally
substitutable as falling under the general rubric of sporting facilities,
whereas schools and churches are just different kinds of things, such
that you cannot compensate people for not having access to one
by giving them access to the other. The cultural understandings tell
us that the broader-grained 'access to sporting facilities' is a better
metric than the finer-grained 'access to football pitches' while the
finer-grained 'access to schools' is a better metric than the broader-
grained 'access to enlightenment' which I suggested is what someone
would need to invent if they wanted to argue that the two villages
were equally endowed in the second case.

If we look at how this question is answered within nation-states—
in other words at how the general idea of equal opportunity is

cashed out in terms of more concrete forms of equality—then what we find is that a number of specific types of resource and opportunity are singled out as significant, and these are not regarded at substitutable. Included in the list would be personal security, education, health care, mobility, and so on. Finer-grained distinctions within these categories are not regarded as relevant. So, for instance, while it is regarded as an essential part of the educational package that every child should have the opportunity to learn foreign languages, it is not regarded as a source of inequality if one school offers Russian and another offers Italian. Mobility opportunities might mean underground trains for some people and rural buses for others, and so forth. At the same time, any attempt to use a broader-grained metric—to suggest, for instance that poorer health facilities could be compensated by better educational facilities when opportunities are measured—would be strongly resisted. The public culture marks education and health out as different kinds of goods in respect of each of which citizens should have equal opportunities.

What happens if we try to carry this understanding of equality across to the global level? We run into serious difficulties created by the fact that we can no longer rely on a common set of cultural understandings to tell us which metric or metrics it is appropriate to use when attempting to draw cross-national opportunity comparisons. We face difficulties both within the familiar categories and across them. If education, for instance, takes different forms in different places, how can we judge whether a child in country A has better or worse educational opportunities than a child in country B? And even if we can make judgements of that kind, how can we decide whether it is appropriate or inappropriate to merge specific metrics into more general ones? Suppose, for instance, that we can find a measure of education such that people in Iceland plainly have better educational opportunities than people in Portugal, but that people in Portugal equally plainly have superior leisure opportunities than people in Iceland (sunny beaches, swimming pools, etc.). Is it legitimate to say that people in one of these places are better off (in a global sense) than people in the other, or can we say only that according to metric E Icelanders are better off while according to metric L the Portuguese are better off, and nothing beyond this?

Global egalitarians faced with this challenge will probably respond that the most urgent cases are cases of *gross* inequality where no reasonable person could doubt that the resources and opportunities available to members of A are superior to those available to members of B. We are not primarily concerned about Iceland/Portugal comparisons, but about comparisons such as those I introduced at the beginning of this chapter, between, say, any of the more developed EU member-states, and any sub-Saharan African country. Two things are worth noting about this response. First, by taking countries as the opposite ends of the development scale, and using the components of the HDI as our metric, it may indeed be possible to conclude that the set of opportunities open to a typical citizen of Niger, say, is strictly smaller than the set open to a typical citizen of France—there is no basic dimension along which the former has greater opportunities than the latter. But this does not mean that in general we are in a position to make such inter-societal comparative judgements, either within the group of rich societies or within the group of poor societies, and so although we might be able to identify the most egregious forms of inequality, we remain unable to specify what *equality* (of opportunity) would mean. Second, we can agree that the existence of societies scoring very low on the HDI is a global injustice without agreeing about *why* it is an injustice—whether by virtue of the *inequality* between rich and poor societies, or simply by virtue of the absolute level of deprivation experienced by most members of the poorest societies. As I suggested earlier, our moral responses to the global status quo are overdetermined, and so we can agree in practice about what needs to be done most urgently to promote global justice without having to formulate explicitly the principles that lie behind this judgement.

I want to end this section of this chapter by stressing that the problem I have identified is not a technical problem of measurement: it is not that we lack the data that would enable us to compare societies in terms of the opportunities they provide for work, leisure, mobility, and so forth. It is essentially the problem of saying what equality of opportunity *means* in a culturally plural world in which different societies will construct goods in different ways and also rank them in different ways. The metric problem arises not just because it is hard to determine how much educational opportunity an average child has in any given society, but because the meaning of education, and the way in which it relates to, or contrasts with, other goods will vary from place to place. We can only make judgements with any confidence in extreme cases; and in those cases, what seems at first sight to be a concern about inequality may well turn out on closer inspection to be a concern about absolute poverty or deprivation, a concern which suggests a quite different general understanding of global justice.

IV

I have argued in the last two sections that neither equality of resources nor equality of opportunity represents a workable principle of global justice. In neither case can we measure the resources or opportunities available to people in different societies in a way that is neutral as between cultures—and such neutrality seems indispensable in a global principle of justice. But now I want to turn to the dynamic problem: the problem of whether substantive equality of any kind is a defensible principle for a world made up of separate societies each of which aspires to be self-determining. For this purpose, I am going to assume that we have discovered some neutral currency—I shall refer to it simply as 'advantage'—in terms of which a principle of global equality can be couched. Suppose, then, we could bring it about that at a certain moment people everywhere had equal access to advantage: no matter which society a person belonged to, he or she would have the same rights, opportunities, resources, etc.—all the various components that together make up advantage. What happens as we move forward in time, on the assumption that rights of cultural and political self-determination allow societies to make choices and decisions that will affect the level of advantage their members can enjoy in the future? To illustrate the problem, I imagined, in an earlier discussion, two societies starting out from an equal resource base, one of which Affluenza, decides to use up its resource endowment rapidly to sustain a high level of consumption, while the other, Ecologia, chooses to conserve resources by adopting a strict policy of sustainable development; similarly I contrasted Procreatia, which encourages large families and whose population therefore grows rapidly, with Condominium, whose strictly enforced family planning policy achieves a stable population size.[14] Assuming there are no other differences between these societies, the outcome must be that as we move forward in time, per capita resource levels will be greater in Ecologia than in Affluenza, and greater in Condominium than in Procreatia. Whereas at the beginning members of each of these societies enjoyed equal access to advantage, later on this ceases to be true.[15]

In introducing these examples, I am assuming that levels of advantage in each society are determined by domestic factors, and especially by the policies pursued by their respective governments. This is not, in general, a realistic assumption, and later in this book I shall be looking more closely at different explanations that have been given for the relative wealth and poverty of nations. The assumption is made here simply in order to probe what global equality might mean when applied to cases like this. So how could a supporter of global egalitarianism respond to these two-country stories?

One possibility would be to deny that there is any breach of equality, in the relevant sense, as the countries pursue their different paths of development. Provided that they were equally placed at the start, and the surrounding conditions are the same for each, what happens later does not destroy equality. This response corresponds to the version of egalitarianism favoured in domestic contexts by liberal political philosophers such as Dworkin, according to which equality is not compromised when individuals make choices as to how to use their equal initial share of resources, even though later on they are likely to enjoy different levels of resources: equality is satisfied so

[14] See D. Miller, 'Justice and Global Inequality', in A. Hurrell and N. Woods (eds), *Inequality, Globalization, and World Politics* (Oxford: Oxford University Press, 1999). John Rawls uses a somewhat similar pair of examples to undermine the idea of global distributive justice in *The Law of Peoples* (Cambridge, MA: Harvard University Press, 1999), section 16.

[15] In my original discussion I used the two-society parables to challenge equality of *natural* resources as a conception of global justice, and, as Tim Hayward has pointed out, this is compatible with thinking that *overall* per capita resource levels — humanly produced as well as natural — will be maintained in Affluenza and Procreatia over time: see T. Hayward, 'Global Justice and Natural Resources', *Political Studies*, 54 (2006), 349–69. But the parables can easily be recast so that overall per capita resource levels in Affluenza and Procreatia decrease over time, as their citizens enjoy high levels of consumption and reproduction respectively, where 'resources' are all those things that constitute personal advantage. So recast, they present a general challenge to global egalitarianism, understood as requiring equal access to advantage.

long as final inequalities can be traced to preferences and decisions for which the individuals in question can rightly be held responsible.[16] But there are obvious problems in transferring this liberal form of egalitarianism from individual to collective level. Even if all four of our imagined countries are democratically governed, individual citizens in Affluenza and Procreatia may very well dissent from what they see as the prodigal behaviour of the majority of their fellow-citizens. Why, then, is it fair that their level of advantage should be diminished over time by decisions for which they are not personally responsible? And what of those who are not yet born at the time when the egalitarian starting gate is introduced? They enter a world in which the level of advantage they can enjoy has already been partly determined by the actions of their predecessors. In what sense is there equality between them and others who are born into societies that have chosen differently?

Of course these questions also pose a challenge to those like myself who want to defend the idea that nations can be held responsible for the levels of advantage their members enjoy, so in due course they will need to be properly addressed.[17] I introduce them here to show that whatever plausibility initial-equality-qualified-by-choice may have as a conception of *social* justice, it does not transfer to a world in which *collective* choices remain an important determinant of the resource levels available to different societies. In this context, the proposal to implement an egalitarian starting point is simply far too weak as a conception of equality. So how else might global egalitarians respond to the two-country parables?

A second response is to say that justice requires redistribution from Ecologia to Affluenza and from Condominium to Procreatia so as to preserve equal access to advantage over time. But this proposal seems open to two very serious objections. The first is that it leaves very little incentive for states and their citizens to behave in the responsible way that Ecologia and Condominium have done. People in these societies have foregone opportunities for consumption

---

[16] See Dworkin, 'Equality of Resources', esp. 304–6 (*Sovereign Virtue*, 83–5).

[17] For this challenge, see for instance C. Fabre, 'Global Egalitarianism: An Indefensible Theory of Justice?', in D. Bell and A. De-Shalit (eds), *Forms of Justice* (Lanham, MD: Rowman and Littlefield, 2003), 315–30; C. Beitz, 'Social and Cosmopolitan Liberalism', *International Affairs*, 75 (1999), 526–8; and T. Pogge, *Realizing Rawls* (Ithaca, NY: Cornell University Press, 1989), 252–3.

and raising larger families on the grounds that it was important to conserve resources for the future on the one hand and to keep the population at a sustainable level on the other. But why do this, if profligate societies can expect to find themselves compensated from the stocks of resources saved or accumulated by societies that have shown themselves to be more prudent? Why be an ant, if the grasshoppers are guaranteed equal access to your store of winter provisions? A redistributive scheme of the kind proposed would undermine the responsibility a nation has for its own territory and other collective assets. But as Rawls remarks:

> ...an important role of government...is to be the effective agent of a people as they take responsibility for their territory and the size of their population, as well as for maintaining the land's environmental integrity. Unless a definite agent is given responsibility for maintaining an asset and bears the responsibility and loss for not doing so, that asset tends to deteriorate.[18]

Connected to the first objection is a second, which holds that it is simply unfair to tax Ecologia and Condominium in order to restore Affluenza and Procreatia to a position of equality. Citizens in the former societies have made sacrifices—they have consumed fewer natural resources, and raised fewer children than they would ideally have liked—in order to achieve policies that they see as either in their own long-term interests or as in the interests of their successors. They are now being asked to subsidize the shorter-term preferences of the members of Affluenza and Procreatia, who have meanwhile been enjoying their consumption bonanza and their larger numbers of offspring respectively. But justice does not seem to require transfers when inequalities in advantage can be traced back to preferences, whether individual or collective.[19] The only people with a prima facie claim for compensation appear to be those citizens

---

[18] Rawls, *The Law of Peoples*, 8.

[19] There are some riders that need to be added to this claim: preferences that have arisen in certain ways, or that the agent in question would like to rid herself of but cannot, may provide grounds for compensatory transfers. This is not the place, however, to engage with these difficult questions. For discussion, see, for example, the exchanges between Ronald Dworkin and Jerry Cohen: Dworkin, 'What Is Equality? Part I: Equality of Welfare', *Philosophy and Public Affairs*, 10 (1981), 228–40 (reprinted in Dworkin, *Sovereign Virtue*), section VIII; Dworkin, 'Equality of Resources', section III; G. A. Cohen, 'On the Currency of Egalitarian Justice', *Ethics*, 99 (1989), 906–44 section IV; R. Dworkin, 'Equality and Capability', in Dworkin (ed.), *Sovereign Virtue*, sections II–III; G. A. Cohen, 'Expensive Taste

of Affluenza and Procreatia who can demonstrate that they have consistently opposed the policies of their governments and would, if given the opportunity, have voted for and supported policies such as those adopted in Ecologia and Condominium (whether they do in fact have such a claim depends on how we understand collective responsibility for public policy, a topic I shall consider at length in Chapter 5).

Even if the current citizens of Affluenza and Procreatia cannot complain of unfairness as their access to advantage dwindles relative to the citizens of Ecologia and Condominium, what about children born into the first two societies, who have clearly played no part in enacting the relevant policies? Why isn't it unfair that they begin life with lower material prospects than their counterparts in the second two? Notice that if such a charge of unfairness can be laid, it must be directed in the first place against their predecessors who have caused the shortfall, and only secondarily against the current generation in Ecologia and Condominium. But what would the charge be? Assume that resource levels have not fallen to the point where the rising generation are unable to secure minimally decent lives. The charge, then, is that their access to advantage is lower than it might be if the previous generation had pursued more prudent policies, of the kind prevailing in Ecologia and Condominium. But this is not a very weighty complaint: it does not seem to be a matter of justice that our predecessors should leave us with any particular level of per capita resources, so long as the level does not fall below that required to sustain the institutions that make a decent life possible. (Precisely where that level should be set need not concern us here; the point is that it does not depend on the level achieved by the two counterpart societies). The children of Affluenza and Procreatia may, then, regret that their predecessors chose to act in the way that they did, but this by itself is not sufficient to give them a claim on the resources now enjoyed by the citizens of Ecologia and Condominium.

If wholesale redistribution to restore equality would not only create perverse incentives but also be unfair to those who are required to be net contributors, what other options are open to the would-be global egalitarian? One possibility would be to deny nations rights

Rides Again', in J. Burley (ed.), *Dworkin and His Critics* (Oxford: Blackwell, 2004); and Dworkin's reply in the same volume.

of self-determination in all those areas of policy that have an impact on levels of advantage. But since almost any policy decision of any significance will make *some* difference to a society's future resource and population levels, this is tantamount to doing away with self-determination altogether. Notice also that the position cannot be saved by requiring that each *generation*, at least, should be provided with an equal starting point. In this context, the idea that people belong to discrete generations, each of which passes certain benefits on to its successor, is in an important sense a fiction: the real picture is one of continual population replacement. So if we imagine once again a world in which each nation starts out from a baseline of equality, we cannot allow nations to make autonomous decisions over the course of one generation — thirty years, say — and then apply an international tax-and-transfer regime that restores equality for the next generation. In the meantime, all those reaching maturity in nations that pursue wealth-creating or resource-conserving policies will be materially advantaged relative to those reaching maturity in nations with other goals. And the same applies if we consider nations with contrasting population policies.

There is one final egalitarian proposal that we need to consider: we might permit nations to continue making autonomous decisions in areas such as resource conservation and population control, but then require them to provide free access to anyone who wants to join.[20] So long as the costs of moving between societies are relatively small, equal access to advantage would be preserved. People who are born into societies with relatively low per capita levels of resources and the like would now have the choice of moving to better-endowed societies. It is easy to see, however, that this would also undermine self-determination, in any world that we can realistically envisage. For decisions about admission to citizenship are inseparable from other decisions about the kind of society one wants to build. Some nations setting out on a path of rapid economic growth may welcome all-comers, or at least everyone who possesses marketable skills. Other nations with demanding environmental objectives may pursue policies aimed at reducing population growth among their existing members to zero — policies which

[20] For an argument in favour of freedom of movement along these lines, see J. Carens, 'Aliens and Citizens: The Case for Open Borders', *Review of Politics*, 49 (1987), 251–73.

would obviously be undermined if significant number of immigrants were permitted to enter. Yet other nations may want to preserve linguistic or religious aspects of their public culture, implying selection on these grounds among potential candidates for membership. An unlimited right to free movement would pre-empt policy choices of this kind, and in a different way hollow out the idea of national self-determination.[21]

My objections to the last two ways of implementing global egalitarianism—abandon national self-determination, or undermine it by allowing an unlimited right of free movement—do of course depend on the assumption that self-determination is something to be valued and that free movement is not in any case a human right. I shall have more to say about these questions later in this book. But recall here that the dynamic objection to global egalitarianism takes its place alongside two others already advanced: that there is no a priori reason to assume that global justice must be expressed in the form of a principle of equality, and that at least two of the main candidate principles advanced by political philosophers suffer from intractable metric problems. If a coherent, culturally neutral, principle of global equality could be formulated, and if we had strong grounds for believing that such a principle should play a central role in our thinking about global justice, then we might be driven to conclude 'so much the worse for national self-determination'. But since neither antecedent condition has so far been fulfilled, and since people everywhere appear to have a continuing wish to control their own destinies as members of independent nations, the dynamic objection seems to me to have considerable force. Provided that we attach *some* value to the idea that, in a culturally diverse world, political communities should be able to determine their own futures, we have a good reason to allow significant departures from global equality.[22] And this in turn is a good

---

[21] I shall explore this issue in much greater depth in Chapter 8.

[22] As I shall point out in the next section, valuing self-determination also gives us a reason to *limit* global inequality. I assume here that an ethically acceptable form of nationalism must treat self-determination as a universal value. So, on the one hand, national communities must have the opportunity to set their own priorities in terms of economic policy, environmental policy, population policy, and so forth, even though such collective choices will inevitably generate inequality along particular dimensions over time. On the other hand, these decisions may not deprive other national communities of opportunities for self-determination by,

reason for rejecting global egalitarianism as our theory of global justice.

V

I began this chapter by reminding readers of the sheer scale of material inequality in the contemporary world, while at the same time cautioning that we might have a number of different reasons for finding such inequality objectionable. I have now expended some efforts to show why global inequalities should not automatically be treated as unjust, simply because they are inequalities. But I want to conclude this discussion of global egalitarianism by considering some other reasons we might have for wanting the scale of these inequalities to be reduced—reasons, in other words, that are not directly reasons of justice, even though they may involve seeing inequality as indirectly a *source* of injustice.[23]

The first, and probably most powerful, of these is that material inequalities broadly conceived will naturally translate into inequalities of power, which then become a source of ongoing global injustice.[24] This can happen in a number of fairly obvious ways. When rich countries or rich corporations interact economically with communities or individuals who are very much poorer, they can set the terms of exchange and/or employment largely in their own favour, simply because they are far better placed to withdraw from the exchange than are those they exploit. This phenomenon has been

for example, creating global economic conditions in which their choices are almost completely constrained by the demands of economic survival. This need for a balance may justify transferring some powers—say over economic and environmental issues—upwards to international bodies. Valuing self-determination does not mean accepting national sovereignty in its traditional sense.

[23] The more general ideas that equality can be valued for reasons independent of justice, and that inequality can serve as a source of injustice without being unjust in itself, have been explored in T. M. Scanlon, 'The Diversity of Objections to Inequality', Lindley Lecture, University of Kansas, 1996, now reprinted in T. M. Scanlon, *The Difficulty of Tolerance: Essays in Political Philosophy* (Cambridge: Cambridge University Press, 2003), and insightfully applied to the global context in C. Beitz, 'Does Global Inequality Matter?', in T. Pogge (ed.), *Global Justice* (Oxford: Blackwell, 2001).

[24] See also here Debra Satz, 'International Economic Justice', in H. LaFollette (ed.), *The Oxford Handbook of Practical Ethics* (New York: Oxford University Press, 2003).

widely documented, and all that I need to emphasize here is that the principle of justice that is violated by such interactions is not a strongly egalitarian one. To protest when workers in Third-World countries are employed in sweatshop conditions by powerful corporations, one does not have to believe that these workers ought to enjoy the same terms and conditions, or have the same opportunities, as their counterparts in the developed world. The injustice at stake is more rudimentary.

Next, gross inequality between nations makes it difficult if not impossible for those at the bottom end of the inequality to enjoy an adequate measure of self-determination, unless one imagines, counterfactually, that rich nations' interest in self-determination concerns only their own internal affairs, and not what happens in the world outside. In reality, we know that inequalities in wealth and military power place severe constraints on the policies that weaker nations can pursue. So if our vision of a just world includes the idea that each nation should have a fair opportunity to pursue the particular goals that its members value most—the international equivalent of the domestic idea of toleration—then we are bound to be disturbed by inequalities on the current scale.

Finally, large inequalities in wealth and power also make it difficult to achieve what we might call 'fair terms of cooperation' internationally. Given that there are a number of areas in which nation-states need to cooperate with one another to their mutual advantage— environmental policy is perhaps the most obvious—the distribution of costs and benefits in the agreement that emerges is likely to be determined largely by the relative bargaining power of the various parties. If rich countries refuse to cooperate altogether, poor countries have few sanctions that they can deploy to bring the recalcitrants back to the negotiating table. The refusal of the USA to sign the Kyoto agreement is a clear instance of this phenomenon. Since we cannot place the parties behind a veil of ignorance, procedural fairness in practice requires that they should stand to gain or lose roughly the same amount when cooperation succeeds or fails, and large inequalities make this condition impossible to satisfy.

In a domestic context, there are two possible ways of tackling inequality as a source of injustice: reduce the inequality, or prevent it from having unjust consequences. We employ a battery of measures designed to prevent inequalities of wealth, in particular, from

creating injustice, ranging from the regulation of employment contracts, through limitations on the inheritance of wealth, to restrictions on the political uses of money. It is not so easy to envisage
global analogues of such measures. So in this respect, we may have
more reason to worry about global inequalities than about domestic
ones. Of course, for the very same reasons that large global inequalities pose a threat to justice, they are also difficult to counteract.
It is difficult to envisage rich states agreeing to narrow the gap in
wealth and power between themselves and poor states. Perhaps the
most hopeful prospect is of a world in which rich states, or blocks
of rich states, compete with each other on roughly equal terms, and
thereby also check one another's power vis-à-vis third parties. But
rather than speculate further along these lines, I want to turn to two
other reasons we might have for combating inequality, again drawing
inspiration from domestic analogies.

One such reason is the value of what we may call *equality of status*
or alternatively *social equality*. This is the idea of a set of social
relationships within which people regard and treat each other as
fundamentally equal, despite specific differences between them, and
it is valuable because of the quality of the relationships in question:
where it exists nobody has reason to feel subservient or deferential
and on the other hand nobody has cause to be haughty or conde-
scending.[25] Now, whatever one thinks about this idea, it might seem
that it can only apply within a bounded society and not to the world
as a whole. On the other hand, since travel and communication have
broken down perceptual barriers between societies, we do appear
increasingly to be living in a world in which people are likely to
compare their own positions with those of people in wealthier societies, and may find the comparison humiliating or degrading. Thus
it seems that there may be a global version of equality of status,
and that this would give us reason to be concerned about large
inequalities, especially of wealth and income, along dimensions that
give rise to perceived status differences.

Although there is something to this argument, I am inclined to be
sceptical. Equality of status is important among people who are in
daily contact with one another, and who share a common way of life.

---

[25] I have explored this more fully in 'Equality and Justice', *Ratio*, 10 (1997), 222–
37 and in *Principles of Social Justice*, ch. 11.

In so far as people belong to smaller communities and associations which form their main focus of identity, relationships between these subgroups matter less than how people are treated within them, since it is there that they will gain the sense of self-esteem that comes from being treated as an equal (or not as the case may be). Rawls makes this argument in the section of *A Theory of Justice* where he is responding to the objection that a society governed by the difference principle may still give rise to what he calls 'excusable envy':

...we tend to compare our circumstances with others in the same or in a similar group as ourselves, or in positions that we regard as relevant to our aspirations. The various associations in society tend to divide it into so many noncomparing groups, the discrepancies between these divisions not attracting the kind of attention which unsettles the lives of those less well placed.[26]

If this argument applies domestically, it seems it should apply with greater force still internationally, since for most people national boundaries mark out salient spheres of comparison and non-comparison. Admittedly international society lacks one feature which Rawls sees as counterbalancing material inequalities, namely equal citizenship: there is no common public sphere in which global citizens encounter one another as equals. On the other hand, cultural differences between societies make it less likely that people will be drawn into comparing themselves with each other along a single dimension such as material wealth. We might aspire to an international version of Michael Walzer's 'complex equality', where people in different societies derived their self-esteem in part from their society's success in living up to its own standards, whether materialistic or anti-materialistic.[27] I suggest this not in order to defend the existing global order, since extremes of poverty prevent national projects of all kinds from being pursued, but as a way of thinking about what social equality might mean in a culturally plural world.

---

[26] Rawls, *Theory of Justice*, 536–7.

[27] For the original version, see M. Walzer, *Spheres of Justice: A Defence of Pluralism and Equality* (Oxford: Martin Robertson, 1983), esp. chs. 1 and 13, and for discussion my essay 'Complex Equality', in D. Miller and M. Walzer (eds), *Pluralism, Justice and Equality* (Oxford: Oxford University Press, 1995).

Finally, equality is sometimes defended because of its connection to the idea of *fraternity*: if we want people to live together in close, solidaristic relationships, then we should ensure that they live in much the same material conditions. Fraternity on a global scale might seem an impossibility: however a weaker version of the same claim is that if we want a world in which people are willing to cooperate and to settle their differences peacefully, then this must also be a world in which material inequalities are not too great. In support of this, one might cite arguments made in recent years that the ultimate source of international terrorism is the material gulf that exists between the affluent West and the position of nations in the Middle East and elsewhere, giving rise to anger and resentment that manifests itself in hatred of all things Western.

Once again, my response to this argument is somewhat sceptical. What international cooperation requires is indeed not fraternity, but mutual respect between political communities who recognize their differences but also realize that they need to work together in a number of policy areas. And the precondition for this is not equality, but the absence of serious injustice. In other words, we have first to establish what justice requires in international contexts and having done that we can then set down the conditions under which international cooperation is likely to prove feasible. To assume that the relevant principle of justice here is some form of substantive equality is to beg all the questions raised in earlier sections of this chapter.

To sum up, once we have disentangled the issue of global inequality from questions about global justice, and in particular the deprivation suffered by people living in poor societies, we may still be concerned about the effects of large inequalities. But these concerns will be derivative, and will centre mainly on differences of *power* between rich and poor countries, and the likely effects of these on global justice in the future. If we could prevent the conversion of material advantage into political domination, there would be nothing inherently reprehensible about some nations being richer than others, and we might regard such inequality as an inevitable feature of a culturally diverse world.

Over the course of Chapters 2 and 3, I have been offering a critical appraisal of cosmopolitan theories of global justice. These theories are evidently very radical in their implications, if we set their requirements against the existing world order. But I have not rejected them for that reason: maybe global justice *does* require us to transform our world in quite fundamental ways. I have rejected them instead for ignoring the special responsibilities we properly owe to our compatriots, for failing to take proper account of the value of self-determination, for insufficient sensitivity to cultural difference, and so forth—in other words for philosophical and not merely political deficiencies. But I have not yet begun to develop my own alternative view, or in particular to defend the idea of national responsibility which will play a central part in that view. This is the task of Chapters 4, 5, and 6 that follow.

CHAPTER 4

Two Concepts of Responsibility

I

In Chapter 1, I said that an adequate theory of justice, and especially perhaps of global justice, has to strike the right balance between two aspects of the human condition: between regarding people as needy and vulnerable creatures who may not be able to live decently without the help of others, and regarding them as responsible agents who should be allowed to enjoy the benefits, but also to bear the costs, of their choices and their actions. In this chapter, I want to explore the idea of responsibility in greater detail, and to see how it relates to each aspect. More precisely, I want to distinguish two senses of responsibility, the responsibility we bear for our own actions and decisions—I shall refer to this as 'outcome responsibility'—and the responsibility we may have to come to the aid of those who need help, which I shall call 'remedial responsibility'. Both kinds of responsibility have key roles to play in a theory of global justice, but their roles are very different and should not be confused.

My wider aim in this book is to explain and defend the idea of national responsibility. Does it make sense to hold nations, and their individual members, responsible for the benefits they create for themselves and the harms and losses they inflict on themselves and others? If it does make sense, how far does national responsibility extend, and when does it run out? National responsibility, clearly, is a species of collective responsibility: individuals share in it only by virtue of their membership of those large communities we call nations. Many people find the idea of collective responsibility, and thus national responsibility, puzzling or even abhorrent. They believe that someone can only be held responsible for what he or she does or brings about personally. Responding to these doubts and concerns is the task of Chapter 5, where I explain how it is possible to treat nations as responsible agents, and explore under what circumstances such attributions of collective responsibility are justified. But here I want to focus on the idea of responsibility itself, and, in particular, on the distinction mentioned above between outcome and remedial responsibility. In proceeding in this way, I am assuming that when we apply these concepts to collectives such as nations, the concepts themselves are the same as those we apply on a much smaller scale to individuals. So throughout this chapter I shall use individual examples to clarify the two concepts, before turning in the following one to examine forms of collective responsibility.

Why is it necessary to begin with a conceptual analysis of the idea of responsibility itself? 'Responsibility' has proved to be one of the most slippery and confusing terms in the lexicon of moral and political philosophy. Arguments founder as the protagonists slide from one sense of responsibility to another without noticing what they are doing. The sheer variety of claims that can be made using the language of responsibility is nowhere better illustrated than in a well-known passage by Hart designed to demonstrate precisely this:

As captain of the ship, X was responsible for the safety of his passengers and crew. But on his last voyage he got drunk every night and was responsible for the loss of the ship with all aboard. It was rumoured that he was insane, but the doctors considered that he was responsible for his actions. Throughout the voyage he behaved quite irresponsibly, and various incidents in his career showed that he was not a responsible person. He always maintained that the exceptional winter storms were responsible for the loss of the ship, but in the legal proceedings brought against him he was found criminally responsible for his negligent conduct, and in separate civil proceedings he was held legally responsible for the loss of life and property. He is still alive and he is morally responsible for the deaths of many women and children.[1]

Hart went on to classify notions of responsibility under four main headings, hoping in this way to map the concept systematically. My aim here is less ambitious: it is to identify two senses of responsibility that I believe play a key role in our thinking about issues of global

[1] H. L. A. Hart, *Punishment and Responsibility: Essays in the Philosophy of Law* (Oxford: Clarendon Press, 1968), 211.

justice, and to separate these out from other senses of responsibility that are less relevant, if relevant at all. In other words, I want to narrow down the concept of responsibility for purposes of the task in hand, without in any way suggesting that I have given a definitive account of the concept as a whole.

The second reason for exploring the idea of responsibility is to defend it—or at least to defend the conceptions that I want to use—against a familiar critique, which arises from the fact that human agency is immersed in a stream of natural causation. Whenever human beings act, individually or collectively, their actions can always potentially be explained by causes that are not themselves instances of human action and decision, and this may appear to undermine the very notion of responsibility in any of the ways that we usually understand it. This is a deep problem, but I do not think it can be altogether avoided if we want to show that the idea of responsibility is normatively relevant. If we want to say that individuals or groups should sometimes enjoy benefits or suffer harms because they are responsible for creating those benefits or harms, then we need to show that this claim is not undermined by the fact that the benefit-creating or harm-creating decisions and actions can themselves be given a causal explanation. We need, in short, to establish when causal factors remove responsibility and when they do not ('always' and 'never' being the two extreme answers to this question).

Let me then begin by identifying the two concepts of responsibility that are needed for my larger project, and they can be introduced, and contrasted, most easily by means of an example. Imagine a teacher returning after morning break to find her classroom in a state of chaos, with desks overturned and rubbish strewn across the floor, and demanding indignantly 'who is responsible for all this mess?' Her question is interestingly ambiguous. She might mean 'who is responsible for producing this mess—who tipped the desks over, etc.?' or she might mean 'who is responsible for clearing up this mess—whose job is it to get the room ready for the next class?' Of course the same child might be responsible in both senses: Johnny might be responsible for clearing up the room because he is the one who tipped the desks over. But this is not necessarily the case, and even if it is, there are plainly two notions of responsibility in play here. One has to do with agents producing outcomes, and I shall call this idea, following Honoré, outcome responsibility;[2] the other has to do with agents having a duty or obligation to put a bad situation right, and I shall call this idea remedial responsibility. So, Johnny is outcome responsible for the state of the classroom if he is the one who created (under conditions yet to be specified) the mess, whereas he is remedially responsible for the state of the classroom if he is picked out (in ways yet to be specified) as the person whose duty it is to clear it up.

Notice also that in the case of both of these notions of responsibility, we can distinguish between identifying responsibility and assigning it. Identifying responsibility is a matter of looking to see who, if anybody, meets the relevant conditions for being responsible. What these conditions are will depend on the form of responsibility at issue. In the present case, for the teacher to identify Johnny as outcome responsible for the messy classroom, she would at the very least have to establish certain matters of fact, such as whether he had been in the classroom during break. She could get this wrong, and judge Johnny responsible for the mess when in fact it was Katy who was responsible. Assigning responsibility, by contrast, involves a decision to attach certain costs or benefits to an agent, whether or not the relevant conditions are fulfilled. The teacher may lack any concrete evidence about Johnny, but because she harbours suspicions based perhaps on past incidents, and because she feels the need to pin responsibility on someone, she says to him, 'I'm holding you responsible for the state of this room; you'll be in big trouble if it happens again'. Or, in the absence of any information about which child was in fact responsible for the chaos, she might assign responsibility to the whole class and impose some form of collective punishment or liability. Unlike identifications, assignments of responsibility can be justified or unjustified, but they cannot be correct or incorrect.

A parallel distinction can be drawn in the case of remedial responsibility. Remedial responsibilities can be identified where there are reasons for attaching them to one agent rather than another. In the classroom case, remedial responsibility would naturally fall on the children who were outcome responsible for the mess by virtue of

---

[2] See T. Honoré, 'Responsibility and Luck', in T. Honoré (ed.), *Responsibility and Fault* (Oxford: Hart, 1999).

having created it. But perhaps the class have agreed in advance that, because break-time rumpuses are common and the chief culprits are hard to identify, they will simply take it in turns to clear up the room. It may then be the case that George is on this occasion remedially responsible for the state of the classroom. However, the teacher might also simply assign remedial responsibility, picking out one child at random or choosing a child she dislikes. Here she would naturally say 'I'm making you responsible for clearing up this room'. Again such an assignment might be justified or unjustified—it would be unjustified if the teacher kept picking on a particular pupil, for instance—but it could not be correct or incorrect in the way that an identification could be.

It is easy to overlook or blur this distinction. The language of responsibility is partly to blame: we often say that we are holding certain agents responsible, and this can mean either that we are identifying or assigning responsibility. Furthermore, we often want our assignments of responsibility to track identified responsibility: we want to assign outcome responsibility to Johnny because he is, in fact, responsible for messing up the classroom, or remedial responsibility to George because he is indeed remedially responsible, on whatever grounds apply to the case. On the other hand, notice that we can sometimes be justified in assigning responsibility to agents who are not, in fact, responsible for what has happened. A parent who is away for the weekend on which her teenage son is holding a party may say before she leaves, 'I'm holding you responsible if anything gets broken' and the assignment applies even if the son was in no way involved in the upsetting of the china cabinet and could have done nothing to prevent it. Strict liability laws are another example of this: they can act as incentives to people to take particular care in, say, matters of food hygiene, or serve as a convenient way of assigning costs in circumstances where it is very hard to work out who is indeed responsible for the damage in question. Thus a rule to the effect that the driver of any car that runs into the back of another car is to be held responsible for the costs of the accident may be justified on these grounds, even though it will catch some drivers who were driving carefully and could not have avoided the collision, and who were therefore not responsible in the identification sense.

My interest is in responsibility in this latter sense. I want to establish what must be the case for people to be either outcome or remedially responsible for states of affairs like overturned class-rooms. As just indicated, this will help us decide which assign-ments of responsibility are justified and which are not, but it will not always settle the matter conclusively. Looking at responsibility assignments first, as some authors advocate, seems to me to get matters back to front. That is, we might begin by asking what overall social justice or social welfare requires, and then work out how responsibilities have to be assigned to produce these outcomes. We would then conclude that this is what it means to be responsible. Thus, taking the case of outcome responsibility, we would say that some agent A is responsible for an outcome O when we are justified in assigning O to A on the basis of our preferred conception of social justice and the like. But this ignores the fact that judgements of responsibility can have independent weight. We are uneasy about strict liability laws and other devices for assigning responsibility in the absence of actual responsibility, even if we think that on balance they are justified. It is that unease which motivates us to ask ques-tions like 'are agents ever really responsible for the outcomes they produce? If so, under what conditions?' If all that mattered was to find a justified way of assigning responsibility, we could set these questions aside as irrelevant.

II

Let me begin, then, with outcome responsibility, which is both the more difficult of the two ideas and the one that looms largest in debates about national responsibility. What does it mean for an agent to be responsible for an outcome? Responsibility here has a causal component—the agent must in some way have contributed to producing the outcome—but outcome responsibility needs to be distinguished from causal responsibility as such. Causal responsibil-ity is being invoked when we ask the question 'why did O occur?' We want to know which among the many conditions that had to be fulfilled in order for O to occur to single out as the cause of O. As Hart and Honoré among others have pointed out, there is no single correct answer to this question.[3] Which of the conditions

³ H. L. A. Hart and T. Honoré, *Causation in the Law*, 2nd edn (Oxford: Claren-don Press, 1985), esp. ch. 2.

we identify as causally responsible will depend on the nature of our interest: different people with different concerns might single out the behaviour of the driver, the condition of the car, the state of the road, etc., as the cause of a particular car crash. What this example also reveals is that human agency has no special status when causal responsibility is being allocated. We want to know why something happened, what made the difference between O's occurring and its not occurring, and from this point of view an erratic driver and a burst tyre may be equally good candidates, depending on why we are asking the question. Nor, if human agency is identified as the cause, does the nature of the causal chain between A and O matter. A's releasing a butterfly in China might in theory be identified as causally responsible for a hurricane in the Bahamas.

We ask about causal responsibility when we want to know why something happened. In the case of outcome responsibility, our interest is different. We want to know whether a particular agent can be credited or debited with a particular outcome—a gain or a loss, either to the agent herself or to other parties. There is a presumption that where A is outcome responsible for O, then the gains and losses that fall upon A should stay where they are, whereas gains and losses falling upon P and Q may have to be shifted: A may have to compensate P for imposing a loss, and Q may have to return something to A—a word of thanks at least—when she enjoys a gain. As I have already indicated, this presumption can be set aside. There may be overriding reasons why the gains and losses should be distributed differently. Nevertheless, we will not understand outcome responsibility, and how it differs from causal responsibility, unless we grasp this underlying normative concern. As Honoré has stressed, it appears integral to our conception of ourselves as freely choosing agents who can make a difference to the world that we should, in general, both be permitted to enjoy the benefits that our doings create and be required to bear the costs that may ensue.[4]

This can help us understand the contours of outcome responsibility, and especially cases in which causal responsibility and outcome responsibility come apart. First of all, there must be genuine

---

[4] See T. Honoré, 'Responsibility and Luck and 'Being Responsible and Being a Victim of Circumstance', both in Honoré, *Responsibility and Fault* (Oxford: Hart, 1999); also Hart and Honoré, *Causation in the Law*, lxxx–lxxxi.

agency as opposed to inadvertent bodily movement if the agent in question is to be outcome responsible. I am not, for example, outcome responsible for the carbon dioxide that I am producing by breathing as I write this book.[5] This does not mean that outcome responsibility requires intention. I may be responsible for results that I produce negligently—for instance for breaking the figurine that I handle carelessly and drop. What is required here is that there is a foreseeable connection between my action and the result. When I pick the figurine up, I can be expected to foresee that unless I handle it with care, there is a danger that it will break. Handling it roughly is an action of mine that with some probability will produce the result that does occur, so when the figurine smashes the responsibility and the costs fall to me. Moreover, outcome responsibility may be attributable even to agents who have taken some care to avoid the outcome that does in fact ensue. Suppose I decide to light a bonfire in my garden, taking all proper precautions, but unluckily a stray spark sets fire to my neighbour's garden shed. I am responsible for the damage and should reimburse my neighbour for the cost of replacing the shed.

Because the underlying notion is of an outcome being credited or debited to the agent, the nature of the causal chain matters too for such attributions of responsibility. As the chain becomes longer and more tortuous, responsibility dissipates. Thus I cannot claim outcome responsibility for fluky good results, even if I intended to produce them, such as sinking a hole in one on the golf course (I am not Tiger Woods). There has to be some connection between my capacities and the result for outcome responsibility to obtain, although it is hard to specify this precisely. In the case of bad results, the criterion is somewhat different: the result must be one that a person with normal capacities could have avoided producing. This is to cater for the fact that a person who is, say, unusually clumsy can be held responsible for the destruction he wreaks, even though, at the time of the events, he could not have averted them. We expect such a person to be aware of his shortcomings and therefore to stay

---

[5] There may be cases in which I become outcome responsible for the harmful results of such movement if I fail to take precautions that would avert such results—e.g. I am not normally outcome responsible for emitting germs by breathing, but I might become so if I chose not to wear a face mask in a hospital's intensive care ward.

away from shops full of cut glass.[6] Our interest in outcome responsibility arises from our interest in the fair distribution of benefits and burdens between different agents: as far as possible we want people to be able to control what benefits and burdens they receive, but we also want to protect them against the side effects, intended or unintended, of other people's actions.[7] On the other hand, a genuine accident—dropping the figurine because a loud gunshot just behind you causes you to jump—does not produce responsibility, even though the person who is causally responsible by virtue of having chosen to pick it up will no doubt feel in some sense responsible for the loss. It would not be right to ask this person to bear the costs: the causal connection between his action and the result is of the wrong kind.

Outcome responsibility must also be distinguished from moral responsibility, the kind of responsibility which is a necessary precondition for moral praise or blame. The conditions for moral responsibility are more demanding: to be morally responsible for something, you must be outcome responsible for that thing, but the converse does not hold.[8] We can see this most easily by considering the credit side of the ledger first. Suppose a naturally talented athlete produces a record-breaking performance or a naturally talented artist produces a masterpiece. Here the conditions for outcome responsibility will in normal circumstances be met. The athlete intended to run fast and directed her powers to that end; similarly for the artist. The outcome can be attributed to the agent in the right kind of way (it was not inadvertent or a fluke). But we would not hold either athlete or artist morally responsible for what they have done, in the sense

---

[6] Honoré refers to such persons as 'shortcomers'. See the discussion in Honoré, 'Responsibility and Luck'.

[7] I shall not discuss how these two concerns are to be balanced against each other as the limits of outcome responsibility are set. For illuminating critical discussions of Honoré's concept, see S. R. Perry, 'Honoré on Responsibility for Outcomes' and P. Cane, 'Responsibility and Fault' in P. Cane and J. Gardner (eds), *Relating to Responsibility* (Oxford: Hart, 2001) and P. Cane, *Responsibility in Law and Morality* (Oxford: Hart, 2002), esp. ch. 3.

[8] This is true when we are considering actions and the states of affairs that result from them. On the other hand, it seems that we can be morally responsible, and blameable, for forming certain intentions, even in cases where we are prevented from acting on these intentions—for instance, setting out to kill someone, but being forestalled by one's car breaking down on the way. Here there is no relevant outcome to be responsible for.

of being disposed to express moral praise. The outcome depends too much on natural talent, too little on those qualities of intention and will that attract moral assessment.

On the other side of the ledger, consider someone who is a poor gardener. He handles his seedlings clumsily, does not add the right kind of nutrients to the soil, and so forth, and as a result his yield is poor. He is outcome responsible for this bad result, but he is not morally responsible or morally blameable, except in circumstances where he has an obligation to try to produce a better result (say his family is dependent on the crop). His fault is not of the kind that draws moral appraisal. Keeping outcome responsibility and moral responsibility distinct is important for two reasons. First, as I have indicated, outcome responsibility often gives us reason to let gains and losses stay where they fall, or, in the different case where A is outcome responsible for a loss suffered by P, to require A to make compensation or redress. When we make these judgements, we need not be assigning moral praise or blame. A may, for instance, have been acting in a way that is morally innocent or even admirable, and yet may owe compensation to P since he is outcome responsible for a loss to P—for instance, if A damages P's car in the course of rushing Q to hospital. This will turn out to be important in the international context, where we need to keep responsibility-based claims for compensation separate from the question whether nations can be bearers of moral responsibility, and thus potentially subject to moral praise or blame. Second, if we are interested in the causal conditions of responsibility—which causal antecedents of a decision or an action are such as to relieve the agent of responsibility—then again we may find that outcome responsibility and moral responsibility must be kept apart. For instance, it is often said that an agent must have acted voluntarily if she is to be held responsible for what she does. But, assuming this is true, are the conditions for voluntariness the same for outcome responsibility as they are for moral responsibility?

III

This question leads us unavoidably to the deep problem that I mentioned earlier, namely whether the very idea of outcome responsibility is not undermined if we assume that all human behaviour is

explainable in principle by reference to causes that are not themselves instances of human action or decision. In attempting to resolve
it, I shall adopt a strategy that has been used to answer the parallel
problem about moral responsibility.[9] The strategy is this: to look at
those cases in which an agent is relieved of responsibility because
his actions have certain causal antecedents, and then to see whether
those cases generalize in such a way that the notion of responsibility itself is undermined. If the cases do not generalize—that is,
we can explain why certain causal factors undermine responsibility
but others do not—then we can maintain a normative defence of
responsibility along the lines sketched above, one that underlines the
connection between how we see ourselves as free agents interacting
with other free agents, and the idea of taking responsibility for the
outcomes of our actions. In other words, the general strategy takes
the following form: responsibility is something that we want to hold
on to, if we can, for normative reasons. Certain causal explanations
of human action are taken to relieve the agent of responsibility. But
we can give reasons to distinguish these explanations from others
that do not undermine responsibility in the same way.

So when, according to our everyday intuitions, do the causal
antecedents of an action relieve the agent of outcome responsibility
for its effects? First, we have cases which can be lumped together
under the heading of 'derangement', where the agent wasn't, as we
might say, 'in his right mind'. This might be the consequence of
extreme pain—torture, say; of sensory deprivation or the use of certain drugs; or perhaps extreme provocation. Here the agent acts in a
certain way, and may intend his action to have the result that it does,
but the action is not governed by the reasons he would otherwise
have, or by stable character traits. The external cause generates an
emotional response which in turn produces the action, by-passing
normal processes of decision. There is a sense, therefore, in which
the action, although performed by the agent, is not his action. Under

[9] See, for instance, R. J. Wallace, *Responsibility and the Moral Sentiments* (Cambridge, MA: Harvard University Press, 1996). I apologize to philosophers whose
main interest is in the problem of causal determination and responsibility for the
brief and therefore relatively superficial treatment of the problem that follows.
But given the use I make of the idea of responsibility (individual and collective)
throughout this book, I need at least to say where I stand on this underlying
question.

unbearable pain, for example, a normally trustworthy person betrays a friend. We do not consider him responsible because we think that almost anyone would do the same under these circumstances.

Second, we have cases of manipulation, where A induces B to do something she would not otherwise have done by distorting B's process of decision. The simplest case involves B acting on false information she has been given—doing one thing (poisoning P) when she believes she is doing something else (feeding P). Other cases might involve planting reasons in B's head—persuading her that she will go to heaven if she kills P, for instance. To escape responsibility, B must meet certain standards: she must not be unusually gullible, for instance. But if she does meet these standards—if, for instance, there is nothing to suggest that A has any malign intentions in relation to P, and therefore B has no reason to think that the bowl she has been handed contains anything other than nutritious food—then responsibility for P's fate passes from B to A. B, although in one sense an agent, is in reality A's tool. The reasons which direct her action are not hers, but A's.

Third, we have cases of coercion, where A forces B to do something by issuing a serious and credible threat: a bank robber holding a sawn-off shotgun tells a cashier to open the safe. In these cases, unlike those we have already considered, B is usually in command of her actions. She may be terrified by the threat, in which case it will come closer to being a case of derangement, but equally she may be able to weigh up the situation perfectly rationally and decide to comply—for instance she may decide that it is better to hand over the money than run the risk of people being shot. Again, provided her judgement is reasonable—the threat does indeed look serious— she is not responsible for the ensuing loss. Why is this? To simplify matters, let us suppose that A's threat is to kill P and that A is certain to carry this out. Then let us ask what B has control over. She cannot bring it about that the money remains in her safe keeping while P stays alive. She can choose between keeping the money and seeing P killed, or handing over the money and saving P's life. So if she decides to hand over the money, she is not outcome responsible for losing the money per se, but only for bringing about one outcome (money lost + P saved) in preference to another (money saved + P killed). The external cause operates here by narrowing down the options to these two. If we judge that the outcome she has brought about is the better one, then it should be entered on the credit side of her ledger even though it involves a loss of money.

In each case, the key question to ask is what the agent has control over—how far the outcome is within her power. In derangement cases, the agent loses control because of some overriding emotional force—he is maddened beyond reason, delusional, etc. In manipulation cases, control passes to the manipulating agent who acts through the person he controls. In cases of coercion, the area of control is narrowed down to two unpalatable alternatives by the coercer. Three further points are worth adding, however. First, implicit in all these judgements are expectations about the normal powers of agents—for example, their ability to see through deception or to resist very mild forms of coercion. A cashier who hands over the content of the bank vault having been threatened by a water pistol shares in outcome responsibility for the loss. Second, in saying that for responsibility to be attributed, the outcome must be under the agent's control, I do not mean to retract my earlier claim that we can be outcome responsible for some of the unintended consequences of our actions. When I light a bonfire that, as it happens, sets my neighbour's shed alight, this is certainly not something that I intended or expected, but nevertheless that outcome is in the relevant sense within my control. Honoré uses the analogy of betting to throw light on cases like this: in lighting the bonfire, I have taken a reasonable risk, but on this occasion I have gambled and lost. The key point is that I was fully in control when the bet was placed.[10] Third, responsibility can pass back to the agent if he is responsible for getting into the situation where he loses control. For instance, someone who goes out and gets helplessly drunk may be incapable of controlling his actions when he reaches that stage, but is nonetheless responsible for the damage he may inflict on himself or on others by virtue of choosing to, or allowing himself to, become intoxicated.[11]

In the manipulation and coercion cases, it may seem easier to relieve B of responsibility for the outcome because it belongs so obviously to A, the manipulator or coercer. What then of cases in which an agent's options are narrowed down by natural forces or

---

[10] Honoré, 'Responsibility and Luck', 25–7.
[11] This in turn could be defeated in certain cases—for instance, if the person has lost control of his life and his alcoholism is part of that.

occurrences? Suppose, to use a variant on a well-known example,[12] B is a water engineer who is able to divert a flash flood from one stream to another, causing a different village to be inundated in each case. Suppose she diverts the flood towards the village where the damage will be less severe. Given that the outcome here seems in the relevant sense to be within her control, should she not be held responsible for the damage that the flood causes?

Clearly B is not morally responsible for the damage: given the facts as stated, she has chosen the lesser evil and can justify her action, so there are no grounds for blaming her. But we know that outcome responsibility can attach to agents who act justifiably, like the driver who damages another's car while rushing a third party to hospital. In the present case, I think that some trace of outcome responsibility does rest with B. This is revealed by the fact that she may owe it to the inhabitants of the drowned village to explain to them why she had to take the decision that she did. But this responsibility is very weak, as indicated by the further fact that she is not required to make any form of material compensation despite the extent of the damage she has caused. The reason, I think, is the very narrow sphere of control that B possesses: allowing one village or the other village to be flooded. 'I had no real choice', she would naturally say, echoing the words of the coerced bank clerk. So again we see that causation undermines responsibility when it removes or radically restricts agents' control over outcomes.

If this conclusion is sound, then we can infer that causation generally does not threaten outcome responsibility. Consider any normal case in which a person acts to produce outcomes that benefit or harm himself or others, where he is fully in control of what he does. We might in theory offer a causal explanation of his actions, beginning with his genetic make-up, continuing through his childhood experiences, the opportunities available to him in later life, and so forth. Even if this explanation were available, it would not invalidate the claim that the agent was in the relevant sense in control of his actions and the resulting outcomes. He acted for reasons that he grasped, he knew what he was doing, other options were open to

[12] The original being the trolley problem invented by P. Foot and popularized by J. J. Thomson, 'The Trolley Problem', in J. J. Thomson (ed.), *Rights, Restitution and Risk: Essays in Moral Theory* (Cambridge, MA: Harvard University Press, 1986).

him, and so forth. That is a strong enough sense of control to support outcome responsibility.[13] Where particular causal antecedents
appear to undermine responsibility, it is because they invalidate one
or other of these conditions, as they do in the examples we have
considered. There is no reason to suppose that all causal explanation
can be assimilated to the kinds of causation involved in derangement,
manipulation, etc.[14]

My argument here is not meant to imply that identifying outcome
responsibility is a straightforward matter. There are two main areas
of uncertainty. One has to do with identifying more precisely the
causal antecedents that can relieve agents of responsibility. As we
have seen, our judgements about whether a particular person was
responsible for what he did involve holding him to certain normative
standards. If he was put under pressure to act in a certain way, was
the pressure such that we would expect someone to be able to resist
it? Should he have understood that the action he undertook was
likely to have the consequences that it did? Although where we set
the bar will be heavily influenced by what we observe to happen
in the case of most people—if nine others were able to resist the
pressure, then the tenth should also have resisted—there is still room
for setting it higher or lower in general, and for adjusting it to take
account of individual circumstances. What if somebody has an irra-
tional fear of spiders such that threatening her with a spider induces
her to perform some very harmful act? Should we say that this
person ought to have conquered her fear in the circumstances, or that
for her this is a genuine case of responsibility-annulling coercion?
As we see later, parallel questions arise in debates about national
responsibility, for instance when we ask whether whole populations

[13] Here I follow those authors who caution against attempting to make our
concept of responsibility 'metaphysically deep'. As Williams points out, it is one
thing to worry about how we can discover what a particular agent intended on a
particular occasion, whether he was in a normal frame of mind, etc.; quite another to
think that our notions of voluntariness and responsibility are threatened 'by some
opposing and profound theory about the universe (in particular, to the effect that
determinism is true)'. If we try to respond to such a supposed threat, Williams
argues, our concepts will be transformed beyond recognition. See B. Williams,
Shame and Necessity (Berkeley, CA: University of California Press, 1993), ch. 3,
and also M. Matravers, 'Luck, Responsibility and "The Jumble of Lotteries that
Constitutes Human Life"', *Imprints*, 6 (2002), 28–43.
[14] See further T. M. Scanlon, *What We Owe to Each Other* (Cambridge, MA:
Harvard University Press, 1998), ch. 6, sec. 5.

can be held responsible for not resisting oppressive regimes that inflict damage on other peoples.

The other area of uncertainty concerns how far agents can be held responsible for the remoter consequences of their actions. We have seen that outcome responsibility extends beyond the agent's own intentions: we can be judged responsible for outcomes that arose inadvertently or by omission. A natural requirement is that the agent should have been able to foresee the consequences of what he did, or failed to do. But in interpreting this condition we have to steer a mid-course between, on the one hand, asking what the particular person in question could have foreseen, given his actual capacities and state of mind, and on the other asking what was foreseeable in principle, given complete knowledge of the circumstances in which the action occurred. We have, in other words, to apply a standard of reasonable foresight: an agent is outcome responsible for those consequences of his action that a reasonable person would have foreseen, given the circumstances.[15] Thus a man who fires an air rifle in a wood and hits a passer-by cannot escape responsibility by saying that he believed the wood to be empty, or that he did not know that airgun pellets could hurt human beings, even if he says these things in good faith. A reasonable person would know that people can be hidden from view in woods and that pellets can maim them. But again the standard of reasonableness we use here is partly a normative one, and therefore open to dispute.

From one point of view, tort law can be seen as a way of resolving such disputes by assigning outcome responsibility according to well-defined principles. It has other functions too — it provides incentives to people to take proper care when their behaviour is likely to impact on others; it supplies remedies to people whose interests are harmed by assigning responsibility for the harm somewhere, even if this involves a form of strict liability — but in large part it serves to specify when people are to be treated as outcome responsible and when they are not, giving concrete shape to the pre-legal idea of responsibility I have been trying to outline.[16] Unfortunately, there is as yet no real equivalent to this in the case of nations, or nation-states, and

---

[15]   Here I follow A. Ripstein, *Equality, Responsibility, and the Law* (Cambridge: Cambridge University Press, 1999), ch. 4.

[16]   See, for instance, J. Coleman, *Risks and Wrongs* (Cambridge: Cambridge University Press, 1992), Part III; S. Perry, 'The Moral Foundations of Tort Law', *Iowa*

the impacts they make on outsiders, so in developing the idea of national responsibility we have to rely on intuitive (and therefore partly contestable) judgements of reasonableness when it comes to assigning consequences.

There is one further aspect of this worth mentioning before we turn to the idea of remedial responsibility. When calculating the consequences of someone's action for the purposes of allocating outcome responsibility, we have sometimes to consider the response of other people: in particular, what steps did they take to avert damage to themselves? Tort law includes the idea of contributory negligence, where A's liability to P whom he has injured is reduced or even eliminated when it can be shown that P's conduct was defective in some way—that he was behaving recklessly, for instance. This idea seems sound if we think of outcome responsibility as a basis for assigning costs and benefits fairly among agents each of whom is capable of governing their own behaviour. Why should A bear all the costs of his action when they would have been less had P behaved sensibly? So outcome responsibility does not necessarily extend to the actual consequences of behaviour, but in some cases at least to the consequences that would have occurred if other agents had responded reasonably. Again, we encounter a normatively laden notion of reasonableness, which may give rise to disagreement. Must P's response have been the optimal response to A's action, or does responsibility remain with A so long as P's response was at least adequate by some standard? It requires no great leap of imagination to see how questions of this kind can arise about national responsibility: if nation A changes its trade policy in a way that is damaging to P, what can we reasonably expect members of P to do in return if responsibility for the damage is to remain with A?

IV

I turn now to the second concept of responsibility distinguished at the beginning of this chapter, remedial responsibility. Responsibility of this kind is clearly quite different from outcome responsibility. With outcome responsibility we begin with an agent whose

Law Review, 77 (1992), 449–514; Ripstein, *Equality, Responsibility, and the Law*, chs. 3–4.

action produces beneficial or harmful consequences, and we ask which of these consequences can be credited or debited to the agent. With remedial responsibility we begin with a state of affairs in need of remedy, like the overturned classroom, and we then ask whether there is anyone whose responsibility it is to put that state of affairs right. If there is, then we require that person to act and stand ready to apply sanctions of one form or other if she fails. What needs to be explored here is how remedial responsibilities arise, and what relationship they bear to the other kinds of responsibility (causal, moral, and outcome) we have already discussed.

As the classroom example illustrates, the idea of remedial responsibility potentially applies whenever we encounter a situation in need of remedy. My particular interest, however, is in cases where the remedy is owed to a person or a group of people who are unjustifiably deprived in some way. They fall below some threshold in terms of material resources, or they are in danger or distress. They may, for example, be victims of famine or a natural disaster, or they may have been humanly deprived by robbery or civil war. On a much smaller scale we might think of the person who collapses in the street or is stranded by a rising tide. For the time being I want to bracket off questions about the source of their deprivation. What matters for remedial responsibility is that the situation is one that demands to be put right: it is morally unacceptable for people to be left in that deprived or needy condition, and there is no overriding justification such as that they are being fairly punished for some wrongful deed. So initially it seems that there is a moral requirement that falls on everybody else to provide the help or the resources that are needed. It is not necessary for present purposes to decide whether this moral requirement is better interpreted as a matter of justice or, for instance, as a humanitarian duty. All that matters is that we find it morally unacceptable if the deprived person is simply left to suffer.

The problem that arises, however, is that an undistributed duty such as this to which everybody is subject is likely to be discharged by nobody unless it can be allocated in some way. We need to pick out one person or several people (or perhaps an organized group) as having a special responsibility to put the situation right. This is what it means to be remedially responsible: to have a special responsibility, either individually or along with others, to remedy the position of the deprived or suffering people, one that is not equally shared with all agents; and to be liable to sanction (blame, punishment, etc.) if the responsibility is not discharged. Unless remedial responsibilities are identified, then even well-meaning people are likely not to intervene, either on the grounds that their intervention would be superfluous, or for the less generous reason that they do not see why it is their job to pick up the pieces when so many others are spared that cost.

Since deprivation is often severe, and since the problem I have just identified is pervasive, human societies have evolved mechanisms for assigning remedial responsibilities. People are given jobs or roles that carry such responsibilities with them, so that if we ask who is responsible for safeguarding this particular battered child, the answer is likely to be the social worker who has been assigned to the case. But unfortunately there are many instances in which no such mechanism exists—who should go to the aid of a person who collapses in the street, for instance?—and where we must therefore try to discover reasons of principle to identify responsible agents.[17] Indeed, at global level, the absence of such mechanisms is all too evident: no one is formally assigned the responsibility to rescue the victims of famine or civil war, for instance, so it becomes crucially important to see whether we can have good reason to hold particular governments or nations responsible in such cases.

I want to propose what I shall call a 'connection theory' of remedial responsibility.[18] The basic idea here is that A should be considered remedially responsible for P's condition when he is linked to P in one or more of the ways that I shall shortly specify. The nature of the link varies greatly: in some cases, as we shall see, it provides a substantive moral reason for holding A remedially responsible, whereas in others it simply picks A out as salient for non-moral reasons. We might think, therefore, that some forms of connection

---

[17] I have discussed the general issue raised here in greater detail in ' "Are They My Poor?": The Problem of Altruism in a World of Strangers', *Critical Review of International Social and Political Philosophy*, 5 (2002), 106–27, reprinted in J. Seglow, *The Ethics of Altruism* (London: Frank Cass, 2004).

[18] I first put this forward in 'Distributing Responsibilities', *Journal of Political Philosophy*, 9 (2001), 453–71, but have revised it in several respects in the meantime.

should always be given priority over others; I shall argue, however, against this. The point to bear in mind is that the weight of justification is borne by the pressing need to relieve P, and the necessity of identifying a particular agent as having the obligation to provide the relief. The fact that some of the links appear morally flimsy when taken by themselves matters less when this point is grasped.

I shall suggest six ways in which remedial responsibilities might be identified. The first three look backwards and correspond to forms of responsibility discussed earlier in this chapter; the second three are of a sharply contrasting kind.

1. *Moral Responsibility*: The agent who is remedially responsible for P's condition is the agent who is morally responsible for bringing it about. This way of identifying remedial responsibility is intuitively very powerful. In order to be morally responsible for P's condition, A must have acted in a way that displays moral fault: he must have deprived P deliberately or recklessly, or he must have failed to provide for P despite having a pre-existing obligation to do so (e.g. he had promised to feed B, but then defaulted on his promise by doing nothing). So A is to be blamed for P being in the state that she is, and by holding A remedially responsible for P we not only create a mechanism for getting P out of that condition but we also help to put right the moral imbalance between A and P (to put the balance completely right, more has to be done—for instance, A may have to apologize to P for the original act or omission, as well as remedying the effects of that act or omission). It would be wrong to say that we are punishing A by holding him responsible, but making him pay the cost of helping P is a natural way of expressing blame for what he has done. So we have strong, independent moral reasons for wanting to assign remedial responsibility on this basis.

2. *Outcome Responsibility*: As we have seen already, A can be outcome responsible for P's condition without being morally responsible for it. This will be the case, for example, if P's deprivation is a side effect of some action of A's, that is morally neutral or even justified. A might enter into fair economic competition with P, causing her in the process to go bankrupt. So long as the outcome is not due to P's negligence—it happens because A is better at business than P, or has more luck—it will be A's responsibility. The same applies to our earlier example of a bonfire that sets fire to a neighbour's

shed, despite all reasonable precautions having been taken. If in cases like this, P's subsequent condition calls out for remedy, then it will seem natural to pin the responsibility on A, who has brought about the deprivation, albeit inadvertently. Is there an independent moral reason for doing this? I think there is, although the reason is less compelling than in the case of moral responsibility. When we act as free agents among other free agents, we expect to keep the benefits that result from our actions, and so we should also expect, in general, to bear the costs. Of course we do not always assign costs in this way: people who drive others out of business in the course of fair competition are not expected to provide compensation, nor are athletes who win races expected to comfort the losers. But if the costs are heavy—the defeated shopkeeper becomes destitute, or the losing athlete becomes suicidal—then remedial responsibilities cut in, and, other things being equal, they fall to the agent who was outcome responsible.[19]

3. *Causal Responsibility*: What if A is the cause of P's deprivation, but in such a way that he cannot be regarded as outcome responsible for P's condition? How could this be? There are cases in which A is not acting in the sense that outcome responsibility requires—for example, I move backwards in a crowded bar to avoid somebody else who is pushing forward and as a result knock over someone else's drink. There are also cases in which the causal link between action and result is so bizarre and unpredictable that it would be unreasonable to hold A (outcome) responsible—for instance, I walk round the corner of a street, causing a workman standing on a ladder to start and fall off the ladder. And there are cases where A acts under coercion or constraint—B says he will kill P, unless A first punches her in the face. Here, then, the only link between A and P is one of physical causation. Nonetheless, this may be enough to trigger remedial responsibility in certain cases. The causal relationship suffices to pick A out from the universe of others who might also come to P's

---

[19] Not everyone shares my intuition that in these competitive examples the winners may have remedial responsibilities to the losers when the latter suffer serious harm. Of course, we can establish practices that assign these responsibilities elsewhere—we can set up social safety nets for bankrupt shopkeepers and counselling services for defeated athletes—and there may be good reason to do this. My argument is that in the absence of such practices primary responsibility lies with the agent who is outcome responsible for the harm.

aid. The mere fact that it was I who caused the workman to start identifies me as the person who should attend to see whether he has been injured in the fall.

Admittedly, it can be difficult to separate pure causal responsibility from relationships of outcome and/or moral responsibility on the one hand, and what I shall shortly describe as capacity on the other. That is, we might be inclined to see the person who steps backwards in the bar and upsets a drink as to some degree negligent, and therefore morally responsible; we might think that causing workmen to fall off their ladders is one of the hazards that goes with being a pedestrian, and therefore assimilate that example to outcome responsibility. Equally, the person who is causally responsible for P's condition may also be the best placed to help him subsequently: if I stumble in the street and knock a fellow pedestrian down, then by virtue of physical proximity it will normally be easy for me to help him up. Nonetheless I am inclined to treat causal responsibility as an independent source of remedial responsibility, one that continues to be relevant even in the absence of the other factors just mentioned. My stumbling in the street might have been unavoidable; there may be many others who are equally well placed to pick up the person I have knocked over; nevertheless, the bare fact that I have caused him to fall connects me to him in a special way and *ceteris paribus* makes me remedially responsible. Or consider someone who under coercion injures another. If the coercer himself disappears from the scene, causal responsibility falls on to the person who has been made to inflict the injury, and with it the responsibility to care for the injured party. There is of course no moral reason why agents who are causally responsible and nothing else beyond that should be judged remedially responsible for the conditions they have caused. But in the absence of other forms of connection, the importance of fixing remedial responsibility somewhere explains why bare causation can count.

4. *Benefit*: Suppose that A has played no causal role in the process that led to P's deprivation. He has nonetheless benefited from that process—for instance, resources that would otherwise have gone to P have been allotted to A. In these circumstances, A is not responsible for P's condition in any of the three ways we have so far identified, and yet indirectly he is linked to that condition. He is

an innocent beneficiary, let us assume, but the benefit would not have arisen unless P had been deprived. This may be sufficient to make him remedially responsible for P. Suppose that the agents who have deprived P have vanished from the scene or are no longer capable of helping P. A, however, is not in need himself and can restore resources to P. There is a moral reason for him to do this — he has been unjustly enriched by the train of events that led to P's being deprived, even though he himself has not behaved unjustly. In general, the reason invoked here is not particularly strong: we do not think innocent beneficiaries always have an obligation to return their gains. It is also important to distinguish benefit from capacity, the next criterion to be considered. Sometimes beneficiaries, by virtue of having been advantaged, are also the people most capable of supplying the remedy without incurring significant costs. It seems nonetheless that benefit by itself can serve as a ground of remedial responsibility: being a beneficiary of the action or policy that has harmed P establishes a special connection with P of a kind that stands independently alongside the other forms of connection that make up this list, and that may in certain cases provide a decisive reason for A to remedy the harm that has befallen P.[20]

5. *Capacity*: One rather obvious way of identifying an agent who can be held responsible for bringing relief to P is to establish who is capable of supplying the remedy. If A is uniquely in this position, then he is remedially responsible for P: if I am the only person walking along a river bank when a child falls in, then it is my responsibility to rescue the child. In other cases, where several agents are to different degrees capable, we may assign responsibility to the most capable, or divide it between them along the lines of the classic principle: 'From each according to his abilities, to each according to his needs'. The rationale for this criterion is evident: since the whole purpose of identifying remedial responsibilities is to get help to P, picking the agent who is actually able to provide that help makes obvious sense.

---

[20] For a thorough exploration of the circumstances under which benefiting from wrongdoing may give rise to remedial responsibilities, and more generally responsibilities to compensate, see D. Butt, 'On Benefiting from Injustice', *Canadian Journal of Philosophy*, 37 (2007), 129–52.

On closer inspection, however, the capacity principle seems to blend two different factors which may not always point in the same direction. One has to do with the effectiveness of different agents in remedying the situation; the other has to do with the costs they must bear in the course of doing so. Suppose there are a number of people standing on the river bank when the child falls in. We may think that whoever is the strongest swimmer should go to the rescue. But suppose that person is also fearful of strong currents (so that although he is an effective rescuer, the rescue causes him considerable distress)—or perhaps he simply dislikes the kind of attention that goes along with a successful rescue. If A is slightly stronger than B, but A's costs are also much higher, is it obviously the right solution to hold A responsible for rescuing P? In this context, judging capacity may involve us in trading off effectiveness against cost in identifying the relevant agent.

6. *Community*: The final criterion that I want to consider for attaching remedial responsibility to A is that he should be attached to P by ties of community. This term is used loosely here to cover the great variety of bonds that link people in groups—ties of family or friendship, collegiality, religion, nationality, and so forth. Communitarian relationships are in general independent of and prior to the fact of P's deprivation. But because it is integral to these relationships that they involve special obligations to fellow-members, when P stands in need of assistance, an obvious place for her to look is to agents linked to her in this way. If a child goes missing, for instance, not only her family but also neighbours, the local community, etc., will feel a special responsibility to try to find her. They are in no way causally responsible for her disappearance, have no special capacity, etc., but the fact of community picks them out as bearers of responsibility. In some cases being connected to P by ties of community will also mean having certain kinds of expertise that will help in relieving her condition: if A and P share the same language or cultural background, for instance, A may be better able to work out what P needs. So here community is connected with capacity. But this is a special case, and it would be a mistake to try to reduce community to one of the forms of connection already discussed. It stands on its own feet as an independent source of remedial responsibility.

V

Up to this point, my analysis of remedial responsibility has been primarily descriptive, in the sense that I have sought to identify the criteria that are, as a matter of fact, called into play when remedial responsibilities are distributed, and briefly considered to what extent they have independent moral force. But the analysis is somewhat indeterminate in so far as it gives no normative advice as to what to do when the different criteria conflict. Suppose A is morally responsible for P's condition, but B has far greater capacity than A to remedy it: who should then be assigned remedial responsibility for helping P if only one such agent is needed? If A has pushed P into the river, but is a weak swimmer, whereas B, a passer-by, is an experienced lifeguard, who should carry the primary responsibility for rescuing P?

   Let me explore two possible ways of responding to this question. One would be to attempt to arrange the criteria we have explored in rank order: we look first for an agent who fits the criterion we judge to be the strongest, then if there is no such agent, we move on to the next criterion in order of strength, and so forth. Such an approach might seem plausible in the case of the first three criteria in the above list. If we can identify someone who is morally responsible for P's condition, we should hold them remedially responsible; failing that, we look for someone who is outcome responsible for P's condition; failing that again, we look for someone who is merely causally responsible. But this does not generalize plausibly when we bring the other three criteria into the picture. Consider the case of the person pushed into the river. We might think that the person who pushed her should also be responsible for rescuing her. But moral responsibility can come in degrees: carelessly pushing someone into a river is blameworthy, but not as bad as pushing them deliberately. Are we to say that a careless pusher who is also a weak swimmer should be held responsible for the rescue in preference to the lifeguard who can make the rescue easily and safely? Getting P out of the river seems more important here than enforcing the moral responsibility of the pusher. Or think of a case where A is outcome responsible for a serious loss borne by P, but the main beneficiary is not A but B—A is employed to harvest fruit belonging to P, but because of incompetence on A's part most of the fruit ends up scattered on land belonging to B. Depending on the specifics of the case, we may believe that either A or B should be primarily responsible for covering P's loss. It is not plausible to say, in general, that outcome responsibility trumps benefit or vice versa.

Another response would be to challenge the idea of remedial responsibility as I have been using it. Someone might argue that two quite different phenomena are being conflated in this discussion. On the one hand, we have the idea of making redress to someone who has been wronged; on the other, we have the idea of bringing aid to someone who is in need. In a particular case these might overlap, but they remain conceptually distinct. Returning to my six-part list, the first four criteria belong under the first heading—they represent different ways of redressing a wrong or an injustice—whereas capacity and community belong under the second—they are relevant as ways of determining who should help people in need, irrespective of whether they have been wronged.

There is some truth in this challenge, in so far as it draws attention to the fact that in explaining the moral force of the various criteria, we invoked quite different considerations. It is also true, and worth recognizing, that moral responsibility and outcome responsibility can ground claims for redress even in cases where the injured party is not deprived in some absolute sense. If I deliberately or carelessly ruin one of your paintings, I owe you compensation even though, without the painting, you are still in a perfectly comfortable state overall. Your position is not one that calls out for remedy, except in the sense that there is an injustice that requires redress. I am outcome responsible for your loss, but not remedially responsible in the sense in which I have been using the term.

Despite this concession, I want to defend the idea of remedial responsibility I have been examining. Although we can imagine simple cases such as the one just described in which redress and deprivation come apart, in many cases they are intertwined. We become concerned about redress only because the person who has suffered the loss is thereby deprived in a way that causes independent moral concern. Suppose you have a large apple tree on the border of your land, and I own the neighbouring field, which I cultivate in such a way that the yield of your tree is reduced. What, if anything, do I owe you? If the crop is still amply big enough to meet your needs, then although you might still have some legal case for compensation, the moral case seems vanishingly weak. The case changes radically if you are dependent on the crop and will go hungry if the yield is reduced.[21] My outcome responsibility now matters because of the absolute level of deprivation I have brought about.

In many, probably most, real-world cases of deprivation, assigning remedial responsibility involves applying multiple criteria, which are also somewhat opaque. It may be uncertain how the deprivation came about, and whether the roles played by individual agents in that process are such that they bear moral or outcome, as well as causal, responsibility. Questions of capacity may be equally problematic, particularly when relative costs are taken into account. If we take a complex case, such as poverty in developing nations, all of these questions arise, and it may seem that fixing remedial responsibilities is impossible. Such cases certainly show us why having formal mechanisms for assigning responsibility are so vital—in the absence of such mechanisms, everyone can find a plausible reason for shifting the burden of responsibility elsewhere. In designing the mechanisms, however, we have no alternative but to consider each of the agents— primarily states and international institutions—able to provide a remedy and then to assess how strongly each is connected to the impoverished group. Sometimes the upshot will be to assign responsibility to one agent who stands out as most closely connected; in other cases remedial responsibility will be shared between several agents. There may be disputes about how the different sources of connection should be weighed against each other—for instance how far the historical impact of the As on the Ps should be weighed against the greater present capacity of the Bs. As far as I can see, there is no algorithm that could resolve such disputes. We have to rely on our intuitions about the relative importance of different sources of connection.

---

[21] It may also change somewhat if the previous large crop has come to play a significant role in your life, for example if you are known in the neighbourhood for the delicious cider that you generously offer your friends and acquaintances. Under such circumstances my action harms you and I may have remedial responsibilities.

VI

In this chapter I have been outlining two concepts of responsibility that appear to play a crucial role in debates about national responsibility and global justice. As we have seen, they are conceptually quite distinct, and yet normatively closely connected— outcome responsibility provides us with one important way of identifying remedial responsibility. Outcome responsibility starts with agents and asks how far they can reasonably be credited and debited with the results of their conduct. Remedial responsibility starts with patients—people who are deprived or suffering—and asks who should shoulder the burden of helping them. As I suggested at the beginning, these two kinds of responsibility reflect contrasting aspects of the human condition: on the one hand, we are vulnerable creatures whose lives may not be worth living unless others are willing to come to our aid and supply us with resources. These needs impose obligations of justice on all those who are able to help, but because these obligations are initially so diffuse, we need the idea of remedial responsibility to make them specific and effective. On the other hand, human beings are choosing agents able to control their actions and to take responsibility for the results. For such agency to exist they must be willing to bear losses and enjoy gains, whether these fall immediately on themselves or on others. The idea of outcome responsibility permits that. It prevents one person, or group of persons, imposing losses on other. At the same time, where losses are self-imposed, it frees other agents from having to make good the deficit.

In our thinking about responsibility, we have to keep these two aspects of the human condition in proper balance. This applies both to questions of social justice and to questions of global justice. If we focus too narrowly on outcome responsibility, then when confronted by situations in which people are in desperate need, but where responsibility for this appears to lie with them, or with no one at all (as in the case of natural disasters), we will fail to see injustice. If we focus too narrowly on remedial responsibility, we may encourage a victim mentality and deny people who are in need of help the status of agents who can, and ought to, take control of their lives. We need each concept to play its proper role in our thinking about justice, and the obligations that it imposes.

Although in this chapter I have occasionally used examples in which responsibility is attributed to collectives, my primary focus has been on the responsibilities of individual agents. But can the concepts developed here really be applied to collective bodies, and communities such as nations? This is the issue that I take up in the chapters that follow, where I investigate the idea of national responsibility.

CHAPTER 5

National Responsibility

I

In everyday political discourse, we often make judgements that seem to involve holding nations responsible for their actions, or for the consequences that follow from those actions. We say that Russians are responsible for the civil war in Chechnya, Israelis for the fate of Palestinian refugees, and Americans for their excessive contribution to global warming. We also make judgements about events that have occurred in the national past: we hold Britons responsible for the deaths of one million Irish people in the potato famine, Turks for the Armenian genocide, and Germans for the Holocaust. But against who or what are these judgements directed? In particular, are they directed against *nations* or against *states*? Is it the British people or the British state that we hold responsible for the Irish deaths?

In this chapter, I want to show that judgements of national responsibility are not only defensible (under appropriate conditions), but are also more basic than judgements of state responsibility. Often, when states are held responsible for the outcomes they produce, they are being judged as agents of the people they are supposed to serve. State responsibility might seem easier to establish, since where states are involved we can point to specific institutions— governments, legislatures, armies, and so forth—as the bearers of responsibility, and we can also point to particular acts—passing legislation, signing treaties, or declaring war—for whose consequences states can be held responsible.[1] But to limit responsibility to states

---

[1] See, for instance, T. Erskine, 'Assigning Responsibilities to Institutional Moral Agents: The Case of States and Quasi-States', *Ethics and International Affairs*, 15 (2001), 67–85.

considered as formally constituted bodies would have several disadvantages. One of these is that if we divorce state responsibility
from national responsibility, it then becomes difficult to show how
individual people can share in the responsibility to compensate those
whom the state they belong to has harmed, whereas if we treat states
as acting on behalf of nations, such collective responsibility will be
easier to establish. Another is that we may want to hold nations
responsible for actions performed by states that no longer exist, as
in the case of the continuing responsibility of the German people for
acts carried out by the Nazi state that was destroyed and replaced
in 1945. A third is that, although nations may act through states,
in which case national responsibility and state responsibility may
coincide, in other cases this may not happen. Think, for example,
of a stateless nation whose quest for self-determination leads it to
carry out a terror campaign against the people holding it in subjec-
tion. For these reasons, it is important to show that our practice of
holding nations responsible, for both the 'self-regarding' and 'other-
regarding' effects of their actions, is philosophically defensible.

The sense of responsibility that is immediately at stake here is
outcome responsibility. As we saw in Chapter 4, judgements of
outcome responsibility can in some circumstances ground judgements of remedial responsibility: if A is outcome responsible for P's
deprivation, A may have a remedial responsibility to help P. But this
does not always follow, since remedial responsibilities can be distributed on other grounds as well. Perhaps some resistance to the idea
of national responsibility arises because it is thought automatically
to entail remedial responsibility, especially in the case of poverty-
stricken peoples: if nation A is responsible for its own dire economic
condition, as a result of civil war or disastrous public policy, then
no one else has a remedial responsibility to go to its aid. But this
does not in fact follow, for reasons that were laid out in the second
half of Chapter 4. Moreover, outcome responsibility will in most
cases be shared between nations in an interdependent world. So we
should not foreclose the discussion of national responsibility on the
grounds that it is bound to produce repugnant conclusions about
global justice, with poor nations abandoned to their fate. How far
national responsibility extends is a large issue that the present chapter will not try to resolve decisively. Its aim is more modest: to show
that national responsibility, as a species of collective responsibility,

makes (ethical) sense, and therefore that the people who make up a nation may sometimes properly be held liable for what their nation has done.

This chapter's scope is limited in one further way: it is concerned with national responsibility in the present, that is with the outcome responsibility of those who currently belong to the nation for what the nation does now. Responsibility for the national past is a separate matter, to be dealt with in Chapter 6. Clearly, many judgements made in practice about national responsibility presuppose that the present generation of compatriots can be held responsible (in some sense) for what their predecessors did; at the very least they may be remedially responsible for harms caused by earlier generations, through colonial expansion, warfare, slavery, etc. Such judgements raise difficult questions about the inheritance of responsibility that cannot be answered using the apparatus I shall deploy below. We might therefore see the complete argument for national responsibility as involving three separate steps. First, we need to explain and justify the idea of collective responsibility in general. We must show that it makes sense to hold collective groups—teams, crowds, corporations, and so forth—responsible for the effects of what they do in such a way that the individual members of those collectives can properly be held liable for the ensuing costs.[2] Second, we must extend the argument to nations, understood at this point as contemporaneous groups of people; we must show that nations have features such that the general analysis of collective responsibility applies also to them. Third, we need to develop a further argument

---

[2] Some authors consider it important to distinguish between groups that have a formal structure—with a defined membership, a fixed procedure for making decisions, and so forth—and those whose members are more loosely associated. This affects assignments of collective responsibility—for instance, Cane ascribes 'group responsibility' to corporations and other such rule-governed bodies, but 'shared responsibility' to individuals acting in concert. He argues that in the former case but not the latter, responsibility and the ensuing liability to pay costs remains with the group and does not descend to individual members. See P. Cane, *Responsibility in Law and Morality* (Oxford: Hart, 2002), ch. 5. Others have challenged this view: see, for instance, L. May, *The Morality of Groups: Collective Responsibility, Group-Based Harm and Corporate Rights* (Notre Dame, IND: University of Notre Dame Press, 1987). I prefer to use the idea of collective responsibility to cover all these cases, leaving it an open question for the moment what difference the presence or absence of a formal structure makes when responsibility is assigned. In the case of nations, I address this question in Section III of this chapter.

that can apply to nations considered now as extended in historical time—we need to show, in other words, that it makes sense to hold present-day nations responsible for the actions of their forebears in such a way that their current members can be held liable to bear the (self-regarding or other-regarding) costs of those actions. Each step is of course challengeable and needs careful argument. In this chapter, I try to justify steps one and two, and in the one that follows, step three.

II

To help our thinking about collective responsibility generally I want to elaborate two models, which I shall call the like-minded group model and the cooperative practice model. These are to be thought of as ideal types to which real groups may approximate to different degrees, and that may in practice overlap—a real group, that is to say, may have some features that belong to the like-minded group model and some that belong to the cooperative practice model. I do not want to claim that it is a necessary condition for ascribing collective responsibility to a set of individuals that they should display like-minded group or cooperative practice features. It has been argued with some plausibility that there are circumstances in which we are justified in holding even randomly assembled collections of individuals responsible for the outcomes of their actions.[3] But I think that these are the models that are most relevant in thinking about national responsibility; I shall argue later that we are justified in holding nations responsible in so far as they display like-minded group and/or cooperative practice features. So let me begin with the idea of a like-minded group.

It is easiest to introduce this by means of an example. Consider a mob rampaging through a neighbourhood, terrifying the residents, destroying property, and looting shops. Different participants in the mob act in different ways. Some actively attack persons or property; others shout abuse or issue threats; yet others play a more passive role, running alongside the activists, urging them on and contributing generally to the atmosphere of excitement and fear. If after the

[3] See V. Held, 'Can a Random Collection of Individuals be Morally Responsible?', *Journal of Philosophy*, 68 (1970), 471–81.

event we had to apportion individual moral or legal responsibility for what has happened, we should need to identify the precise causal role that each had played in creating the damage. But it is also the case, I want to argue, that the whole mob bears collective responsibility for the effects of the riot, and together they can be held liable for the cost of repairing the damage to persons and property. The specific intentions of each participant at the beginning of the riot may have been different: some may have started out meaning to inflict physical damage; others may have wanted to make a political point; and so forth. What matters is that each person took part with the same general attitude—'teaching them a lesson', 'showing them that we mean business', etc.—and each made some causal contribution to the final outcome, whether this involved engaging directly in destructive acts, or merely in supporting and encouraging those who did. Indeed, we may not be able to disentangle individual contributions. Consider several members of the mob throwing bricks at a plate-glass window at roughly the same moment: we cannot say that any particular brick thrower was (causally) responsible for smashing the window, but we *can* say that the group as a whole is outcome responsible for the damage they brought about.[4]

What justifies us in saying not only that the mob *as a collective* is responsible for the damage that it has caused but also that its individual members share in the collective responsibility?[5] Recall that our interest in outcome responsibility derives at least in part from our

[4] See Michael Zimmerman's argument that where more people than were necessary to bring about O all acted in a way designed to bring about O, no participant can escape responsibility by claiming that his or her actions were inessential to O's occurring. (M. Zimmerman, 'Sharing Responsibility', *American Philosophical Quarterly*, 22 (1985), 115–22.)

[5] For a thoughtful discussion of the circumstances in which the collective responsibility of groups either does or does not descend to their individual members, see J. Feinberg, 'Collective Responsibility', in J. Feinberg (ed.), *Doing and Deserving: Essays in the Theory of Responsibility* (Princeton, NJ: Princeton University Press, 1970). Feinberg takes as an example of group responsibility without individual responsibility the case of a car full of railway passengers who fail to prevent an armed bandit robbing the train. Acting together the passengers could have overcome the robber, but this would have been heroic, since one or two would probably have been shot in the course of doing so. It seems to me, however, that the group of passengers is only responsible for not preventing the robbery in a *causal* sense. There is no collective *outcome* responsibility, in the sense used here, since as we saw imputations of outcome responsibility depend on judgements about what it is reasonable to expect of normal people. It was not reasonable to expect the

interest in remedial responsibility. We want to know whose responsibility it is to clean up the vandalized neighbourhood. Attributing responsibility to the mob as a collective will not help unless responsibility also descends to the individual members, because these are the people who will actually have to bear the clean-up costs (we might imagine them contributing their labour or their money to the clean-up operation). But we also have to show that attributing responsibility to individual rioters is justified, and this we can do by recognizing that they contributed to a collective activity that was certain to inflict damage on other people, whether they specifically intended the overall outcome that actually occurred. Recall that outcome responsibility does not in general require intention: we hold people responsible for the consequences of their actions that a reasonable person would have foreseen, whether these consequences were intended and whether they were actually foreseen by the person in question. This condition was surely met in the case of the riot; anyone participating should have foreseen what a hostile crowd entering a vulnerable neighbourhood was likely to do.

Given that the responsibility of the collective descends to its individual members, why not dispense with the notion of collective responsibility altogether, and instead focus entirely on the outcome responsibility of each individual? As I indicated earlier, it may be impossible to assign specific shares of responsibility for what has happened to individual members of the mob. We may not know what causal contribution each made to the final outcome, and even if we did, it might still be controversial how responsibility should be divided (if there are recognized community leaders among the group conducting the rampage, should they be assigned a greater share of responsibility simply by virtue of that fact?). So our starting point must be that the group is collectively responsible, that other things being equal they are remedially responsible for restoring the damage they have caused, and that every participant bears an equal share of that responsibility. It may then be possible for the participants themselves to make finer-grained allocations of responsibility, depending on what is known about the activities of each member,

---

passengers to tackle the bandit, and so they should not be asked to bear the loss of property that their inaction entailed.

whether some can be identified as ringleaders, and so forth.[6] This, however, is irrelevant from the point of view of achieving a fair distribution of costs and benefits between the rioters and their victims. From this perspective, all that matters is that the rioters as a group can be held collectively responsible for the damage they have caused, and are therefore liable to bear the costs of repairing that damage. Similarly, when nations behave in ways that are harmful either to themselves or to others, our primary concern will be to establish collective outcome responsibility for what has happened, in so far as this bears on the allocation of costs between nations. Within each nation, particular individuals or particular subgroups may then be identified as bearing a special responsibility, depending on the circumstances. I shall not attempt to investigate principles for distributing responsibility *within* nations.

Returning now to the like-minded group model, this applies to groups who share aims and outlooks in common, and who *recognize* their like-mindedness, so that when individual members act they do so in the light of the support they are receiving from other members of the group. This is particularly clear in the case of the mob. As students of crowd behaviour have long recognized, people in crowds behave *differently* precisely because of the contagion of those around them.[7] Groups that exemplify this model are not then just collections of individuals who happen to have aims in common; they are groups whose members interact in such a way that even those who play no direct role in producing the outcome that concerns us may nonetheless properly be brought within the scope of collective responsibility. And this allows us to widen the model to take in cases that are less obvious than that of the rioting mob, but that bring us closer to the idea of national responsibility.[8]

---

[6] c.f. here Larry May's argument that when groups are responsible for harm, the share of responsibility that descends to each member should depend on the causal role played by that person in bringing about, or failing to prevent, the harm. See L. May, *Sharing Responsibility* (Chicago, IL: University of Chicago Press, 1992), chs. 2 and 6.

[7] See the analysis in May, *The Morality of Groups*, chs. 2 and 4.

[8] The rioting mob example illustrates how individuals can share in collective responsibility for outcomes that they did not specifically intend, which is one important aspect of national responsibility, but in other ways it works less well as a model of national responsibility. It involves a specific event, limited in time, and it also allows for a relatively clear demarcation between those who share in the responsibility and those who do not: to escape responsibility, in normal

A good example is provided by Feinberg's discussion of racism in the post-bellum American South.[9] Acts of violence against blacks, Feinberg suggests, were carried out in a context in which Southern whites generally passively sympathized with such acts, even if they were not actively involved in perpetrating them, as a result of a widely shared culture of racial inequality. In these circumstances, it makes sense to hold all Southern whites collectively responsible for keeping blacks in a state of subjugation. Feinberg argues that this includes whites who did not approve of the beatings and lynchings on the grounds of their solidarity with the majority who did. This distinguishes the example from the case of the rioting mob, where I claimed that relatively passive rioters who shared in the general aim of the riot but took no physical part in inflicting damage on persons and property nonetheless were collectively responsible for that damage. The argument in the case of the post-bellum American South is that where a community of people shares a set of cultural values, one of whose effects is to encourage behaviour that results in outcome O, then everyone who belongs to the community shares in the responsibility for O, even if they disapprove of it.[10] By participating in the community they help to sustain the climate of opinion in which the actions in question take place, even if they voice their opposition to the actions themselves.[11]

This of course raises the question of what individuals have to do in order to *escape* from collective responsibility for the results of the actions of groups to which they belong. I shall postpone discussion of this important question in order to introduce my second model of group responsibility, the cooperative practice model. Again, an example may help to bring out its main features.

---

circumstances, all one has to do is to stay at home. I therefore extend the model to include cases that exhibit neither of these features.

[9] Feinberg, 'Collective Responsibility', 247–8.

[10] See also here the discussion in May, *Sharing Responsibility*, ch. 2, section 4.

[11] For another example, consider the collective responsibility of the Roman Catholic Church for the sexual abuse of minors by priests. There is little doubt that the overwhelming majority of Church members condemn this behaviour. Yet the general mindset of Church officials has been such that effective measures to prevent such abuse have not been put in place. We could say that the Church has tolerated the abuse even while not condoning it. So while individual responsibility clearly rests primarily with the small number of priests who have taken advantage of their position to abuse minors, we can hold the Church collectively responsible for the general ethos that allowed this to happen.

Consider an employee-controlled firm whose manufacturing process has unwanted environmental effects—it involves depositing chemical substances in a river, for instance. Members are divided on whether this practice should continue, or whether a different, more expensive, technology should be used, but when the matter is discussed the majority favours staying with the existing process. The employees, I want to claim, are collectively responsible for the environmental damage they are causing, and if they are required to pay the costs of cleaning up the river, these costs should be borne collectively by all the members. Why does collective responsibility extend to the dissenting minority? They are the beneficiaries of a common practice in which participants are treated fairly—they get the income and other benefits that go with the job, and they have a fair chance to influence the firm's decisions—and so they must also be prepared to carry their share of the costs, in this case the costs that stem from the external impact of the practice. Here again we see the difference between holding people *morally* responsible for the results of their actions and holding them outcome responsible. It would not in general be right to blame (or punish) members of the minority for what their firm has done to the river—they could quite properly defend themselves by saying that they spoke out against the manufacturing process that caused the pollution. But it is right to hold them, along with others, liable for the damage they have caused.

The cooperative practice model goes further than the like-minded group model in one direction, because there is no requirement here that the group in question should share a common identity or have aims in common; participating in the practice and sharing in the benefits may be sufficient to create responsibility. In another way, however, it is more restrictive, because it imposes fairness requirements that the like-minded group model need not impose. Change our example in such a way that the decisions about which technology to use are taken by a small clique who keep the rest of the workforce in the dark about the whole issue, or skew the distribution of rewards in such a way that one section of the workforce could reasonably claim to be working on exploitative terms, and collective responsibility no longer extends to all members, but at most to the decision-makers or the leading beneficiaries of the practice.[12] The like-minded

[12] One can envisage intermediate cases here, and one might also explore further the question whether *both* procedural and substantive fairness are necessary in

group model does not depend in this way on substantive fairness. So long as the group in question is genuinely like-minded, its collective responsibility does not depend on how it allocates power, status, or other benefits among its members. We can therefore see these models as indicating two complementary sources of collective responsibility which may, as I have indicated already, overlap in particular cases. You can share in collective responsibility for an outcome because you form part of a like-minded group that has brought the outcome about, or because you are a participant in a cooperative practice that produces the outcome, or for both reasons at once.

My analysis of the sources of collective responsibility may however set liberal alarm bells ringing. For it implies that in certain circumstances membership in a group may be sufficient to establish responsibility for acts performed by other members of that community even when one is opposed to those acts, and this goes against an intuition that it is only what a person does herself that can make her responsible for harmful outcomes.[13] If membership is sufficient for responsibility, then it seems that no one can escape responsibility except by physically removing himself from the group in question, a course of action that it may be very difficult if not impossible for the person to take. So we need to take a closer look at the conditions under which a member *can* legitimately claim that he has acted in such a way that he bears no personal responsibility for the harmful consequences of the policies and practices of his group.

As already suggested, mere inactivity will not, in general, relieve members of their group-based responsibility. A member who stands by and does nothing still provides passive support to other members of his group (in the like-minded group case) or still receives his share of the benefits (in the cooperative practice case). Nor is it sufficient

order for the cooperative practice model of responsibility to apply, but I shall restrict my analysis to the simple cases.

[13] This intuition is not universally shared. Indeed, paradoxically, it may occur more often to liberal observers looking in from the outside than to those on the ground who find themselves included in collective responsibility. For a robust statement of the opposite view—that mere membership may be enough to implicate someone in collective responsibility no matter what she does—see H. Arendt, 'Collective Responsibility', in J. W. Bernauer (ed.), *Amor Mundi: Explorations in the Faith and Thought of Hannah Arendt* (Boston, MA: Martinus Nijhoff, 1987). Arendt, does, however distinguish collective responsibility in this sense—she calls it 'political responsibility'—from moral and legal responsibility, in much the same way as Karl Jaspers (see n. 21 below).

simply to voice your opposition to the activities that are imposing the costs. Speaking up is better than doing nothing, of course, but as our discussion of Southern white racism revealed, even someone who voices opposition to certain of her community's actions may still, by virtue of her membership, contribute to the climate of opinion in which those actions take place, because she subscribes to the community's values in general, reinforces them in her daily activities, and perhaps supports the community in material terms. Nor, if the group has a formal procedure for reaching decisions, will voting against the action or policy in question necessarily exempt you from responsibility. Democratic procedures work on the basis that people who find themselves on the losing side of a vote must regard themselves as bound by the result, unless that result is so morally offensive, or so far outside the competence of the decision-making body, that some form of civil disobedience (or its equivalent) is justified. Just as a member of the minority must, except in these special circumstances, comply with the majority's decision even though she strongly dislikes it, so she must bear her share of the costs if the decision turns out to have costly consequences. After all, were she in the majority, she would expect the losing minority to pay *its* share.

So what must a dissenting member do to escape from collective outcome responsibility? Unfortunately, it is difficult to say anything more precise than that he or she must take all reasonable steps to prevent the outcome occurring. What is reasonable in a particular case will depend on how seriously harmful the prospective outcome is, and what costs different courses of action will impose on the dissenter. Consider the case of the post-bellum American South. Anyone who joined the NAACP or one of its predecessor organizations, who took part in public demonstrations against white racism, and so forth, and who by virtue of these activities faced hostility from his neighbours in the white community would surely have met the condition. Equally someone who embarked on these activities but was then deterred by serious threats from racist groups to the safety of her home and family should also be exempted from responsibility—this is not a cost that we can reasonably expect an average person to bear in the course of trying to stop racist attacks on blacks (some people may turn out to be willing to bear the costs, but in doing so they reveal themselves to be heroic: our imputations of responsibility must be based on [admittedly imprecise] judgements about what can reasonably be expected of people in general, not on what exceptional individuals are able to achieve).

But what if the most effective way to combat the outcomes that you oppose is to work inside the relevant group or practice, rather than adopting a stance of outright opposition? In the racism case, for instance, a person opposed to violence towards blacks might believe, with justification, that he would have greater influence by staying within the white community and gently shaming it into adopting more liberal attitudes, whereas by actively opposing the community he would simply be written off as a 'nigger-lover' whose opinions could henceforth be ignored. Or again, where a group governs itself through democratic procedures, the most effective way to change its policies may be to stay within democratic parameters — accepting rather than contesting decisions when you find yourself in a minority — since this will increase your influence in the long term. In cases like this, it may be ethically better to accept a share of collective responsibility for a bad outcome than to seek to avoid responsibility by distancing yourself from the group or the practice that produces the outcome. This is not a paradox, provided we keep it in mind that we are talking about outcome responsibility rather than moral responsibility of the blame-incurring kind. The person who with good reason decides that he should use his position as an insider to try to change the way that the collective behaves does the right thing and is not morally blameable for the ensuing harm (when his efforts fail or only partly succeed), but he does render himself liable to pay his share of the costs.[14]

Is it an objection to the view of collective responsibility advanced here that it makes people responsible for outcomes simply by virtue of their membership of certain groups, or their participation in certain practices, even though they may not have chosen to be in that position? A liberal Southern white may bitterly regret that he

[14] A more elaborately described example in support of the conclusion that individuals can be held responsible for the results of practices that they oppose can be found in J. Raikka, 'On Disassociating Oneself from Collective Responsibility', *Social Theory and Practice*, 23 (1997), 93–108. Raikka, however, attempts to argue that the individuals involved in such cases may be morally blameworthy even though they are acting rightly, all things considered. I believe that blame is inappropriate here, and that a different sense of responsibility is at stake, as argued in the text.

finds himself in a community that supports violence against blacks, with the result that he has to choose between radical opposition that relieves him of collective responsibility, and working within the community to change attitudes while continuing to share in responsibility for the violence. Bear in mind, however, that in other, less controversial, cases people can become responsible for outcomes as a result of chance factors over which they have no control. Virginia Held gives the example of three pedestrians who happen on the scene of an accident. In order to save the victim they must act in concert. It is only chance that brings them together in that place, and yet, confronted by the accident and being the only people able to rescue the victim, they become collectively responsible for the harm he suffers if they fail to form a team and act.[15] This may be unlucky for them: they may have to miss appointments or dirty their clothes to get the victim to safety, but this is luck of an unavoidable kind. We would not be impressed if one of the pedestrians asked 'why me?', not just as an expression of frustration at having to miss the concert he was hurrying to attend, but as an attempt to dodge responsibility for the situation that now confronted him. In a similar way, I may see it as regrettable bad luck that I belong to a political community many of whose members are willing to support policies with terrible outcomes, making it incumbent on me to get my hands dirty and help to create a majority for some less objectionable (but still objectionable) alternative. My responsibilities are thrust on me by my circumstances, but they do not cease to be my responsibilities because of that.

The claim that people who belong to like-minded groups or who participate in cooperative practices are collectively responsible for the results of their behaviour does not, then, depend on the assumption that entry into such groups or practices was voluntary or consented to. This is going to be important when we turn our attention to nations in the following section, because, exceptional cases apart, people do not choose to belong to national communities: they are simply born into them. What I have tried to do in this part of this chapter is to sketch two models of collective responsibility, two cases in which people can justifiably be held liable for the costs incurred by

[15] Held, 'Can a Random Collection of Individuals be Morally Responsible?', 479.

groups of which they are members. The next step is to see whether the conclusions we have reached can be applied to nations. Granted that nations are communities of some kind, do they display the features that would justify ascribing collective responsibility to their members?

III

What, then, is a nation, to repeat Renan's famous question?[16] It is first of all a group with a common identity: belonging to the nation is partially constitutive of the identity of each member (partially constitutive because national membership does not exclude belonging to other communities of identity, such as religious or ethnic groups). In other words, nations are not merely collections of individuals who happen to be juxtaposed in physical space, in the way that the three pedestrians were in Held's example referred to above. They are groups of people who feel that they belong together because of what they have in common. Second, among the things they have in common is a public culture, a set of understandings about how their collective life should be led, including principles that set the terms of their political association (a principle of political equality, for instance), and guide, in broad terms the making of political decisions (a principle of individual rights, for instance). This shared public culture does not exclude significant cultural differences among subgroups within the nation, nor does it mean—this is important to stress—that there is no political disagreement among the members. On the contrary, people who share a public culture can disagree quite radically about what the principles embedded in that culture entail in relation to particular issues. Third, nations are groups whose members recognize special obligations to one another, so that in that respect they are not like groups formed on a contractual basis to realize the predetermined aims and objectives of the members, where the reason for becoming and remaining a

---

[16] E. Renan, 'What is a Nation?', in A. Zimmern (ed.), *Modern Political Doctrines* (London: Oxford University Press, 1939). My concern in the paragraph that follows is to highlight features of nationhood that are relevant to the question of collective responsibility rather than to distinguish national communities from other social groups. For the latter, see my discussion in *On Nationality* (Oxford: Clarendon Press, 1995), ch. 2.

member is entirely instrumental. Fourth, the continued existence of the nation is regarded by the members as a valuable good, so that even if we could imagine the instrumental benefits of membership, such as personal security, being provided in some other way, they would regard with horror and dismay any suggestion that the nation should be disbanded and its individual members assimilated to other national groups, or that the whole nation should simply be absorbed into a larger unit without its distinct identity being preserved.

If these four features are necessary for a group of people to constitute a nation, one might wonder whether any nations do, in fact, exist. Nationality should not be confused with common citizenship: the citizens of a given state may bear two or more national identities. But even when that possible source of confusion is removed, we still need to ask whether every co-national does in fact share the set of beliefs and attitudes I have listed in characterizing nationality. Must every French person believe that he or she has special obligations to co-nationals, or that the continued existence of France is intrinsically valuable, if there is to be a French nation? If so, it seems very unlikely that this or any other nation actually exists.[17]

But the condition just proposed is too stringent. What is necessary to the existence of a nation is that the beliefs and attitudes in question should be generally held (and believed by those who hold them to be correct), not that they be held by every single member. This is true of communities of all kinds. For a religious community to exist, for example, its members must hold certain beliefs in common, and behave in certain ways towards each other, but it can survive the presence of a few dissident members whose beliefs are heterodox or whose behaviour violates principles of reciprocity. One cannot say precisely how much dissidence can occur before the community ceases to exist as such, and similarly with nations there must come a point where indifference towards the national identity, or unwillingness to acknowledge national obligations, would mean

---

[17] Could not one sidestep the problem by defining as French only those people who held the beliefs and attitudes in question? The problem here is that the full-fledged French will want to include the deviants as part of the French nation, partly on the grounds of cultural commonalties, and partly because they think that these others *should* recognize special obligations and so forth. They regard the deviants as reprobates rather than as outsiders, in other words. So one cannot simply adopt a narrower criterion for being French.

that the nation in question had become something else—a group of people who just happened to share a language or some other cultural traits, perhaps. So when speaking of nations I am making a broad empirical assumption that there exists, among many peoples, a sufficient degree of convergence in attitudes and beliefs that the four conditions are met for the great majority of members.

Belonging to a nation also involves a fifth feature: the aspiration to be politically self-determining. But in the real world this aspiration is met to very different degrees. There is a spectrum of possibilities here, of which three in particular are worth singling out. A nation may lack self-determination entirely, as when it is subject to imperial rule from outside. Next, it may possess its own state, but have a despotic or authoritarian form of government, where the ruler or ruling elite is drawn from the people and claims to be acting in their name, but there is no mechanism that subjects them to popular control. Finally, the nation may be governed democratically with major decision-takers answerable to the citizen body as a whole at periodic elections. We need to distinguish these cases in order to decide how far nations can be regarded as collective agents who might be held responsible for the consequences of what they do. Nations can be said to act collectively in two different senses. First, because their members share an identity and a public culture, both the practices that they follow and the behaviour of individual members can be seen as expressions of that common identity and culture. We say, for instance, that Germans are hard-working, meaning that the way individual German workers behave reflects a shared norm of industriousness that forms part of the public culture of Germany. Or we find that the pattern of family relations in a particular country, and the number of children who are on average produced, corresponds to the religious or other cultural values of the nation in question. Here there is no deliberate decision to behave in a particular way or to adopt a particular practice, but nevertheless what happens reflects the national culture in a fairly direct sense. Second, where a suitable political structure is in place, the political decisions that are taken will embody to a greater or lesser extent the articulated beliefs and attitudes of the nation in question. The closer we come to the democratic end of the spectrum, the truer this will be. So we have two forms of collective national action: action that is deliberately concerted through political channels, and action that is undertaken by individuals, or groups of individuals, but that reflects some ele-ment in the national culture.[18]

How closely do nations conform to either of the two models of collective responsibility outlined in Section II? Does it make sense, first of all, to regard them as like-minded groups liable to bear the consequences of their actions? Since members share both a common identity and a public culture—the first two features noted above—there is prima facie reason to regard them as meeting this condi-tion. But it is clearly crucial to establish that their collective actions are a genuine embodiment of the shared beliefs and values that go to make up the national culture. Here the distinction just drawn between different levels of self-determination becomes significant. Where nations are subject to outside rule, any ascription of national responsibility becomes problematic. The nation is governed in a certain way, but it does not *act* politically at all. And even where we witness forms of collective behaviour that significantly affect the well-being of members or impose burdens on outsiders, it will be difficult to say which of these are authentic expressions of national culture, and which are merely the work of individuals who claim that what they are doing reflects that culture. In the absence of a political forum in which national aims and values can be articulated and debated, it will be difficult to establish how far the population as a whole is implicated in support for the activities in question.[19]

[18] Is the second case a genuine case of collective action, sufficient to ground collective responsibility? Clearly, the fact that a number of individuals follow the same norm in their private or economic lives does not by itself allow us to say that they are engaging in collective action. But where the prevalence of the norm is common knowledge, and it is regarded as a component feature of national identity, then the fact that the behaviour in question is not formally coordinated does not mean that it cannot be regarded as a form of collective action. Compare here the cases of the rioting mob and white culture in the post-bellum American South discussed in the previous section.

[19] This is not to say that we can *never* attribute responsibility to nations that lack political self-determination. The clearest cases may be those that resemble the racism of Southern whites discussed earlier. Suppose two peoples, A and B, locked together under the same system of imperial rule, feel mutual hatred and contempt for each other, and this results in genocidal acts perpetrated by certain As against the Bs. Under these circumstances, it would not be wrong to hold members of nation A collectively responsible for these savage acts, on the basis that almost everyone belonging to A contributed to a climate of opinion in which such acts were regarded not as morally reprehensible but as permissible, if not justified. Of course, before making this judgement we would need evidence that the attitudes in question were

At the other end of the spectrum, we have nations that are democratically self-governing. Here the policies pursued by the state can reasonably be seen as policies for whose effects the citizen body as a whole is collectively responsible, given that they have authorized the government to act on their behalf in a free election (I shall return later to the question whether political dissenters can also be held responsible).[20] And even where the consequences flow from patterns of behaviour that are not the direct result of political decision, these patterns of behaviour are open to democratic control. Suppose, for example, that the dominant religion encourages large families, and that as a result the population is increasing at a rate that causes social problems of various kinds. It is open to the government to adopt a population policy that gives incentives for parents to limit the size of their families. If after democratic debate such a policy is rejected, then we can legitimately say that the nation in question is collectively responsible for the consequences of population growth: its culture is such that it prefers large families to, let us say, less crowded roads and cities.

What now of the case where the nation in question is governed autocratically by an individual or a small elite drawn from within? It is certainly harder in these circumstances to lay responsibility at the feet of the ordinary subjects. Yet two considerations must be taken into account even here. One is that the rulers may hold beliefs and values that correspond more or less closely to those of their subjects even though they are not formally accountable to them. To the degree to which their authority depends on that fact, we can say that they are supported by the people, and that when they act, or fail to act, the consequences flow from beliefs and values that are common national property. Suppose for instance that the state is a theocracy, and that its rulers issue a decree that results in the death

indeed very widely shared; we would also need to be sure that large sections of the population were not being bullied into offering their support for the killers. But such evidence could in principle be found.

[20] I leave aside here the difficult question of how far (if at all) democratic elections can be seen as authorizing the governing party to carry out the policies contained in its manifesto. Clearly, if the government acts in ways that were not announced beforehand, and that could not reasonably be foreseen by the voters, responsibility for these policies does not automatically extend to the citizens generally, though my comments below about responsibility under autocratic regimes apply here too.

of some person deemed to be an apostate. If the issuing of the decree stems from religious beliefs and practices that are generally adhered to throughout the population, then some share of responsibility falls on the nation as a whole, even if we want to say that it rests primarily with members of the ruling group.

The second consideration is that subjects of the autocracy may have a duty to resist it in the event that it begins to act in ways that are manifestly wrong, whether the wrongness takes the form of injustice to outsiders or simply of policies that are seriously damaging to the common interests of the nation itself. Mere passivity is then not sufficient to escape responsibility for the policies in question. Everything will turn on whether resistance is feasible, what the costs of resistance are, and whether sufficient numbers of people can act together to make their resistance effective. Unfortunately, correct judgement on these matters may be difficult to achieve, particularly for outsiders who have no experience of living under a repressive regime. How far, for instance, should we hold the Serbian people as a whole responsible for ethnic cleansing in Kosovo, given that they had no avenues of direct control over Milošović and the army that he directed? Should they have been expected to make greater efforts to coordinate their opposition to his regime (we know that it was divisions among the opposition parties that helped him to stay in power for as long as did)? Or were the costs of effective opposition greater than the average Serbian could be expected to bear? The difficulty in answering these questions should make us hesitate before we jump to the conclusion that responsibility spreads beyond the ruling elite to the nation as a whole.[21]

---

[21] Writing in the immediate aftermath of the Second World War, Karl Jaspers took a harder line in *The Question of German Guilt* (Westport, CT: Greenwood Press, 1978). Jaspers distinguishes between legal, political, moral, and metaphysical guilt, where political guilt implies 'having to bear the consequences of the deeds of the state whose power governs me and under whose order I live' (31). In Jaspers's view all citizens share in this political guilt, irrespective of the nature of the regime that governs them, and so it seemed clear to him that all Germans should be expected to pay reparations after the war. 'We are politically responsible for our regime, for the acts of the regime, for the start of the war in this world-historical situation, and for the kind of leaders we allowed to rise among us. For that we answer to the victors, with our labor and with our working faculties, and must make such amends as are exacted from the vanquished.' (78) This included those who had opposed the regime, and those who stood wholly aloof from politics. 'The sense of

Another reason for hesitation is the possibility that the ordinary subjects of the autocracy were effectively brainwashed into holding views that support the policies in question. Attributions of national responsibility depend on the idea that the activities that nations engage in express beliefs and values that are genuinely shared by their members. This does not require that each member should have thought it all out for herself, so to speak; it does not exclude normal processes of socialization whereby individuals are exposed to certain values and practices as they grow up, and come to adopt and identify with those values and practices. But where current political attitudes can be directly traced to sustained propaganda efforts by an autocratic regime that allows no dissenting voices to be heard—attitudes of extreme hostility, say, towards a neighbouring community—it is much less plausible to hold ordinary people responsible for the consequences that follow. Just as we cannot expect people to make superhuman efforts to oppose a regime, so we cannot expect them to stand firm against the propaganda barrage that descends on them (a few individuals will, just as a few individuals may be willing to bear extreme costs to fight the regime, but our judgements about responsibility should be based on what we can reasonably expect of the average person).

What this shows is that the more open and democratic a political community is, the more justified we are in holding its members responsible for the decisions they make and the policies they follow. National values will still to a large extent be inherited in practice, but they will be discussed and debated, alternative views will be expressed, and so forth. There seems little objection in these circumstances to requiring the members to bear the costs of what they decide to do. But what of those who find themselves in a dissenting minority? Here we need to turn to the second of our two models of collective responsibility, the cooperative practice model. For as we saw in the previous section, those who are engaged in cooperative practices from which they benefit can be held responsible for the outcomes of those practices despite their opposition to the policies which produced those outcomes. So how far can we justifiably represent nations as cooperative practices writ large?

political liability lets no man dodge.' (62) Jaspers thought, rightly, that ascriptions of legal and moral guilt must be more discriminating.

The case for so regarding them rests on two claims. First, as indicated earlier, nations are communities whose members see themselves as having obligations of mutual aid that are more extensive than the aid they owe to human beings generally. (I do not address here the question how far these circumscribed practices of mutual aid are *justified*; I am simply indicating that this is how fellow-nationals standardly understand their relationships to one another.) These obligations are typically discharged by creating and supporting institutions that provide protective and welfare services on which each member can call as the need arises. To the extent that there is fairness in the way that these services are funded and provided, we can say that each member belongs to and benefits from a cooperative practice.[22]

Second, nations provide their members with a number of public goods, foremost among which is protection of the national culture itself. I am assuming here that, as indicated in my sketch of nationality at the beginning of the section, people value their national membership and want it to continue. They must also value, therefore, those cultural features that lend their nation its distinct character—the national language, for instance, the physical appearance of cities or landscape, cultural traditions that mark them off from other nations, and so forth.[23] These features are often subject to erosion by outside forces, and so members have to invest resources and accept restrictions on their own behaviour to preserve their cultural heritage. Again we see that nations exhibit the features of a large-scale cooperative practice: each member makes certain sacrifices in order to support a national culture from whose continued existence each is presumed to benefit.

---

[22] In practice, protective and welfare services are normally provided to all citizens of the state in question, regardless of national identity. But their justification—in particular the justification of their redistributive elements—rests on the idea that they are a way of discharging obligations that fellow-nationals owe to one another. In multinational states there is a marked tendency for welfare services especially to be devolved to national subunits, in so far as it is feasible to do so.

[23] These features need not be valued individually by *everyone* who belongs to the nation—it is possible both to recognize some aspect of culture as a distinctive national trait and to dislike it and wish to change it (American gun culture may be a good example of this). What is necessary is that the *ensemble* of cultural features should be valued positively by the nation's members.

So now let us return to the question whether responsibility for the outcomes of political decisions and policies can be extended to those who dissent from, and oppose, the decisions and policies at stake. Even if they cannot be said to play any causal role in the genesis of those policies (as the like-minded group model requires), are they nonetheless involved in a cooperative practice that implicates them in collective responsibility? There are two issues to consider. The first is whether the nation in question does indeed distribute the benefits and burdens of membership fairly, including the opportunity to participate in political decision-making. Where a minority group is exploited, or is excluded from a significant range of benefits that members of other groups standardly enjoy, it will be hard to justify the claim that their membership alone makes them responsible for the consequences of national decisions. Whereas a group that loses on a particular issue in a democratic forum can be included in responsibility for the result on the ground that it will win on other occasions, and therefore benefits from an ongoing practice that allows collective decisions to be taken, no such argument applies to a group that is excluded from decision-making altogether or that forms a permanent and oppressed minority. Thus the position I am defending does not lead to absurd conclusions such as that German Jews share in responsibility for the effects of the Nazi regime or that Iraqi Kurds share in responsibility for the actions of Saddam Hussein. State membership itself does not entail collective responsibility if the conditions for a cooperative practice are not met.

The second issue is the extent to which the dissident group shares with the majority the beliefs and values that constitute the national culture. The analysis I am offering here is an analysis of *national* responsibility, and it therefore does not apply in any direct way to *states* that house two or more conflicting national groups whose public cultures scarcely overlap. In these circumstances protection of the culture of either group ceases to be a genuine public good for both communities. But even if we leave aside radically divided states, it remains an open question how much cultural overlap there is between majority and minority. One important issue here is whether the national culture of the majority includes elements that collide with the ethnic or religious cultures of particular groups, as, for instance, German national identity during the Nazi period embodied notions of racial superiority that made it repugnant to Jews and other ethnic minorities. So we need to draw a distinction between dissenters who oppose the majority view on a particular issue—say a pacifist minority vehemently opposed to a war that the majority supports—while continuing to subscribe to other aspects of national culture, and dissidents who reject that culture in an across-the-board way, and therefore see no value in policies designed to promote it. In the latter case, the idea of the nation as a cooperative practice fails, at least so far as this involves contributing to public goods from which every participant subsequently benefits. It is difficult to judge how often this case occurs in reality: to the extent that national identities are liberalized, in the sense that they are purged of ethnically or religiously exclusive elements, and are constituted instead by political and cultural values that are accessible to all, outright alienation from national culture will be rare.[24]

I have been concerned in this part of this chapter both to defend the idea of national responsibility and to identify its limits. To take the limits first: where nations are subject to external or to autocratic rule, it is usually difficult to identify acts undertaken by individual members or by the state as genuinely national acts, and so it becomes inappropriate to spread responsibility for those acts throughout the population in question. Furthermore, where cultural divisions run deep, we may decide that talk of a single nation (in the sense outlined at the beginning of the section) is out of place. These cases aside, I have argued that where nations act in ways that impose burdens on themselves or on others, responsibility for such burdens falls on every member, even on those who opposed the decisions or policies in question. The argument turns on the sharing of beliefs and attitudes that characterizes national communities, and on the benefits that membership brings with it. So I conclude that we

---

[24] Are there any cases in which a nation has fractured along purely political lines, meaning not just that people disagree sharply over concrete issues, but they find that they also lack any common principles in terms of which they can seek a resolution of their differences? Even where the disagreement is deep and long lasting, as in the case of slavery in the USA, the two sides can still subscribe to many common values. But if, hypothetically, we can imagine such a fractured community, then we would not have a nation in the sense I am presupposing. Instead, we would have a variant of the multinational case: a political association formed between two distinct peoples, in this instance two peoples divided by their basic political principles. In such a case, it would be wrong to hold the whole association responsible for what one of its constituent communities had decided to do.

are not wrong, in general, to hold contemporary fellow-nationals responsible for actions performed in their name. But the bearing this has on questions of global justice is not yet clear. For one thing, nations can be held responsible not only for the benefits and burdens they create for their own members, but also for the impact that their actions have on outsiders. For another, we have seen that outcome responsibility, the focus of this chapter, has to be understood alongside remedial responsibility, the responsibility we may have, as individuals and as members of collective bodies, to respond to human deprivation, including global poverty. So by accepting the idea of national responsibility, we have not foreclosed the question what global justice demands of us. The next step, however, is to establish whether national responsibility can be extended to cover responsibility for the national past—especially responsibility to make good the injustices that earlier generations of compatriots have perpetrated. This is the task of Chapter 6.

CHAPTER 6

Inheriting Responsibilities

I

The idea that people today can be held responsible for what their forebears did has gained a significant foothold in contemporary politics. Various groups who claim that they are the victims of historical injustice have made legal or political demands for redress against the bodies taken to be responsible for the injustice—governments, corporations, banks, and so forth. These claims have been quite diverse in character, whether in terms of the nature of the groups involved, the basis for their claims, or the kind of redress that is being sought, so it may be helpful to begin by citing some examples of demands of this kind—some that have met with success and some that have not.[1] Their common feature is that the present generation, or their representatives, are being asked to make good injustices that occurred before most of them at least were born. Consider, then, the following cases:

1. The payments that have been made by the German government to Jews as reparation for the Nazi holocaust, mainly in the form of transfers to Israel, and estimated to be in the order of 80 billion Deutschmarks.
2. The demands made by members of the Australian Aboriginal community for compensation and for a national Day of Apology for the so-called 'stolen generation' of Aboriginal children

---

[1] I have drawn upon E. Barkan, *The Guilt of Nations* (New York: W. W. Norton, 2000) and R. L. Brooks (ed.), *When Sorry Isn't Enough: The Controversy over Apologies and Reparations for Human Injustice* (New York: New York University Press, 1999), where detailed evidence on the cases that follow can be found.

taken from their families and brought up in white homes or orphanages.

3. The compensation of $122 million awarded by the US Supreme Court to the Sioux Indians for the occupation by whites in the late nineteenth century of the gold-rich Black Hills area that had previously been reserved to the Sioux by treaty.

4. Demands that Japan should pay compensation to 'comfort women' taken from other East Asian countries (especially Korea) and forced into prostitution by the Japanese military, giving rise to official apologies and the creation of an Asian Women's Fund to offer compensation to the women involved.

5. Demands that items of symbolic significance seized from their original owners should be returned to those owners or their descendants, for instance the demand that the Parthenon Marbles should be returned to Greece, or the demand by some aboriginal peoples that the bones of their ancestors now held in museums across the world should be sent back to them for reburial.

6. The many and varied demands that have been made in the USA as forms of redress for black slavery, from land settlements for blacks, to financial compensation to the descendants of slaves, to affirmative action policies, to formal apologies for slavery on the part of Congress or the president.

To many people, claims of this kind appear inherently problematic. Some of the problems are specific to particular cases, such as those having to do with establishing what exactly took place in the past to justify the claim that is being made in the present, or having to do with the identity of the would-be beneficiaries (who should count as a Sioux or a victim of slavery?). But there is also an underlying problem, namely that meeting such demands appears to require the present generation to accept responsibility for events that took place before their birth, and this immediately severs the link between agency and responsibility which, as we have seen, is so central to the idea of outcome responsibility in particular. Whether as individuals or as members of collectivities, we can only be held responsible, it is thought, for those outcomes that we have contributed to producing. The discomfort many people feel with the idea of inheriting responsibility can be seen in the reluctance of politicians, in particular, to issue apologies for past events. One might believe that the issuing of an apology, in contrast to providing material compensation, was a fairly costless act, but although apologies *are* sometimes offered (a few years back the Queen apologized to the Maoris for the wrongs they had suffered at the hands of the British, for example[2]), in general we find considerable reluctance on the part of political leaders to admit responsibility for historical injustice. Asked to make a formal apology to the Aborigines, the Australian Prime Minister John Howard stated 'Australians of this generation should not be required to accept guilt and blame for past actions and policies', and likewise President Clinton, under pressure to apologize officially for slavery in the USA, but aware of how controversial such an action would be for many voters, found a form of words that was something less. 'Going back to the time before we were even a nation, European-Americans received the fruits of the slave trade and we were wrong in that', he told an audience of schoolchildren in Uganda, adding that it was more important to look to the future than to dwell on the past.

Our question, then, is whether it is possible to overcome this reluctance, and extend the idea of national responsibility in such a way as to encompass responsibility for the national past. Defending the general idea of inherited collective responsibility does not of course settle which, if any, of the claims cited above are valid ones. Philosophers writing on this topic have focused mainly on the claimants' side of the issue, asking what must be shown in order to justify their demand for some form of historical redress. Here questions arise such as how a present-day group can prove that they are the legitimate inheritors of the group that was wronged in the past; how land and property titles are established, and how these titles are affected by the passing of time; how one should calculate compensation for historic losses, given the many uncertainties about what might have happened between now and then had the injustice not occurred; whether past practices can properly be judged by the principles of justice we adhere to today; and so forth.[3] These are all

[2] For some other cases, see M. Cunningham, 'Saying Sorry: The Politics of Apology', *Political Quarterly*, 70 (1999), 285–93.

[3] See, for instance, J. Waldron, 'Superseding Historic Injustice', *Ethics*, 103 (1992–3), 4–28 and 'Redressing Historic Injustice', *University of Toronto Law Journal*, 52 (2002), 135–60; G. Sher, 'Ancient Wrongs and Modern Rights', in Sher, *Approximate Justice: Studies in Non-Ideal Theory* (Lanham, MD: Rowman and

good and important questions, and unless we can give satisfactory answers it will be impossible to formulate coherent principles to regulate the practice of historical rectification. But they all bear on the issue of whether the alleged victims of injustice have a claim to redress, not on the issue whether another group has an obligation to meet that claim. There are, after all, circumstances in which person P or group P has been wronged or harmed, but there is no person A or group A whose responsibility it is to rectify the wrong or the harm. If I beat you up and then, stricken with remorse, decide to kill myself, there may be no one you can turn to to ask for compensation for the damage I have caused (I shall come back later to legal doctrine in cases such as this). So even if we are able to overcome the several difficulties noted above, and establish that claimant groups have a justified demand for compensation of some kind, it is still necessary to investigate whether other groups, or institutions, have a responsibility to meet such a demand.

Before asking where such responsibility might be located, it is worth dwelling on the very diverse nature of the claims for historical redress that are being made, which also suggests that their ethical force may vary significantly. We can, I think, distinguish roughly between four kinds of demands, each with a different logic. First, we have claims for restitution, for example the handing back of land, art treasures, or sacred objects. Here the claim is simply that the objects in question rightfully belong to group P, but that at some historic moment they were wrongfully appropriated by group A and remain in the possession of the As. Second, we have claims based on the idea of unjust enrichment, for instance those made by the descendants of victims of exploitation such as slaves or colonial peoples. The claim is that over some historical period the As exploited the Ps and retained the benefits of exploitation, benefits that have been passed down to their descendants; so descendants of the Ps now demand the equivalent of what was taken from their ancestors. Third, we have claims based on the idea of a compensable historic wrong—for

Littlefield, 1997); A. J. Simmons, 'Historical Rights and Fair Shares', in Simmons, *Justification and Legitimacy: Essays on Rights and Obligations* (Cambridge: Cambridge University Press, 2001); J. Thompson, *Taking Responsibility for the Past: Reparation and Historical Injustice* (Cambridge: Polity Press, 2002), esp. chs. 7–9; S. Kershnar, *Justice for the Past* (Albany, NY: State University of New York Press, 2004).

instance the internment of Japanese-Americans by the US government during the Second World War, or the taking of comfort women by the Japanese military in the same period. In such cases it is alleged that acts of injustice occurred which harmed their victims in one way or other (without necessarily benefiting the perpetrators or their descendants), and which can be compensated for, at least in part, by money payments or other forms of material compensation either to the victims themselves or to their descendants. Fourth, we have demands which involve simply asking the perpetrators to set the historic record straight and acknowledge their responsibility for historic injustice—usually in the form of a public apology by a representative figure such as a president or a monarch. Here, those who identify with the original victims of the injustice, whether by virtue of biological descent or cultural affiliation, claim that the continued refusal by representative bodies to offer an apology is psychologically damaging to them; their present status is undermined by the failure to accept responsibility and provide appropriate (usually symbolic) redress.

It is important to keep the differences between these claims in mind as we proceed, because each involves a different understanding of how people in the present might take responsibility for the past. They may of course be run in tandem in particular instances: arguments for the redress of slavery often assert both that the slaves and their descendants were wronged, and that slave owners and others were unjustly enriched. Nevertheless there are two distinct claims being made here, and it is possible that one will succeed while the other fails. It is also important to distinguish all four of these claims from a fifth, which differs from them in having a less exclusively backward-looking character. This is a claim that starts from the fact that some group P is now living below some morally significant threshold of material resources, health, etc., and then assigns remedial responsibility to group A on the grounds of the past interactions between A and P. As we saw in Chapter 4, remedial responsibilities are often assigned in this way, by reference to past history. However what is at stake here is not the remedying of historic injustice for its own sake, but the lifting of the Ps above the threshold in question, and the corresponding need to find an agent with the responsibility to do this. Arguments of this kind need to be kept distinct partly because they may appeal to those who think that redressing historic injustice has no intrinsic value (or is impossible to achieve),[4] and partly because the conditions for attributing responsibility to the As here may be less demanding than in redress cases proper. That is, it may be enough to show *some* causal impact of the As on the Ps—enough to distinguish the As from other groups that might provide remedy to the Ps—without having to establish that the As acted unjustly, were unfairly enriched, etc. Thus we might think that colonial nations have special remedial responsibilities to their impoverished former colonies without delving into contested questions such as whether colonialism unjustly enriched the metropolis at the expense of the periphery.

Although remedial responsibilities are a central concern of this book as a whole, in the present chapter I want to look more specifically at historical rectification as an aspect of global justice, and as indicated to focus on the question whether nations can be held responsible for the deeds of their forebears, so that claims of the four kinds identified above can legitimately be addressed to them. What could bind the past and the future together in such a way that responsibilities to provide redress can be inherited?

One way to sidestep this question is to focus on *states* rather than *nations* as the potential bearers of inherited responsibilities.[5] States, as formally constituted bodies, persist over time despite changes in their personnel, and therefore there is no problem of inheritance in the strict sense: it seems that a state can now be held responsible for actions performed by that same state in the year 1800, say, just as an individual can be held responsible for deeds performed much earlier in his life. I shall discuss one state-centred approach to historic responsibility in Section II, but let me now just indicate why I prefer to focus attention on nations, despite the greater difficulties with this approach. One reason is that many historic injustices are not in fact perpetrated by states, but by peoples, or by individuals acting in the name of peoples. This can be seen most clearly where

[4] See, for instance, R. Vernon, 'Against Restitution', *Political Studies*, 51 (2003), 542–57.

[5] There are other possibilities too. Chandran Kukathas has argued that responsibility for remedying past injustice should be assigned to *associations* more generally—corporations, churches, universities, etc., as well as states. See C. Kukathas, 'Responsibility for Past Injustice: How to Shift the Burden', *Politics, Philosophy and Economics*, 2 (2003), 165–90.

no national state yet exists but a nation is struggling to establish one, or to break away from an existing state. But even where a nation has a state of its own, it seems to me somewhat artificial to hold the state responsible for everything the nation does. Colonial adventures, for example, may require the tacit blessing of the relevant state, but what then occurs is largely determined by the colonizers themselves, and through them by the interests and the world view of the nation from which they are drawn.[6] A second reason is that demonstrating the identity of states over time is generally much more problematic than the state-centred approach assumes. The UK and the USA are unusual in having states whose evolution has been gradual and unbroken. Of how many other European countries, for instance, could one say that they are governed by the same state that governed them in 1750, in the light of the radical disruptions that have occurred meanwhile, including territorial expansion and contraction as well as regime change?

I prefer, therefore, to locate the problem of inherited responsibilities in nations rather than in states—states are often the bodies that should discharge the resulting liabilities, but they are not the primary bearers of historic responsibility. So let us return to the question whether the idea of inheriting responsibilities makes sense at all. Why do we find ourselves pulled in opposite directions on this question, sometimes wanting to affirm and at other times to deny that we can be held responsible for what our ancestors did? We can understand this, I believe, in terms of a conflict between liberal and communitarian intuitions. On the liberal side, we are drawn to the idea that we are only implicated in responsibility when as agents we have made some causal contribution to the outcome for which we are being held liable, and behind that stands the idea that we want to be in control of what happens to us: if we are held responsible for what other people, past or present, have done, then in one important respect we lose control of our lives.[7] On the communitarian side,

---

[6] This is most obviously true of the earlier colonial period of European history; nineteenth-century imperialism, by contrast, was usually driven by state interests and implemented by state personnel—armed forces and civil servants.

[7] I do not wish to endorse the liberal intuition in this form; as a moment's inspection will show, it is inconsistent with the account of collective responsibility developed in Chapter 5. Nevertheless I recognize the pull that it exerts on people in contemporary liberal societies especially.

we have identities that connect us to larger groups of people, and we often feel vicarious pride or shame in what they do. For instance, when I see English football fans terrorizing the inhabitants of foreign cities, I feel not only anger but also shame at what is happening, and want to rush out to apologize to the people whose lives and neighbourhoods are being invaded. With pride and shame comes responsibility: if the shops and the street furniture need repairing, then obviously the fans should be asked to pay up first, but if they cannot or will not, then we — the British taxpayers — should cover the cost. This communitarian intuition runs backwards in time in so far as our identity stretches backward to include our ancestors. Alasdair MacIntyre has expressed this well:

... we all approach our own circumstances as bearers of a particular social identity. I am someone's son or daughter, someone else's cousin or uncle; I am a citizen of this or that city, a member of this or that guild or profession; I belong to this clan, that tribe, this nation. Hence what is good for me has to be the good for one who inhabits these roles. As such, I inherit from the past of my family, my city, my tribe, my nation, a variety of debts, inheritances, rightful expectations and obligations.[8]

The debts and obligations are a natural corollary of identifying oneself in social terms, as standing in a particular relationship to transgenerational communities such as families, professions, and nations. But as MacIntyre immediately goes on to note:

this thought is likely to appear alien and even surprising from the standpoint of modern individualism. From the standpoint of individualism. ... I may biologically be my father's son, but I cannot be held responsible for what he did unless I choose implicitly or explicitly to assume such responsibility. I may legally be a citizen of a certain country; but I cannot be held responsible for what my country does or has done unless I choose implicitly or explicitly to assume such responsibility.[9]

In other words, the communitarian intuition that supports the idea of inherited responsibility runs straight up against the liberal intuition that we can and should choose the relationships from which responsibilities spring, and this intuition is as firmly embedded as the other. To justify taking responsibility for the past, we need to do

---

[8] A. MacIntyre, *After Virtue* (London: Duckworth, 1981), 204–5.
[9] MacIntyre, *After Virtue*, 205.

more than simply point out that de facto people do often feel pride and shame in what their ancestors have done, and are sometimes willing to bear the resulting costs. We need to find *arguments* that will support the communitarian intuition, or at least its consequences, to the detriment of the liberal one.

II

I want to begin by examining the most sustained attempt that I know of to justify inherited responsibilities, Janna Thompson's recent book *Taking Responsibility for the Past*.[10] Thompson's aim is to show that nations have duties of reparation for the unjust acts of their predecessors, and she takes cases such as those I cited earlier to illustrate this thesis. However, for reasons that will shortly become apparent, she uses 'nation' in a different sense from mine. For Thompson, a nation is a political community with an institutional structure that allows it to make laws for itself and agreements with other communities—in other words it is a state, or a state-like entity. (Thompson prefers 'nation' to 'state' because she wants to include, for instance, aboriginal communities whose political structure is less formal than that of a modern state.) As indicated in Chapter 5, I use 'nation' to refer to a body of people who share a common national identity, involving cultural values, attachment to a territory, and so forth, and who *aspire* to institutions of political self-determination which they may or may not actually enjoy.[11] For Thompson, it is a contingent matter whether the citizens who form a nation in her sense also form a nation in my sense; for me, it is a contingent matter whether a nation in my sense has a political structure that allows it to make laws and commitments and therefore qualifies as a nation in Thompson's sense. So the argument she develops has a different catchment area, so to speak, from mine, though there will be overlap in the case of countries such as Britain, France, or the USA which will count as nations on both our definitions.

Why does Thompson define 'nation' in the way that she does? Her argument hinges on the idea that nations are bodies that make

[10] J. Thompson, *Taking Responsibility for the Past: Reparation and Historical Injustice* (Cambridge: Polity Press, 2002).

[11] For a fuller definition, see D. Miller, *On Nationality* (Oxford: Clarendon Press, 1995), ch. 2.

trans-generational commitments, and so she needs to focus on bodies that *can* make such commitments, especially formal commitments to other nations through treaties. Her idea is that if we can understand why we ought to honour the commitments that earlier generations made, we shall also understand why we ought to make reparations for their acts of injustice, including, but not limited to, their breach of treaties and other agreements.

Thompson observes that when treaties are made, these are supposed to last indefinitely, and not to lapse when the generation that signed them passes away. They might be affected by changed circumstances, but not by the passage of time alone. She argues that when the present generation makes treaties, it intends them to bind its successors, and so it participates in a practice that commits it to honouring the treaties made by previous generations, at least so long as these meet certain criteria of justice. This looks at first sight as though it has the form of a fair play argument: a generation that wants to enjoy the benefits of entering into binding intergenerational treaties must also accept the costs in the form of the treaty obligations it inherits from the past—to do otherwise would be to take unfair advantage of a prevailing practice. But she recognizes that this argument would not apply in the case of a generation that made no treaties, or made no treaties that were intended to bind succeeding generations. Her response is as follows:

> Our moral commitments do not depend on what we actually do or refrain from doing. They depend on our judgements about what ought to be done in cases real or merely possible. . . . The moral practice we think we ought to adopt in relation to the promises of our predecessors is determined not by whether we actually make posterity binding promises, but by what we think our successors ought to do were we to make them.[12]

It would clearly be hypocritical to believe that our successors ought to honour any commitments that we make while we ourselves refuse to honour the commitments made by our predecessors. But what if we say that it is entirely up to our successors whether they honour the promises we make, and entirely up to us whether we honour the promises made by our ancestors? We would then be neither inconsistent nor hypocritical. Thompson's argument at this point depends

---

[12] Thompson, *Taking Responsibility for the Past*, 18.

on assuming what has to be shown, namely that later generations ought to honour the promises made by earlier generations. If that is assumed, then of course we will judge that our successors ought to keep any promises we make, and that we ought to keep the promises made by our predecessors. But no argument has been given for the assumption itself.

Of course it might be said that the practice of making intergenerational treaties is a valuable one, because it allows nations (in Thompson's sense) to stabilize their relations with one another, to form expectations about how other nations will behave, to avoid violent conflicts, and so forth. Given that the practice exists, we ought to support it by fulfilling whatever treaty obligations descend to us. But Thompson is unwilling to deploy that argument because she thinks it cannot convince 'proponents of democracy who think that citizens should collectively be able to determine what burdens they will assume'[13]—in other words people who are willing to honour the promises that they make collectively themselves, but do not want to engage in the practice of trans-generational promise-making. Such people place political autonomy above stability and security. But if this argument is set aside, then Thompson is left with nothing beyond the bare assertion that honouring trans-generational promises is morally required.

Thompson also has to show how the case for honouring treaty obligations can be extended to cover reparation for acts of injustice that may or may not involve a breach of treaty commitments. She attempts to do so by introducing the idea of mutual respect between nations—the idea that nations that wish to be treated with respect themselves must treat other nations that deserve respect *with* respect. This is said to ground not only the obligation to enter into agreements with other nations when circumstances require it, but also the requirement not to engage in acts of injustice such as territorial invasion or disrupting the nation's common life. If our predecessors have defaulted on these requirements, then in order to restore mutual respect we must make reparations to the injured parties or their descendants.

This way of thinking about the problem may provide good pragmatic grounds for redressing past injustice: it may well be that acts

---

[13] Thompson, *Taking Responsibility for the Past*, 7.

of restitution, compensation, or apology pave the way for future good relations between the nation providing the redress and the community that benefits from it. But the connection between redress and maintaining or creating mutual respect is here only contingent, and Thompson admits as much when she says that 'it may not always be *necessary* to make reparations for past wrongs in order to establish or re-establish relations of respect'.[14] It may be enough to behave in ways that show that you intend to act respectfully from now on. So Thompson's argument here does not show that nations have an obligation to provide redress for the injustices perpetrated by past generations; what it shows is that providing redress may sometimes be a valuable way of creating good international relations in the future. Her underlying aim is not justice but *reconciliation* — or to put it more exactly, the redress of past injustice as a means of achieving reconciliation. This is a worthwhile aim, certainly, but it bypasses the question whether we can inherit responsibilities that impose *obligations of justice* on the present generation.

More generally, both Thompson's more specific argument about honouring treaties and her wider argument about reparation involve turning backward-looking arguments into forward-looking ones. Instead of saying that we have responsibilities now simply by virtue of what happened in the past, she says that taking responsibility for the past is a way of achieving something valuable in the present: upholding the practice of trans-generational promise-making, maintaining mutual respect among nations. It is analogous to the claim that the reason I should keep a promise is not simply that I made it but that by keeping it I am upholding a valuable practice. Thompson is driven in this direction by her belief that straightforward backward-looking arguments would not be acceptable to democratic citizens with liberal instincts, who will ask why they should be held responsible for repairing injustices that they had no part in making. But, as is often the case, when the argument gets reconstructed in this way, it no longer directly addresses the original question.

It is worth underlining here that the harms and injustices for which redress is being sought when historic responsibility claims are made need not leave the victims very badly off in absolute terms. No doubt some claims are being made on behalf of individuals or groups who are absolutely deprived. But this does not apply, for

---

[14] Thompson, *Taking Responsibility for the Past*, 35.

instance, to the descendants of Jewish victims of the Nazi holocaust; the payments made to Israel are not going to people whose lives now fall below some absolute poverty threshold. As indicated earlier, we need to distinguish between claims for redress of historic injustice *per se*, and claims about remedial responsibility for people whose condition *is* one of absolute deprivation. When remedial responsibility claims are advanced, what's doing the work is the forward-looking consideration that nation A can relieve nation P or group P's suffering, and we look to the past only to single A out from other nations who might also bring relief to P. In contrast, the logic of historic redress is straightforwardly backward-looking: because of what happened at some past time T, group P is now worse off in some respect, materially or psychologically, than it ought rightly to be, and the present members of nation A inherit the responsibility to correct that injustice. They must do something now *because* of what happened at T: we Britons should give the Parthenon Marbles back to Greece *because* Lord Elgin had no right to take them, not because it will make the Greeks happier to have them back, or because our future relations with Greece will improve, even if these things are true. The forward-looking benefits of redressing historic injustice are an incidental bonus, not the reason for doing it.

III

This diagnosis of what has gone wrong in Thompson's argument does, however, still leave us with the task of explaining *how* the present members of A can be held responsible for what previous generations have done. Why should responsibility descend in this way, rather than dying with the original perpetrators? Can we learn anything here by switching attention for the moment from nations to individual people, and considering whether people can be held responsible for the misdeeds of their personal forebears? If my father has robbed, injured, defrauded or slandered your father, can you now claim restitution, compensation or apology from me, his only heir? What does the law have to say about this, and does morality say anything different?[15]

---

[15] What follows is not intended to be a detailed account of legal doctrine, but an interpretation of the principles that appear to inform what the law has to say about

If we begin by looking at how English common law has evolved, we first encounter the general rule that actions for redress are extinguished by the death of the wrongdoer. This rule, however, is by no means absolute, and has always been qualified in various ways. One immediate qualification is that it does not apply to the taking of property: if A wrongfully takes P's property and holds it until his death, then afterwards P or P's successors can take action to recover the property. Another qualification concerns contracts entered into by A that remain unfulfilled at the time of his death. But in the case of other torts, the law historically has embodied a presumption that liability cannot be inherited but rather ceases upon the death of the tortfeasor. The rationale for this was stated by Blackstone in the following terms:

And in actions merely personal, arising *ex delicto*, for wrongs actually done or committed by the defendant, as trespass, battery, and slander, the rule is that *actio personalis moritur cum persona*; and that it never shall be revived either by or against the executors or other representatives. For neither the executors of the plaintiff have received, nor those of the defendant have committed, in their own personal capacity, any manner of wrong or injury.[16]

We need to take the two parts of this explanation separately. First, Blackstone says that the wrongdoer's executors have committed no wrong or injury themselves, which is plainly true. Legal historians have suggested that common law doctrine as embodied in this passage from Blackstone was influenced by the criminal law associations of the idea of trespass: if one thinks of trespass as a type of crime, then only the perpetrator is liable to be punished, and to take action against his successors would be plainly unjust.[17] But if we look at the other part of the explanation, the analogy fails. Why should

---

inherited responsibilities. I shall not discuss the question whether there is a legal basis for collective historical reparations, for instance in the case of slavery in the USA. The different grounds on which such reparations claims might be advanced have been analysed in a symposium published in the *Boston University Law Review* for 2004: see especially H. Dagan, 'Restitution and Slavery: On Incomplete Commodification, Intergenerational Justice, and Legal Transitions', *Boston University Law Review*, 84 (2004), 1139–76.

[16] W. Blackstone, *Commentaries on the Law of England*, intro. J. H. Langbein (Chicago, IL: University of Chicago Press, 1979), book 3, 302.

[17] P. H. Winfield, 'Death as Affecting Liability in Tort', *Columbia Law Review*, 29 (1929), 239–54.

we assume that the plaintiff's successors have not been harmed or injured by the wrong? This may seem a reasonable assumption in the case of slander, but it is less obvious in the case of battery, and far less obvious in the case of trespass, which may include torts such as damaging the plaintiff's property or wrongfully imprisoning him. Here it seems natural to say that where his successors can prove that they have been injured by the wrongdoing, materially or in some other demonstrable way, then they have a prima facie case for redress, as they have in cases of wrongfully taken property or breach of contract. The case would be conclusive when the wrongdoer's own successors can be shown to have benefited from the wrong to such an extent that providing redress would leave them no worse off than they would have been had the wrong not been committed. Common law since Blackstone wrote has moved in this direction: following an act of 1934 'all causes of action subsisting against or vested in any person on his death, except causes of action for defamation, now survive against, or, as the case may be, for the benefit of his estate'.[18] In other words, the only wrong for which in principle P's successors cannot claim redress is A's defamation of P. There are of course time limits within which actions for redress must be taken, as there are for all wrongs whether the perpetrator has died or not, but these should be seen in my view as reflecting the utilitarian consideration that resource holdings should as far as possible be stabilized and not upset because of events long past. Time limits do not contradict the principle of redress itself.

If we switch our attention from common to Roman law, we find a more explicit acceptance of the idea of inherited responsibility.[19] The law of succession revolved around the idea of the *heir*, who it has been said 'stepped into the shoes' of the deceased person, and was assigned both the benefits and most of the burdens arising from the estate. There was no guarantee that the inherited assets would be sufficient to cover all of the costs, in which case the heir was required to pay up out of his own pocket, and so as Roman law evolved nominated heirs were given time to decide whether to take on the

---

[18] W. V. H. Rogers (ed.), *Winfield and Jolowicz on Tort*, 10th edn (London: Sweet and Maxwell, 1975), 499.

[19] I have relied here on W. W. Buckland, *A Text-Book of Roman Law from Augustus to Justinian* (Cambridge: Cambridge University Press, 1932), ch. 7 and W. W. Buckland and A. D. McNair, *Roman Law and Common Law* (Cambridge: Cambridge University Press, 1936), ch. 5.

office. But once the heir had assumed that role, he was responsible not only for paying debts and restoring property but also for other liabilities incurred by the person whose heir he was, for example breaches of contract committed by the deceased.

Both common and Roman law, then, accept the core idea that those who inherit from wrongdoers are potentially liable to make compensation for the wrongs committed. What has to be shown is that the victims or their descendants are themselves made worse off by the effects of the wrong—it is the failure of this condition that presumably excludes defamation as a cause of action under common law. On the other hand, the law insists that inheritors not be *punished* for what their predecessors did, and so this sets an upper limit to the compensation that must be paid. The common law does this by interpreting the claim for compensation as a claim against A's estate: A's successors are not liable to contribute resources that they own independently of the inheritance. Roman law dispensed with this safeguard, but instead allowed the designated heir to decide whether to assume that office. (Heirs who chose to act knowing that on balance they would lose as a result presumably did so out of a sense of honour, to protect the good name of the deceased.)

If we ask what ethical rationale might be given for these legal practices, the balance of argument must count against the *actio personalis moritur cum persona* rule, and in favour of allowing those who suffer from wrongs to claim redress notwithstanding the death of the wrongdoer. The moral case for inheritance is after all fairly weak: the person who inherits has, in general, done nothing to deserve the gain she receives, so she has no strong ground for complaint if that gain is reduced by the need to compensate the victims of wrongdoing, any more that she would have if there were straightforward debts to be paid out of the estate. In the case where A has wronged P and P now makes the claim against A's successors, this argument seems decisive. What if it is P's successors who make the claim? Here it might be said that they no more deserve to inherit from P than A's successors deserve to inherit from A, so if their claim is allowed we are merely swapping one morally arbitrary distribution for another. However the right of A's successors to inherit might seem especially questionable, since they will in part be the beneficiaries of injustice—they will be benefiting from that portion of the estate which ought to have been transferred to P by way of redress. So it seems that in the case of individual inheritance, both law and ethics support the general principle of holding people responsible for making good the wrongful harms brought about by their predecessors.

IV

Let us now return from individual inheritors to nations and consider the idea of national inheritance. In what sense can we describe nations as inheriting assets of various kinds from their predecessors? It seems perfectly natural to say that the present generation has inherited territory, institutions, physical and cultural capital, and so forth from earlier generations. Although there is no distinct moment of inheritance, since the membership of nations is in constant flux, still each incoming generation enjoys benefits that would not have existed but for the activities of previous generations in settling and defending territory, building up industry, creating schools and hospitals, and so on. Moreover the present generation controls these assets and decides who is to profit from them and on what terms. It claims the right to exclude aliens from national territory; it decides how much of the income generated from inherited capital should be used for foreign aid—in other words it asserts virtually unlimited rights over its inheritance. Some political philosophers would object to these claims, maintaining that inherited resources should be treated as a common asset to be shared among the world's peoples according to some principle of equality.[20] I have argued, however, in Chapter 3 that such principles are unacceptable, even if we could find some culturally neutral way of defining equality of resources. No meaningful form of national self-determination is possible unless nations are given sufficient control of their assets to be able to make decisions about their own future priorities, and this inevitably means that resource levels will vary over time as a result of these decisions. This does not entail the view (which I suggested above is widely held at present) that nations are entitled to regard their inherited

[20] For instance H. Steiner, 'Territorial Justice', in S. Caney, D. George and P. Jones (eds), *National Rights, International Obligations* (Boulder, CO: Westview Press, 1996); B. Barry, 'Humanity and Justice in Global Perspective', in B. Barry (ed.), *Democracy, Power and Justice* (Oxford: Clarendon Press, 1989); C. Beitz, *Political Theory and International Relations* (Princeton, NJ: Princeton University Press, 1979), Part 3, section 2.

assets as exclusive property on which no one else has any kind of claim. But it does support the idea of collective national inheritance as a prima facie right that stands up to the point at which strong competing claims are advanced by outsiders—for instance claims based on urgent need.

Let us assume, then, that the national inheritance of assets is legitimate, subject to the qualification in the last sentence. The question that arises is whether nations can inherit assets without at the same time inheriting responsibilities to redress past injustice. At this point, we must revert to the fourfold distinction between types of redress claims that I drew in Section I, because the argument has to proceed somewhat differently in each case.

Consider first, then, restitution claims for objects or resources that have been unjustly seized by nation A in the past—pieces of territory with symbolic or strategic importance, culturally significant artefacts, etc. Assume that at the time of the appropriation members of nation P had a good title to the items in question. Then the generation of As who acquired the items had no right to do so, and so cannot pass a valid title down to the present generation. The As' national inheritance comes encumbered with the claim of the Ps to have the items that are rightfully theirs returned to them.

Such claims appear uncontroversial because the underlying principle seems clear: in the face of competing claims, you cannot bequeath goods to which you do not have a valid title. In practice, however, there may well be controversy either about how titles to land or other assets are established, or about the effect of the passage of time on the respective claims of present-day As and Ps.[21] That is, present-day As may challenge the original title of the Ps and claim that their ancestors did no wrong in appropriating the resource that is at issue; or they may acknowledge the wrong but argue that by holding the resource over time they have established a claim to it that is now stronger than the purely historical claim of the Ps. This underlines a point I made earlier, that in order to adjudicate any specific claim for historic redress, we need to have elaborated principles to govern such matters such as territorial rights and how the passage of time affects them. But assuming that we have such principles and by using them are able to establish that the Ps now have a valid claim to the

---

[21] See the contributions listed in fn. 3 earlier.

land or the artefact in question, it then follows that the As' title by inheritance is invalid and the resource in question must be returned to the Ps.

Can we extend this argument to cases of the second kind, where the historical injustice we are concerned with does not consist in the taking of some identifiable object such as a piece of territory, but in some form of exploitation of the Ps by the As, resulting in the unjust enrichment of the As? In the case of imperialism, for instance, the main charge that is usually laid is not that the empire-builders physically removed assets that belonged to the subject peoples, but that they established political and economic relations whose effect was to profit the imperial metropolis at the expense of the periphery. Once again I want to leave aside the question of how such charges of exploitation are established in order to focus on the principle at stake. By analogy with our first case, the claim for redress on the part of the Ps would be that some part of the present-day assets of the As derives from the historic exploitation of their predecessors, even if there are no specific assets of which we can say that without the exploitation these would not now be in the hands of the As. The claim is that, had the exploitation not occurred, the As' present stock of capital would be reduced by some, no doubt hard to determine, amount—again, I shall leave aside the issue of how the relevant counterfactual could be validated.

The question here is whether the As' claim to their national inheritance can be defended if it turns out that part of that inheritance was unjustly acquired by their predecessors, in this case through exploitation rather than unjust acquisition. It seems to me that it cannot, and that the differences we find between this case and the first have to do with establishing that unjust transfers took place and in settling on the appropriate level of compensation, and not with the underlying principle involved.[22] Where physical items have been taken, the fact of the taking will be relatively clear, and it is also relatively clear what historical redress demands—the return of the

---

[22] Bernard Boxhill has advanced an argument of this kind to justify paying reparations to American blacks for slavery. Boxhill claims that the descendants of slaves have inherited a claim for reparation against the assets making up the collective inheritance of white Americans, stemming from the injustice of slavery. See B. Boxhill, 'A Lockean Argument for Black Reparations', *Journal of Ethics*, 7 (2003), 63–91.

items in question. Where exploitation occurs through economic relationships, to show that the relationships are indeed exploitative you
must appeal to a theory of exploitation, which may be controversial.
This is particularly the case where both the As and the Ps gained
something from their relationship, and the dispute is about whether
the gains were fairly or unfairly shared between them. Moreover
what should now be offered by way of compensation if injustice
is established is contestable, for all the reasons that Waldron and
others have identified. But this difference should not conceal the
similarity of underlying principle, namely that a claim to inherit
must depend on the bequeathers having a valid title to the assets they
are bequeathing.[23]

The third category of cases are those in which the As have
wronged the Ps in the past, but not in such a way as to leave the
present generation of As unjustly enriched—cases, for instance, in
which the Ps were simply oppressed to no benefit of the As, or in
which the original advantage reaped by the As has long since been
dissipated: think of seizing some resource that is then allowed to
decay to the point where it is worthless. We cannot in these cases
argue that the As' claim to their national inheritance is compromised because there is some part of it to which they have no valid
title—the wrongful act has left no valuable residue. So can we show
that they nevertheless inherit a responsibility to put the injustice
right?

To answer this question, we need to reflect more deeply on
what justifies the idea of national inheritance in the first place.
We have to think of nations as intergenerational communities in
which the present generation acknowledges responsibilities both
to respect the memory of past generations in various ways—for
instance to protect their achievements or to continue unfinished
projects that were important to them—and to enrich the lives of
future ones. I do not want to suggest that in either case the content
of these responsibilities is clear and simple—there can and should be

---

[23] I do not mean to suggest that paying the present generation of Ps the compensation that would have been due to their ancestors by virtue of the original acts of
injustice is always sufficient to wipe the moral slate clean. It may be that adequate
redress must include apology for the wrong as well as material compensation. I shall
discuss the question of apology below. Here I am trying to identify what seem to
me to be the more straightforward aspects of inherited national responsibility.

lively debates about how best to respect our ancestors and benefit our descendants—but unless we accept this picture the very idea of national inheritance becomes morally unsupportable (as I have acknowledged, some would consider it unsupportable for independent reasons: my point here is that *if* we are going to say anything to defeat the arguments of those advocating global equality of opportunity or something similar, it can only be by appealing to the picture I have sketched). In a just world, then, we could explain the position of each present-day national community in terms of what they and their ancestors have achieved—the set of resources available to each community would reflect the labours, practices, political decisions, and so forth of succeeding generations. Now introduce into the story some unjust policy practised by an earlier generation of As to the detriment of the Ps. In the cases we are presently considering, unlike those discussed earlier, the effect of these policies is no longer beneficial to the As, though it continues to harm the Ps, who have fewer resources, broadly conceived, than they would have in the just world scenario. The question is whether present-day As can disown these policies on the grounds that they receive no benefit from them—there is nothing they 'have', as it were, that rightfully belongs to the present-day Ps. And it seems to me that they cannot disown the policies in question while continuing to 'own' those other policies and practices of older generations of As that now provide them with advantages. Suppose, to take a very simple and stylized example, that Victorian Britons had pursued just two policies with significant present-day effects: domestic industrialization and imperial expansion. And suppose that the effects of imperial expansion were harmful to the subjects of imperial rule and their descendants but brought no lasting benefit to Britain (there was a lively debate about this at the time), whereas domestic industrialization generated valuable capital for future generations of Britons. Then it seems to me inconsistent for present-day Britons to claim the resources produced by industrialization as part of their national inheritance while refusing to acknowledge any responsibility for the consequences of imperialism. The picture of nations as intergenerational communities that supports the claim to advantages also imposes the liability.

I do not want to deny that the liability in cases like this is somewhat weaker than in the earlier cases where the nation that had perpetrated the injustice also continued to benefit from it, because in those cases the actual history departs from the hypothetical just history in two directions: the As now have more than they should and the Ps have less, so there are two injustices to put right— there is unjust enrichment as well as unjust deprivation. But even where there is no unjust enrichment, a nation that wants to claim the advantages created by previous generations must also accept a responsibility to offer redress for the injustices they inflicted. As a general matter, claims to compensation do not depend on the agent who committed the injustice continuing to benefit from it—if I steal your car and then write it off, you still have a claim for compensation against me. So in the case we are considering, all that needs to be shown to ground a claim for redress is that the present-day As can properly be treated as the heirs of earlier As for this purpose. My argument is that it is unjustifiable to treat them in that way when what is at stake is the inheritance of benefits, but not when what is at stake is the inheritance of liabilities.

What finally of cases in which the injustice for which redress is being demanded does not affect the present-day position either of the As or of the Ps, or at least not in any material way that can be demonstrated? It might seem that there can be no such cases, because the very fact that someone or some group is demanding redress proves that they are suffering in some fashion from the effects of the injustice. However I am inclined to draw a line between those who can be seen to bear the impact of the injustice, either in terms of deprivation of resources or in terms of its psychological consequences, and those for whom redress matters for symbolic reasons. So, for instance, Aboriginal children whose lives were ruined by being 'stolen' and their own children who had to grow up living under that shadow would fall on one side of the line, whereas later Aboriginal generations for whom a failure by the Australian state to offer an apology or compensation continues to rankle will fall on the other side. I do not deny that people who are not materially affected may still feel very strongly about the injustice: we see this in parallel cases involving individuals, for instance people who are prepared to go to great lengths to see their parents or grandparents, now dead, cleared of crimes they did not commit. However there does seem to be a morally relevant difference between cases that fall on either side of the line, which is why this final category needs separate consideration.

Since *ex hypothesi* both the present-day As and the present-day Ps have the resources and other advantages they ought to have in a historically just world, what is at stake is the issuing of an apology by the As for a historic injustice or, if compensation is involved, it is not compensation owed to the present-day Ps, but owed to their ancestors and paid to the present generation as their representatives.[24] Some have challenged the idea of compensating the dead, but I shall assume that the idea itself makes sense in order to focus on the question whether the responsibility to do this is one that can be inherited.[25] If material compensation and not just verbal apology is involved, then what matters is the symbolic significance of the compensation — the resources that are handed over are meant to demonstrate the depth of the apology rather than to bring the present generation up to any particular level of advantage.

Thinking once again about individual cases, the idea of vicarious apology clearly makes sense.[26] We frequently apologize for what our children do, and, rather less often, apologize for the misdemeanours of our forebears. But we have to proceed carefully here. If I discover that my father has behaved very badly towards another person, perhaps in a way that does not have material consequences — needlessly insulted him, for instance — then it may well be right for me to apologize on his behalf. However for this to make sense it seems that I have to identify in a certain way with my father; I have to think that this was a lapse on his part, that he would have wanted to apologize if he had been given the opportunity. Suppose on the contrary that I disidentify with him more or less completely, I

[24] Richard Vernon has argued that apologies should not be seen as (backward-looking) cases of what he calls 'restitution' and I am calling 'redress', but as statements designed to extend recognition and respect to victim groups — their underlying purpose is to include these groups in equal citizenship. I agree that the motivation behind an apology may be as described, but I want to insist that the actual content of the apology involves the vicarious acceptance of responsibility for what occurred historically. See Vernon, 'Against Restitution', pp. 544–6.

[25] For a defence of the idea of making reparations to the dead, see M. Ridge, 'Giving the Dead their Due', *Ethics*, 114 (2003–4), 38–59.

[26] See the analysis of the conditions necessary for something to qualify as an apology in K. Gill, 'The Moral Functions of an Apology', *Philosophical Forum*, 31 (2000), 11–27. The key condition here is that 'for an act to count as an apology, it must be true that...someone is responsible for the offensive act, and either the person offering the apology takes responsibility for the act or there is some relationship between the responsible person and the apologizer that justifies her taking responsibility for offering an apology' (13).

thoroughly disapprove of the way that he conducted his life, and so forth, then although I can still apologize for his behaviour—much as one might apologize for a cat that has just fouled a neighbour's lawn—I cannot apologize on his behalf. The latter involves standing in his shoes and saying the things that I believe he would have wanted to say, which requires identification.

If this is correct, then it does impose some limits on what can be done to redress 'pure' historic injustice, injustice that does not leave material traces in the present. If the source of the injustice is the fact that our predecessors acted on moral beliefs very different from our own, then that very fact may make it difficult for us to identify with them in a way that makes apology possible.[27] I conjecture that this may be the reason why politicians and statesmen today are often reluctant to issue apologies, as noted earlier. This may be expressed, as in the case of the statement by John Howard I cited, as a reluctance to accept 'guilt and blame' for past actions and policies. If guilt and blame were the issue, then it would be simple enough to point out that people who make vicarious apologies do not acknowledge guilt and blame *themselves*. But perhaps the underlying thought is that in making an apology we are also identifying ourselves with the perpetrators of the injustice—we are recognizing commonalties between our beliefs and values and theirs, with the implication that we too might have committed the injustice if we had been in their position.[28] Conversely, the politician who resists making the apology is attempting to draw a firm line between them and us, between then and now.

Demands for apologies in the absence of continuing material injustice do then seem to presuppose ties of identification and not just the inheritance of benefits between the present generation and its national predecessors. All that can be required here is consistency. One cannot, morally speaking, identify with the positive past

---

[27] For instance, I may regret the slaughter of Muslims that took place following the capture of Acre by Richard I in 1191, but to apologize for that event I would have to be able to identify with a group of Frankish-speaking crusaders in such a way as to recognize a line of descent from them to me—something that seems very difficult if not impossible to accomplish.

[28] For further reflection on the connection between the perpetrators of injustice and those in the present who are being asked to offer an apology, see L. Radzik, 'Collective Responsibility and the Duty to Respond', *Social Theory and Practice*, 27 (2001), 455–71.

achievements of one's nation and take pride in them without at the same time acknowledging responsibility, and the need to apologize, for past actions that were harmful to others.[29] Since national pride is a widespread phenomenon, so too is the potential scope of national apology. No nation, of course, understands its own history from a purely detached perspective. National history is written and rewritten in the light of the interests and concerns of the present, and one purpose that such history serves is to hold up the past as a model to be emulated in the present—to recall the triumphs and achievements of previous generations as setting standards that we must now live up to.[30] So there is some incentive to airbrush discreditable episodes from the historical record. But it is also possible to interpret the past as offering salutary lessons about how the nation should *not* behave, and it seems to me a mark of a mature nation that it is able to come to terms with both the good and the bad parts of its historical record—think, for example, of how ongoing reflection on the Holocaust and its sources has helped to strengthen Germans' commitment to their present democratic constitution. So it is not only morally necessary but also psychologically feasible to identify with past generations while at the same time remaining critical of the injustices they perpetrated. Sincere apology, as I suggested above, requires both identification and disidentification—identification with the agent for whose misdeeds one is apologizing, but disidentification with the deeds themselves, which are condemned by principles that the agent ought to have accepted. So the limits of national apology are determined by how the present generation understands the national past, not by material factors such as the proportion of inherited national capital that can be attributed to the effects of past injustice.

V

The argument about national apologies becomes particularly problematic in the case of those whose ancestors migrated to the nation that is now being asked to apologize after the events in question took place. Descendants of immigrants can say, reasonably enough, that

---

[29] This argument is developed in F. Abdel-Nour, 'National Responsibility', *Political Theory*, 31 (2003), 693–719.

[30] I have discussed this function of national history in *On Nationality*, ch. 2.

they identify with their own ancestors, not with the perpetrators, and so it is inappropriate for any apology to be issued on their behalf. It might seem that this argument applies not only to apologies but to all claims for redress that refer to events in the remoter past. Why should immigrants or descendants of immigrants be asked to contribute towards restitution or compensation for injustices that their ancestors played no part in bringing about?

A possible line of reply here is to say that when immigrants join a nation they give their consent to many requirements, including the requirement to offer redress for past injustice if that turns out to be necessary. By way of analogy, someone who joins a corporation or a business partnership takes on a share of responsibility for the debts and liabilities of the firm, including debts and liabilities that were not apparent at the moment she joined (for instance the possibility of being sued for the harmful side effects of products manufactured in the past). But the analogy is not a strong one. One problem is that even if the original immigrants can be shown to have given their consent, this does not extend to their descendants, whose membership in the nation in question is clearly involuntary. Another problem is that immigrants may be driven by necessity—by the fear of persecution, for example—and not by free choice. So I think it would be a mistake to incorporate immigrant minorities into national responsibility by appealing to their presumed consent to national debts and liabilities.

A more promising way forward is to apply the general argument for inherited responsibilities sketched in the previous section to immigrants as well. Here the salient fact is that immigrant minorities typically share in the national inheritance: they benefit from the physical, human, and cultural capital accumulated by previous generations.[31] The extent of their benefit depends on how effectively they are included within the scope of institutions of social justice that treat all citizens equally. In Chapter 5, I argued that, in so far as nations can be regarded as cooperative practices in which costs and benefits (including the opportunity to participate in decision-making) are fairly distributed among the members, each member falls within the scope of collective responsibility, even if on a particular occasion she dissents from the decisions that are taken or

---

[31] For a similar point made in relation to reparations for slavery in the USA, see Boxhill, 'A Lockean Argument for Black Reparations', 77.

the actions that result. This argument, I believe, can be extended to national responsibility for the past. In the case of minority groups, the issue is not how far their ancestors were causally responsible for the historic injustices that concern us, but how far they are now receiving a fair share of the national inheritance, in the form of the goods and services that inherited capital provides. Groups that are currently marginalized—for instance aboriginal groups in many cases—should not on this understanding of the question be asked to contribute towards the rectification of historic injustice; on the contrary, they would be among the potential beneficiaries of such redress. Depending on the circumstances, the same may apply to guest workers or refugees who are not granted full rights of citizenship. Immigrant groups that have prospered, by contrast, should pay their fair share of the costs of rectification.

My argument in this chapter has been that anyone who is prepared to accept the general idea of national responsibility ought also to accept the idea of responsibility for the national past. The key, I have suggested, is to reflect on the benefits that membership in a national community can provide, primarily tangible benefits in the form of inherited territory and capital, but also intangible benefits in the form of pride in the national past. My claim is that one cannot legitimately enjoy such benefits without at the same time acknowledging responsibility for aspects of the national past that have involved the unjust treatment of people inside or outside the national community itself, and liability to provide redress in whatever form the particular circumstances demand. Such redress is by no means the whole of global justice, nor have I taken any stand on the question how we should weight obligations of historical redress against other obligations such as those owed to the global poor irrespective of past history. But it is certainly one part of the picture, and one that no theory that takes the idea of national responsibility seriously can afford to dismiss.

CHAPTER 7

———

Human Rights: Setting the
Global Minimum

I

Over the course of Chapters 4–6, I have been exploring the idea of responsibility, and more especially national responsibility: I have tried to show why, and when, we can hold nations responsible for the material condition of their members and for the external costs they impose on others. The main focus has been on what I have been calling outcome responsibility, the idea that where we can identify A as the agent who has produced a certain outcome O, we have reason to let A enjoy the benefits or suffer the harms associated with O, and at the same time to indemnify others who have been damaged by O. But I also commented, in Chapter 4, on another form of responsibility that is relevant to debates about global justice— remedial responsibility, the responsibility we may have to come to the aid of those who are deprived or suffering in some way. In that chapter, I discussed some of the problems involved in assigning remedial responsibilities, in cases where there is a plurality of agents who might come to the aid of a particular deprived P. I return to this question, as applied to the case of global poverty, in Chapter 9. Here I want to investigate a prior aspect of the problem: how are we to decide when a person's deprivation or suffering is bad enough to trigger remedial responsibilities in others, in particular if we are thinking about the question at a global level? To put the question in more familiar terms: what do we owe to the world's poor? When does their poverty impose obligations on us, leaving aside for the moment the issue of how those obligations are to be assigned as between all of the agencies who might come to their aid?

I propose to answer this question by giving an account of *basic human rights*. I shall suggest, in other words, that when basic human rights go unprotected, any agent, individual or collective, who is able to help protect them may in principle bear remedial responsibilities. The language of human rights is appropriate here because it serves to emphasize the moral urgency of the situation of the person or group whose rights are being denied. Having a right denied is more serious than just having a claim unmet or a desire unfulfilled. This urgency means that other agents can be placed under enforceable obligations to protect the right.[1] But at the same time the notion of human rights is somewhat vague, and open to multiple interpretations, as we shall see shortly. In particular, it is liable to be stretched in a way that diminishes the moral urgency of the claim that it advances. I therefore speak of *basic* human rights to underline the point that the rights I have in mind are a subset of those sometimes listed under this heading, distinguished by the compelling moral force of the claims they represent.[2]

I shall be interested in the question of how basic human rights are to be justified: what has to be shown in order to vindicate the claim that human beings everywhere have a right to something—to subsistence, to free speech, and so forth. This question has attracted a lot of attention, and it becomes especially pressing when human rights are being used, as here, as part of a theory of global justice. Since the human rights of people in one place may impose remedial obligations on people, or states, elsewhere, it seems important that they should be justified in a way that has universal reach. In other words, the justification we give should be valid across the

---

[1] I do not want to say that whenever we identify a human right, we must at the same time identify an agent who bears an obligation that corresponds directly to the right. I examine this correspondence claim, which has been advanced in particular by Onora O'Neill, later in this chapter. The point for now is that human rights are always *potentially* obligation-imposing, and must therefore represent strong moral claims on the part of the right-holders. Not until the end of this book do I examine how large are the sacrifices that rich nations must be prepared to make to honour these claims.

[2] Here I follow, among others, Henry Shue for whom 'basic rights ... are everyone's minimum reasonable demands upon the rest of humanity'. See H. Shue, *Basic Rights: Subsistence, Affluence, and American Foreign Policy*, 2nd edn (Princeton, NJ: Princeton University Press, 1996), 19.

different religious, moral, and political cultures that we find in the contemporary world.[3] Of course, it may not be possible to find such a justification. But if we fail, this has potentially damaging implications. Where serious breaches of human rights are taking place, or being threatened, there may be no alternative but to intervene forcibly in the society in question, disrupting local practices and removing regimes with significant local support. If outsiders do this, it is important that they should be able to justify their actions by reference to principles that those in the society have reason to accept (many of the insiders may not currently embrace these principles— if they did, the rights violations would probably not be occurring— but at least they can be given a justification that connects to beliefs that they already hold). In this way, we show respect for the people whose rights we are attempting to protect.

Finding a justification for human rights that meets this condition is not easy, and I shall shortly review various justificatory strategies that have been proposed. But first I need to say a little more about how my conception of basic human rights differs from some other interpretations of that idea. Human rights are often now thought of as components of international law, which is indeed how they were conceived in the original UN *Universal Declaration of Human Rights* in 1948 and the various later covenants and treaties that have amplified that document. As so interpreted, the purpose of human rights is to set standards with which all states are expected to comply. There is, however, an ambiguity as to how this standard-setting role is to be understood. On the one hand, human rights might serve us as a minimal standard, a way of demarcating the morally tolerable from the morally intolerable. In this role, they would also serve as a necessary, but perhaps not sufficient, condition of political legitimacy. Any state that perpetrated, or permitted, widespread violations of human rights within its borders would no longer be regarded by

---

[3] Here I am assuming a view about moral justification that may be controversial. Others might say that if a reason is a good reason for holding a belief, this must be a good reason for everyone, no matter what they think. So a justification for human rights, if it is sound, must by that token be a justification for human beings everywhere. But this view of justification seems implausible to me. What counts as a justification for someone, at least in the field of practical reason that concerns us here, must depend on the beliefs that they already hold. So there is no a priori guarantee that the justification for human rights that we propose, even if valid in our own terms, will have universal reach.

other states and by international institutions as a legitimate state, and it would therefore lose its normal immunity against outside intervention.[4] Whether such intervention should in fact occur, and what form it should take, is another question. What, on this interpretation, human rights are doing is identifying conditions that states must meet if they are to enjoy standard rights of sovereignty and self-determination. On this understanding of their purpose, we would expect the list of human rights to be fairly short. Only *essential* rights, such as rights to life and physical security, belong on a list whose aim is to set a minimum standard separating the tolerable from the intolerable.

On the other hand, human rights might be understood as setting a target, something to which all peoples and all states should *aspire*. They would constitute one component, perhaps the most important component, of a just political regime. On this understanding of their purpose, states that failed to meet the target would not necessarily be regarded as illegitimate, especially if their failure could be attributed to economic underdevelopment, say, but other states should encourage them—through aid, through financial incentives, through offers of membership of international bodies such as the EU, and so forth—to move closer to the goal. In the light of this purpose, the list of human rights could properly extend to include many items that would not appear on the basic list, for instance extensive rights to liberty, democratic rights, and rights to non-discrimination—rights, in other words, that we would see as fundamental to the constitution of a just political regime.

As I have indicated, my own purpose in setting out a theory of basic human rights is different from either of these. My aim is to identify a list of rights that can specify a global minimum that people everywhere are entitled to as a matter of justice, and that therefore may impose obligations, on rich nations especially. It will include rights that would not belong on a list whose purpose was simply to define conditions of political legitimacy. Rights to subsistence are a good example. States cannot always provide their citizens with an adequate level of subsistence: natural disasters, for example, may prevent them from doing so. So long as they make reasonable

---

[4] Such a position is developed in A. Buchanan, 'Recognitional Legitimacy and the State System', *Philosophy and Public Affairs*, 28 (1999), 46–78.

attempts to provide subsistence, they should not be judged illegitimate if they fail, and so subsistence rights should not be included on a list whose rationale is to provide conditions of political legitimacy. Yet in these circumstances outsiders will have remedial responsibilities to come to the aid of the citizens in question, and by including subsistence on our longer list of human rights, we highlight these responsibilities.

On the other hand, basic human rights as I shall understand them do not extend to the complete list of rights that we would wish to include in our description of a fully just political regime.[5] For most readers of this book, that description will reflect liberal political principles, and will therefore include rights of the kind that feature in the constitutions of liberal states, or in treaties between such states such as the European Convention on Human Rights. Although the language of human rights has become well-entrenched in this context, it might be better to describe such rights as rights of citizenship, in recognition of the fact that the rights included can reasonably vary from one society to the next. The relevant point here is that if a society fails to recognize a right that we would regard as a right of citizenship—say a right to equal participation in politics— this does not generate remedial responsibilities in outsiders (and this is not merely because it may be impossible in practice for outsiders to enforce such a right). We are not obliged to take steps to implement citizenship rights, as we understand them, in the society in question, even though we may be justified in encouraging its members to move, in due course, towards recognizing them. Put another way, the fact that different societies may recognize and enforce different sets of citizenship rights does not in itself constitute a global injustice, even if we believe that (social) justice would be enhanced if all societies were eventually to converge on roughly the same set of rights.

In drawing this line between basic human rights and the longer list that can be found in some human rights documents, I am assuming that only certain rights-violations are urgent enough to trigger remedial responsibilities in outsiders: being denied material subsistence triggers such responsibilities, whereas being denied equal

---

[5] For cautions against extending human rights to cover all the requirements of justice, see J. Griffin, 'Discrepancies Between the Best Philosophical Account of Human Rights and the International Law of Human Rights', *Proceedings of the Aristotelian Society*, 101 (2000), 1–28.

participation in politics does not. This could be disputed, of course, and to counter the objection I need to explain what distinguishes basic human rights from others that are better called rights of citizenship. At this stage, I am simply trying to indicate the role that my theory of human rights is meant to play, and to explain why for other purposes the relevant list of human rights may be either shorter or longer. Equally there is no single correct answer to the question: 'How are human rights to be justified?' The justification we give depends on what we want our theory of human rights to do.

II

With that in mind, I want now to proceed by contrasting three general strategies that have been used to justify human rights. The first I shall call the practice-based strategy. This asserts that we do not need to look for deep philosophical foundations for human rights. Instead, we should go directly to the *practice* of human rights, that is to the various official declarations and covenants, and the way these have been implemented in international law, in the foreign policies of governments, and in the day-to-day work of human rights organizations, and extract a theory of human rights from that practice. The second strategy, I shall call the search for an overlapping consensus. The idea here is that we can find multiple foundations for human rights by going in turn to each of the major world religions, or to significant non-religious world views, and showing that each of these supports a common list of human rights. In this case, unlike the first, human rights would have philosophical foundations, but the foundations would be different for different people, depending on their underlying values. The third strategy involves finding a common foundation in features of human beings—basic human needs are the feature I shall appeal to—that (so it is claimed) must be recognized as morally compelling by people everywhere whatever their own particular religious or secular world view. Human rights are justified by showing that they provide the necessary conditions for such needs to be fulfilled (or, e.g. in another version of this strategy, for certain human capabilities to be realized). I shall call this the humanitarian strategy, and it is the one that I want to defend after having shown where the first two go wrong.

The practice-based strategy is initially very appealing, and a large part of its appeal is that it tells us to put aside all the worries about the allegedly sectarian character of human rights.[6] Since human rights can be shown to work, in the sense that they form the basis for an ever-growing international practice of claiming, recognizing, and enforcing human rights, why worry too much about their philosophical foundations? Justification, after all, has to stop somewhere—nothing can be justified all the way down. So why look beyond a practice that appears to be in good order, and that has given human rights a reasonably clear role in international politics? If somebody asks whether a particular alleged right should be counted as a human right, we answer him by seeing whether this right fits with the other rights that are already included in the practice. Can it function in the way that these other rights do? A theory of human rights is best understood, from this point of view, as an interpretation of the practice—as a statement of the principles that are latent in the practice itself. As the practice evolves, so too should our understanding of human rights—this, according to the defenders of the first strategy, is an advantage, for it allows the list of human rights to expand in response to technological or other changes in conditions of life. As Charles Beitz puts it:

International human rights are not even *prospectively* timeless. They are standards appropriate to the institutions of modern or modernizing societies coexisting in a global political economy in which human beings face a series of predictable threats...the composition of the list of human rights is explained by the nature of these threats. As the economic and technological environment evolves, the array of threats will change, and so, over time, will the list of human rights.[7]

Such pragmatism must surely be welcome to those of us who think, about moral and political values in general, that they do not embody timeless truths, but are concepts that have to be understood against the background of particular forms of social life. Ideas of justice, for example, are contextually specific, as I have argued elsewhere.[8] A

---

[6] For a good account of human rights that uses this strategy, see C. Beitz, 'Human Rights as a Common Concern', *American Political Science Review*, 95 (2001), 269–82.

[7] C. Beitz, 'What Human Rights Mean', *Daedalus*, 132 (2003), 44.

[8] In D. Miller, 'Two Ways to Think about Justice', *Politics, Philosophy and Economics*, 1 (2002), 5–28.

value or a principle may be justified, even if the justification involves connecting that concept or principle to a particular set of social circumstances, with the implication that if those circumstances were to change, the justification would no longer apply. So why refuse the practice-based strategy for justifying human rights?

The justification works only if the practice really is in good order, in the sense of there being a widespread, unforced agreement to implement a set of human rights. Recall that we are aiming for a justification of human rights that will provide everyone everywhere with a good reason to observe them. This does not, of course, mean that we must discover a universal will to respect human rights concretely — if that happy state of affairs were to obtain, we would hardly need the doctrine. But for the practice-based strategy to work, we must be able to observe practical agreement across societies on the set of human rights that it is obligatory for states to respect, and not merely, for instance, agreement among activists who are steeped in the traditions of Western liberalism. Here we are hampered by the fact that there is no authoritative source to which we can appeal if there is a dispute about whether an alleged right is indeed a genuine human right. It is sometimes suggested that the growing body of international law constitutes such an authoritative source. But the content of international law is always to a greater or lesser extent a matter of interpretation, and so we cannot obtain a definitive ruling on, for example, the question whether there is a human right to democracy.[9]

Another source to which appeal has been made in defence of the practice-based strategy are the norms that various national and international bodies — human rights NGOs, for instance — use to judge the human rights records of different countries. But again, we have

---

[9] Thomas Franck has made a persuasive case that a 'right to democratic governance' is in the process of establishing itself within international law, citing, for instance, the many treaties and resolutions in which such a right has been proclaimed, the growing practice of monitoring of elections by international observers to establish that they are free and fair, and so forth. Yet Franck also acknowledges that this right collides directly with the well-established principle of non-interference in the domestic affairs of sovereign states, limiting the extent to which it is enforceable under international law. Thus its present status remains ambiguous, even if, like Franck, we anticipate a future world in which the right has become an enforceable human right. See T. Franck, 'The Emerging Right to Democratic Governance', *American Journal of International Law*, 86 (1992), 46–91.

to ask what standing these norms have. Are they, indeed, norms that could command universal acceptance, or do they represent the particular agendas of the bodies that use them?[10] Amnesty International, for example, takes use of the death penalty as one of the criteria to be used in judging the human rights records of various countries, but it is doubtful whether there is any genuine consensus on the principle that capital punishment, as such, necessarily involves a violation of human rights.

A third element in the practice-based strategy involves looking at the formal human rights documents, given that these, if not unanimously endorsed, have at least been consented to by the great majority of states worldwide. But one has to ask what exactly these states took themselves to be agreeing to when they signed. I am not the first to observe that few of the forty-eight countries that originally signed the Universal Declaration can have supposed that they would actually be *required* to observe its provisions at some later date. Some of the provisions would have been politically unacceptable; others would have far exceeded the capacities of many of the signatories. Presumably signing the Declaration was a symbolic act representing a hope for a better world in the aftermath of the Second World War. Later use of the documents has relied on a working distinction being drawn between basic rights—rights to life, bodily integrity, freedom of expression, etc.—to which appeal is made when the legitimacy of a particular state is being put in question, and other rights that are never used in that way—the right to equal pay for equal work (Article 23), for example, or the right of parents to choose the kind of education their children receive (Article 26). But this distinction could not be drawn simply from a reading of the documents themselves. As documents with signatures attached, the various covenants and treaties may be treated as authoritative, but for their interpretation we need to turn to other aspects of human rights practice, which as I have argued above may turn out to be less than universally endorsed.

To sum up, the practice-based approach cannot really provide an answer to the non-Western critic who may not be completely hostile to the idea of human rights itself, but who regards the human

[10] For a fuller treatment of this question, see M. Ignatieff, *Human Rights as Politics and Idolatry* (Princeton, NJ: Princeton University Press, 2001).

rights regime as it has emerged as very largely an expression of liberal priorities. Such a person might, for example, reject the heavy emphasis placed on civil and political rights at the expense of social and economic rights. Where rival practices, or rival interpretations of the canonical documents, emerge, the practice-based approach cannot adjudicate between them. This may not always matter when human rights are being used as counters in international diplomacy, for instance. Here partial agreement may be sufficient to motivate collective action against regimes that violate human rights across the board. But if we want a theory of human rights to play a central role in our thinking about global justice, we need to be able to say, with some precision, what counts as a human right and what does not. So although the practice-based approach, with its promise of avoiding foundational questions, seems initially very appealing, it cannot deliver what we need in the absence of a high level of practical agreement on which human rights belong on the definitive list.

III

So let me turn to the second justificatory strategy, which I dubbed the overlapping consensus strategy. As its name implies, this recommends arriving at human rights in a way that recalls John Rawls's strategy for demonstrating that there might be reasonable agreement on principles of social justice among people holding different fundamental world views. In the latter case, Rawls suggests that a conception of social justice rooted in the public culture of a liberal society may also find support from within a variety of religious and non-religious conceptions of the good life favoured by individual citizens.[11] In the human rights case, we begin from the major world views, religious and secular, that we find in existence at global level, and then seek to show that adherents of each of these world views has reason to support an agreed doctrine of human rights—the doctrine is, so to speak, implicit in the general beliefs and conceptions of the human good that people around the world already hold.

There are, in fact, two variants of the overlapping consensus strategy. The first tries to find the *substance* of human rights, if not the

---

[11] See J. Rawls, *Political Liberalism* (New York: Columbia University Press, 1993), lecture IV.

concept, explicitly present in the various world views. The best-known example of this is Michael Walzer's so-called 'moral minimalism', which claims that virtually every 'thick' human morality that we have encountered contains within it a core of rules and principles that is common to all. These, he says, will most likely be negative injunctions—'rules against murder, deceit, torture, oppression, and tyranny'—which we in Western societies will express using the language of human rights, though elsewhere other moral vocabularies will be used. Since these standards are universally recognized, Walzer claims, we are entitled to hold other societies to them.[12]

Walzer's claim about the reiteration of the moral minimum across societies is a plausible one that I do not intend to challenge empirically. It suffers, however, from two limitations as a strategy for justifying human rights. First, as Walzer says himself, the content of the moral minimum is likely to consist of a set of prohibitions—of murder, torture, etc.—and therefore not to extend to cases in which the protection of human rights requires positive action on the part of others. Thus a government that deliberately starves some of its subjects to death could be condemned by reference to an injunction against wanton killing, but a government that for ideological reasons pursues a policy one of whose side effects is widespread starvation could not. This latter government has defaulted on a positive obligation to ensure that those living under it have access to the means of subsistence. If we believe that human rights can be, and often are, violated by policies such as this, then Walzer's version of the overlapping consensus will not yield a sufficiently thick list of rights. Walzer's minimalism might suffice if our purpose in appealing to human rights were simply to discriminate between regimes that are morally and politically legitimate and those that are not. But if we think that a government that permits starvation, or other gross forms of deprivation, is also contributing to the violation of human rights, and that international intervention of some kind may in principle be justifiable in such circumstances, then minimalism is not enough.[13]

[12] M. Walzer, *Thick and Thin: Moral Argument at Home and Abroad* (Notre Dame, IND: University of Notre Dame Press, 1994), ch. 1.

[13] I do not mean to imply here that Walzer would dissent from this view. Indeed he would say that when people within a community are starving, outsiders who are able to help have an obligation to do so. But this would be an independently justified obligation of mutual aid, not a corollary of moral minimalism.

Walzer's approach does not give us the resources to make this judgement.

The second limitation inherent in moral minimalism concerns the scope of the injunctions that Walzer lists. Do they have universal scope, in the sense of applying to all human beings, or are they restricted to the society that promulgates them? What, for example, if a society has an injunction against murder or rape, but does not regard the killing or raping of outsiders as covered by that injunction? Moral minimalism seems empirically plausible because it is hard to imagine a society surviving that does not recognize and enforce such basic injunctions among its own members. But, as we well know, this does not mean that the same restrictions will be applied to non-members—or indeed that when a society descends into civil war on the basis of ethnic or religious divisions, to those on the other side of the dividing line. In so far, therefore, as human rights doctrine is meant to apply not only to rights-violations within a society but to acts perpetrated by one society, or its government, against another, that doctrine needs stronger support than moral minimalism can provide. We need to show that it is *always* wrong to murder, torture, or deceive, no matter what the identity of the victim.

Now I turn to the second variant of the overlapping consensus strategy. Whereas the first variant looks for rules and principles that are explicitly present in the moral codes of other societies, Western and non-Western, the second variant tries to extract human rights from the underlying philosophies of these societies, whether their substance is already recognized in first-order morality. In other words, the claim is that all the major world views contain ethical resources from which human rights can be derived. When we appeal to them in order to criticize or condemn prevailing practices in other societies, we can justify our appeal by recourse to ideas and beliefs that members of those societies already hold.

Much effort in recent years has gone into showing how human rights can be grounded in the traditions of Islam, Judaism, Confucianism, Buddhism, and so forth, and politically speaking this strategy has much to be said for it. By searching for an overlapping consensus, we show our respect for these non-Western traditions, and make it easier for those who embrace them to accept human rights doctrine. But we also need to be clear and honest about what is going on here. The interpretive efforts in question do not really start with Islam, or Confucianism, etc., as a whole and ask whether the best reading of these cultures entails recognition of and respect for human rights. Instead, beginning with one or other received list of human rights, they search for elements in the cultures which might be used to ground the list, or certain parts of it. Inevitably this involves a selective interpretation of the culture in question, highlighting certain components and downplaying others. Because each of these major world-philosophies is internally contested and contains different sub-traditions, it will almost certainly be possible to find the connections that are being sought between underlying concepts and human rights. Charles Taylor, for example, has argued that a strand of reformed Buddhism that has gained adherents in Thailand contains a doctrine of non-violence that can ground human rights and democratic values more generally.[14] Joseph Chan has claimed that the central Confucian concept of *ren*, which means something like benevolence, can justify basic civil liberties such as freedom of expression.[15] Similar attempts have been made for the other world views. But being able to tell a plausible story that leads from the selected idea to a list of human rights is not the same as showing that, taking the cultures as a whole, we can generate an overlapping consensus on human rights from within.[16]

---

[14] C. Taylor, 'Conditions of an Unforced Consensus on Human Rights', in J. R. Bauer and D. A. Bell (eds), *The East Asian Challenge for Human Rights* (Cambridge: Cambridge University Press, 1999).

[15] J. Chan, 'A Confucian Perspective on Human Rights for Contemporary China', in J. R. Bauer and D. A. Bell Bauer (eds), *The East Asian Challenge for Human Rights* (Cambridge: Cambridge University Press, 1999), 212–40.

[16] For further problems with the overlapping consensus strategy, see P. Jones, 'Human Rights and Diverse Cultures: Continuity or Discontinuity?', in S. Caney and P. Jones (eds), *Human Rights and Global Diversity* (London: Frank Cass, 2001). The overlapping consensus strategy discussed here needs to be distinguished from a different proposal, namely that having worked out our conception of human rights on independent grounds, we can then develop *interpretations* of the various world views that render them consistent with this conception. Here the direction of justification is reversed: human rights come first, and the preferred reading of a given religious tradition like Confucianism or Islam is the one that allows human rights to be derived from within it. For this proposal, see especially J. Cohen, 'Minimalism About Human Rights: The Most We Can Hope For?', *Journal of Political Philosophy*, 12 (2004), 190–213. As I have indicated, politically there is much to be said for it.

Why am I sceptical that cultures not already imbued with liberal principles will generate human rights that correspond more or less closely to the standard documents such as the Universal Declaration and its successors? Let me suggest two reasons. The first has to do with the liberal belief in equality. Liberals, when asked to justify human rights, will often refer to the equal moral worth of each person, or showing equal respect for every human being, and within liberal cultures these phrases are often interpreted as requiring more substantial forms of equal treatment. Now I do not want to suggest that belief in human equality is completely missing from non-liberal cultures—and here I am including not just non-Western cultures, but also the pre-liberal West—but it is overshadowed by belief in two kinds of inequality. The first is inequality between insiders and outsiders, those who belong and those who do not, whether 'belonging' is construed in religious terms—believers versus infidels or heretics—or in more general cultural terms—civilized people versus barbarians, a contrast that can be found, for instance, in Confucian thought as well as in Western classical sources.[17] What one owes to outsiders is radically different from what one owes to those belonging to one's own cultural community. The second is inequality of status within the community: the community is seen as incorporating a hierarchy of value, and each person has an assigned place within that hierarchy. The most obvious and pervasive case is inequality of status between men and women. In other cases—again Confucian culture provides an example—the key status difference is between fathers and sons. Another very obvious example is provided by cultures that are based on inherited caste differences. In all these cases, there are reciprocal obligations across the status divide, but the content of the upward-looking and downward-looking obligations is very different—there is no sense that everyone within the community is owed treatment *as an equal*.

If we compare cultures that are inegalitarian in one or more of these ways with liberal cultures, and ask about what this implies for deriving human rights from within the culture, the answer is that a number of rights that feature prominently on liberal lists would not

---

[17] See J. Chan, 'Territorial Boundaries and Confucianism', in D. Miller and S. Hashmi (eds), *Boundaries and Justice: Diverse Ethical Perspectives* (Princeton, NJ: Princeton University Press, 2001).

appear.[18] For instance, there will be no right of democratic political participation in the sense that each person's voice or vote should count equally in politics. Either there will be no universal right of participation at all, or else there will be an unequal right where men, say, are given rights denied to women. Or consider the right to equal treatment under the law. Each person who has the same status may be accorded equal rights, but there will be no objection to laws that treat different groups differently, for instance imposing restrictive dress requirements on women but not on men, or imposing different penalties for adultery when committed by men and by women. The general point is that if we start from within the culture, we do not get equal rights, but different rights for each status group that enable the members of that group to flourish in the way the culture lays down.

The second difference between liberal and non-liberal cultures that I want to highlight concerns the liberal belief in autonomy — the importance liberal culture attaches to each person choosing their mode of life, including the beliefs that inform it. To put it at its simplest, most other cultures think that what matters is that people should live a good life (there may be more than one model for this) and do not value choice per se, whereas liberals tend to think that choice matters above all, even if people turn out to lead lives that liberals themselves regard as worthless. This has important consequences for the way one understands rights such as freedom of expression, occupational choice, choice of marriage partner, etc. Liberals will want to give these rights a very strong interpretation: freedom of religious expression, for instance, will be interpreted to mean that all religions should receive equal treatment at the hands of the state, that members of each religion should have the right to proselytize, and so forth. Within non-liberal cultures such rights will be understood much more restrictively.

Once we move beyond very basic rights, therefore — the rights that would feature on Walzer's minimal list, for example — we encounter a tension between taking non-liberal cultures seriously in their own terms, and deriving a common list of human rights, of the sort that could be laid down in an official document. I

---

[18] I am assuming here that rights of some kind can be derived, although this of course may be questioned in the case of cultures that place great weight on human relationships and community. My claim is simply about the substance of these rights, when set against the standard list.

have acknowledged the political importance of interpretive exercises designed to show cross-cultural support for human rights.[19] But if we are looking for justification proper—in particular a justification that would allow us to settle disputed questions such as whether there is a human right to democracy or equality under the law—the overlapping consensus strategy will not provide it.

IV

I turn therefore to the humanitarian strategy, which identifies and justifies human rights by fixing on universal features of human beings that can serve as a ground of these rights. The argument, in other words, takes the form: because human beings have features $F1 \ldots FN$, they possess a corresponding set of rights $R1 \ldots RX$. This argument moves from a descriptive premise to a normative conclusion, so it cannot be deductive. It can nonetheless be a valid moral argument: 'People suffer extreme pain when they are tortured; therefore they have a right not to be tortured' is a valid moral argument, even though it is logically possible to assert the premise and deny the conclusion. I shall take it for granted that such arguments that ground rights in empirical features of human beings are at least potentially valid. My interest is in seeing whether we can discover a feature that can indeed successfully serve to ground human rights.

In the literature on human rights, a number of candidate features have made their appearance. Some authors, for example, have tried to ground rights in the idea of human *agency*;[20] others in human *autonomy*;[21] yet others in human *capabilities*.[22] Rather than reviewing

[19] For a much fuller discussion of this, see D. Bell, *East Meets West: Human Rights and Democracy in East Asia* (Princeton, NJ: Princeton University Press, 2000), ch. 1.

[20] See, e.g., A. Gewirth, *Human Rights: Essays on Justification and Applications* (Chicago, IL: University of Chicago Press, 1982), ch. 1.

[21] See especially J. Griffin, 'First Steps in an Account of Human Rights', *European Journal of Philosophy*, 9 (2001), 306–27, and Griffin, 'Discrepancies Between the Best Philosophical Account of Human Rights and the International Law of Human Rights'. For a critical appraisal, see J. Tasioulas, 'Human Rights, Universality and the Values of Personhood: Retracing Griffin's Steps', *European Journal of Philosophy*, 10 (2002), 79–100.

[22] This approach has been developed in somewhat different versions by Amartya Sen and Martha Nussbaum. For Sen, see especially A. Sen, *Commodities and Capabilities* (Amsterdam: North-Holland, 1985); A. Sen, *Inequality Reexamined*

these attempts, however, I shall present my preferred version of the humanitarian strategy, which appeals to basic human *needs*, and only in passing indicate why I think it is to be preferred to the alternatives. As we shall see, the needs approach has some difficulties to confront, and addressing these will occupy the rest of the chapter.

According to the needs approach, we prove that something is a human right by showing that having that right fulfils the needs of the right-holder. But what does it mean to have a need? To play such a justificatory role, the needs in question must be what I have elsewhere called 'intrinsic' needs, as opposed to merely instrumental needs which get their moral force from the contingent ends that they serve.[23] A person's intrinsic needs are those items or conditions it is necessary for a person to have if she is to avoid being harmed — thus food is an intrinsic need because in its absence people suffer the harms of hunger and malnutrition.[24] This immediately raises the

(Oxford: Clarendon Press, 1992); A. Sen, 'Capability and Well-Being', in M. Nussbaum and A. Sen (eds), *The Quality of Life* (Oxford: Clarendon Press, 1993); A. Sen, *Development as Freedom* (Oxford: Oxford University Press, 1999). For Nussbaum, see especially M. Nussbaum, 'Human Functioning and Social Justice: In Defense of Aristotelian Essentialism', *Political Theory*, 20 (1992), 202–46; M. Nussbaum, 'Human Capabilities, Female Human Beings', in M. Nussbaum and J. Glover (eds), *Women, Culture, and Development* (Oxford: Clarendon Press, 1995); M. Nussbaum, *Women and Human Development* (Cambridge: Cambridge University Press, 2000). For comparisons between the two, see D. Crocker, 'Functioning and Capability: The Foundations of Sen's and Nussbaum's Development Ethic', *Political Theory*, 20 (1992), 584–612, and 'Functioning and Capability: The Foundations of Sen's and Nussbaum's Development Ethic, Part 2', in Nussbaum and Glover (eds), *Women, Culture, and Development*. For the application of the capabilities approach to human rights, see A. Sen, 'Elements of a Theory of Human Rights', *Philosophy and Public Affairs*, 32 (2004), 315–56, and M. Nussbaum, 'Capabilities and Human Rights', *Fordham Law Review*, 66 (1997), 273–300.

[23] So 'I need £500 to buy a new television set' signals a merely instrumental need — meeting the need matters only in so far as it matters that I should have a new TV. See D. Miller, *Principles of Social Justice* (Cambridge, MA: Harvard University Press, 1999), ch. 10.

[24] 'Items or conditions' should be understood in a broad sense. Some needs are needs for physical objects such as food and clothing; but others are needs for freedoms of various kinds — freedom of movement or expression, for instance; and yet others are needs that require inclusion in social practices such as education. One of the charges levelled by Sen against the 'basic needs' approach to development is that is too narrowly focused on commodities (see A. Sen, *Resources, Values and Development* [Oxford: Blackwell, 1984], ch. 20). Reading the relevant texts (e.g. P. Streeten et al., *First Things First: Meeting Basic Human Needs in Developing Countries* [New York: Oxford University Press, 1981]), this criticism seems misplaced, but in any case it should be clear that the concept of need itself is innocent

question whether we can define harm in a way that is genuinely universal, that is not dependent on views of human flourishing that will vary from one society to the next. Answering this question is clearly crucial to a needs-based justification of human rights, but before turning to it let me indicate why starting with needs seems at least plausible as a justificatory strategy.

One reason is that by focusing on needs, we are drawing a distinction between what is essential to human beings and what is non-essential—between food as such, and particular delicacies for which different people will have different preferences, for example. Since human rights are supposed to constitute a kind of moral bedrock—meeting them is a moral imperative, whereas other claims impose weaker duties, or none at all—they should be justified by reference to essential features of human life. Needs possess this kind of moral urgency.[25] Another reason is that needs are not sensitive to the personal choices of those who have them: a person can choose whether to fulfil his needs, but the needs themselves reflect unchosen aspects of human life, for instance the biological fact that we must take in water and breathe oxygen. Again this corresponds to the choice-independent character of human rights. We have these rights qua human beings, not by virtue of the choices we have made as to how we want to lead our lives.

I said that needs, in the relevant sense, were items or conditions that it is necessary for a person to have if she is to avoid being harmed. But if this definition is to be of any practical use, we have to know what to count as harm. The easiest cases will be those where harm can be identified in physical or biological terms: a person is

of 'commodity fetishism'. See further on this question F. Stewart, 'Basic Needs, Capabilities, and Human Development', in A. Offer (ed.), *In Pursuit of the Quality of Life* (Oxford: Oxford University Press, 1996).

[25] In contrast, the idea of human *capabilities* involves no inherent distinction between more or less important capacities that human beings might possess—a capability might refer to the capacity to be adequately nourished or the capacity to eat caviar. Sen and Nussbaum deal with this problem in different ways. For Sen, the idea of human capabilities remains open-ended, although in his writing on poverty, he tacitly introduces a distinction between 'basic capabilities' and the rest; Nussbaum, in contrast, has produced a long and extensive list of 'central human functional capabilities' which, she claims, 'can command a broad cross-cultural consensus' (Nussbaum, *Women and Human Development*, ch. 1, sect. IV). For some doubts about the latter claim, see C. Fabre and D. Miller, 'Justice and Culture: Rawls, Sen, Nussbaum and O'Neill', *Political Studies Review*, 1 (2003), 4–17.

harmed when she suffers pain, or is paralyzed, or has her life cut short, or contracts a disease that prevents her engaging in the normal range of human activities. These judgements rely on a standard that defines what it means to be a properly functioning human being, but the standard is not controversial (there may be controversy at the margins e.g. over what should be considered a normal human life span, but the central cases are sufficiently clear).

Physical-cum-biological conceptions of harm, although important, are not by themselves sufficient to generate needs that can ground an adequate set of human rights. Human beings are social as well as biological creatures, and they can be harmed by being denied the conditions of social existence. I shall capture this idea by saying that a person is harmed when she is unable to live a minimally decent life in the society to which she belongs.[26] A minimally decent life, I should stress at once, is something less than a flourishing life. To live a flourishing life means being able to develop and exercise whichever capacities someone deems to be most important—there are many ways to flourish, and in general they cannot be combined, so a person must choose which form of human excellence she wants to achieve. The conditions for minimal decency, by contrast, are the same for everyone in a given set of social circumstances. Let me give some examples drawn from societies like my own. A person must be able to support herself without begging, that is have access to income sufficient to feed and clothe herself; she must have a secure home to go to; she must have the opportunity to marry and raise a family; she must be able to plan for the future, including her old age, without fearing that she will become destitute; she must be able to move around outside her immediate neighbourhood; she must be able to enter public places without fear of being abused and assaulted; and so forth. These conditions, and others like them, define a baseline that everyone should reach regardless of whether they are able to achieve higher forms of flourishing above it. Someone who only reached the baseline would have a pretty dull life. Nonetheless, unlike those who fell below it, he would not feel degraded, socially excluded, worthless, etc.[27]

[26] Here I follow my earlier analysis in *Principles of Social Justice*, ch. 10.
[27] Does invoking the idea of a minimally decent life help us in explaining needs here? After all one could reverse the order of exposition and say that a minimally decent life is a life in which a person's essential needs are fulfilled. I believe that the

It should be evident that the decency conditions I have just itemized depend on social norms that we should expect to vary to some extent from place to place. Having a secure home is a condition of a decent life in societies like ours, but in nomadic societies, for instance, another norm would take its place. So if we define needs with reference to standards of decency, it seems that they too will vary from place to place. Here we need to distinguish between two ways in which human needs might vary. In the first case, the underlying need remains unchanged, but the items or conditions needed to satisfy it vary from one place to the next. For instance, there is a universal human need for health, but only in certain places will this entail a more concrete need for protection from malaria. Variation of this kind is not, I take it, problematic if we want to ground human rights in needs: we define the human right in terms of the underlying need, and recognize that what is required, concretely, to fulfil the right can be different in different societies.

The more problematic way for needs to vary occurs when the need itself is shaped by the social context in which a person lives. In the example I gave above, shelter from the elements is a universal human need, while in some societies, but not others, this takes the form of a need for a fixed dwelling place—in societies like our own, a homeless person has unmet needs (and is harmed) even if she is adequately sheltered from the elements. But can this socially relative need be used to ground a human right? To deal with this problem, I propose to draw a distinction between *basic needs* and *societal needs*, where the former are to be understood as the conditions for a decent human life in *any* society, and the latter as the more expansive set of requirements for a decent life in the particular society to which a person belongs. Only basic needs can be appealed to in order to ground human rights. Societal needs, by contrast, are used to justify what I earlier called rights of citizenship—the larger set of rights,

---

idea of a minimally decent life illuminates needs because it draws attention to the fact that the needs that matter are not merely the needs of a person considered as a biological creature in isolation from others, as the needs for food and water are. They are also the needs of a person who belongs to a community and who views her life through the lens of that community. If she cannot support herself or appear in public without shame, she will feel excluded from the community and unable to live a human life within it. This is as much a form of harm as is, for example, malnutrition. Thinking about what it means to lead a minimally decent life brings out this social-psychological aspect of many human needs.

possession of which guarantees someone's position as a full member of a particular society, and whose content will vary somewhat from one society to the next. The right to shelter is a human right; the right to a fixed dwelling place is a right of citizenship in most, but not all, societies today. People will in general suffer greater harm if they are denied a human right than if they are denied a right of citizenship that is not also a human right, but this is a contingent fact: the distinction does not depend on the relative urgency of the two kinds of need, but on whether the need is shaped by norms that apply only in particular social settings.[28]

But is it possible to identify the conditions for a decent human life as such without referring surreptitiously to norms of decency that are in fact specific to one society, or a small range of societies, for instance those in the developed West? How might we go about doing this? We might begin by looking at each society in turn, and ask how its members define conditions for a decent life, and thereby define societal needs. Then we would establish what all these definitions have in common: which needs are recognized in every society, no matter what the particular cultural values of its members. We can call this the intersection approach to basic needs: basic needs are defined as the intersection of all sets of societal needs.

The trouble with this approach is that it makes the definition of basic need hostage to what in some cases may be ill-informed beliefs about the conditions for a decent life. This is especially so when what is at stake are the needs of women. Members of some communities, including female members, may believe that women can have a decent life in the absence of certain conditions—access to contraception, or the opportunity to take paid work, for instance— whereas it can be shown, empirically, that women who lack these

---

[28] One might accept the distinction I am drawing here, but deny that it is normatively relevant from the point of view of global justice. A person whose citizenship rights are not respected will be unable to live a decent life in the society to which she belongs: why does this not create remedial responsibilities in outsiders in the same way as an infringement of her human rights? The difference is that societal needs, and the rights they ground, reflect the cultural norms and practices of a particular society, norms, and practices that are in principle open to modification from within. Thus the fact that religious education may be a societal need in a particular place does not impose on outsiders a responsibility to ensure that the need is fulfilled; insiders, by contrast, must, as a matter of justice, either ensure that the need is met, or change their norms and practices so that it is no longer a need.

things do not in general have adequate lives, even within the societies where the beliefs prevail.[29] The intersection approach might not rule out even such barbaric practices as foot-binding or female circumcision if there turn out to be communities whose members believe that these practices do not compromise decency.

So we need to take a more objective approach, one that tries to determine what is *actually* necessary for people to lead decent lives in different cultural contexts, as opposed to what people in those cultures may believe is necessary. And here we must appeal to the fact that there are activities that humans engage in that are reiterated across contexts—activities such as working, playing, learning, raising families, and so forth—so that although the form the activity takes may vary from community to community, the activity itself can be described as universal. Let us refer to these as *core* human activities. Then we can say that a person has a decent life *tout court* when over the course of her life she is able to engage in each of the core activities, given the conditions prevailing in the society she belongs to. She is able to work, play, etc., without having to bear unreasonable costs, and also without having to forgo some other core activity—so that a life would not count as decent if, say, the person in question had an opportunity to work, but only if she gave up the opportunity to raise a family. She may of course choose not to engage in one or more of the core activities, but her life is decent so long as she is able to avail herself of the opportunity if she wants.

Basic needs, then, are to be understood by reference to this idea of a decent human life. They are the conditions that must be met for a person to have a decent life given the environmental conditions he faces. The list of such needs will include (but not be exhausted by): food and water, clothing and shelter, physical security, health care, education, work and leisure, freedoms of movement, conscience, and expression.[30] Although we should generally expect societies to

---

[29] One should not, however, conclude too quickly that women go along with dominant male views about what their needs are. See the powerful argument advanced by Nussbaum in *Women and Human Development* that poor women in India have learnt to value the capabilities that Nussbaum takes as central to an adequate human life.

[30] For a rather similar account of basic human rights as grounded in the conditions for a minimally decent life, see J. Nickel, 'Poverty and Rights', *Philosophical Quarterly*, 55 (2005), 385–402.

recognize these needs, and to incorporate them into their fuller conceptions of societal needs, this may not always be the case. As I have indicated, members of a particular society may fail to see that having X is in fact necessary for all members of that society to lead a decent life. This could happen because of simple empirical error—a society might not recognize a certain bodily condition as generating a need for medical treatment—or because of cultural bias, as the example of a society that fails to recognize that women have a need for work, even though it was demonstrable that without work many women would remain malnourished, shows. A society might also simply set the decency standard too low as a result of adaptive beliefs: if average life expectancy is only 45 years, for example, people in that community may define need as whatever is necessary for the range of core activities but only up to that age. The idea of basic need is to that extent a critical concept, one that can be used to condemn prevailing social practices as well as to ground human rights and international obligations.

V

Basic needs appear to have the kind of moral urgency that we look for in a justification of human rights. What seems more problematic, however, is that the demands that may be generated by basic needs have in principle no upper limit. We take people one at a time and ask what is necessary for each of them to live a minimally decent life. We do not ask what implications satisfying the needs of one person may have for the position of others. In some cases, the cost of satisfying needs may be very high indeed—indeed it may not be possible to satisfy some needs at all. The most obvious examples are cases of medical needs, where in the case of severely ill or disabled people meeting the conditions laid down above for a decent human life may impose enormous personal and financial costs on others. It seems, therefore, that there can be no direct path from basic needs to human rights. For human rights, precisely because they are liable to place others under obligations of justice to fulfil them, have to take account not only of the interest of the right-bearer but also of the interests of those whose behaviour would be constrained by the existence of the right. Theories of human rights characteristically attempt to do this by incorporating a practicality requirement into the existence conditions for a right. In James Griffin's influential account, for example, *personhood* and *practicalities* are presented as twin grounds for human rights.[31] According to Griffin, the existence of a human right 'must depend, to some extent, upon its being an effective, socially manageable claim on others'.[32] The practicalities ground is not spelt out in any detail by Griffin, but the underlying thought is that grounding rights in personhood alone might allow the content of human rights to expand indefinitely. By appealing to practicalities we ensure that rights claims do not exceed what it is feasible for a particular society at a particular point in its development.

Can we say more here? I think we can distinguish several ways in which practical considerations having to do with what can reasonably be demanded from others may place limits on the derivation of rights from needs.

1. What is needed cannot be provided by human agency. Consider diseases for which there is at present no known cure, such as several forms of cancer. People who develop these cancers are likely to suffer severe pain and to die prematurely, so they clearly need a form of treatment that does not yet exist to live a minimally decent life; but it makes no sense to say that they have a right to this form of medical aid. Or to put it differently, their general right to medical treatment does not include, at present, a right to the specific treatment that would halt the cancer. Not only does no one actually have an obligation to supply them with that treatment, but no one could have such an obligation. Their right to health care may, however, ground a further obligation, namely an obligation on the part of governments to devote some portion of their medical research budgets to efforts to find a cure for cancers. This is an example of a phenomenon I shall return to later, where a need does not ground a right with the same scope, but rather a different right whose fulfilment might be expected to satisfy the need, in whole or in part.

[31] Griffin, 'First Steps in an Account of Human Rights'; Griffin, 'Discrepancies Between the Best Philosophical Account of Human Rights and the International Law of Human Rights'.
[32] Griffin, 'First Steps', 315.

2. What is needed cannot be demanded of other human agents.[33] Some human needs can only be met through the unforced responses of others: needs for love and respect are the obvious examples. These may be important elements in a minimally decent life, but because love and respect only count as such if they are voluntarily bestowed on their objects, no one can have an obligation to show love and respect to others,[34] nor can there be rights to be loved or respected. It is true, on the other hand, that needs such as these can be appealed to indirectly to ground rights. The right to marry, which is cited in the Universal Declaration (Article 16), can be justified as a human right partly on the ground that the institution of marriage provides a framework within which people can form relationships that are loving and respectful: it is neither a necessary nor a sufficient condition for these needs to be met, but it contributes positively to their fulfilment. Equally the right not to be subjected to cruel, inhuman, or degrading treatment (Article 5) is justified in part by observing that such treatment violates the human need for respect. So basic needs play some role in grounding human rights such as these. But there is no simple one-to-one entailment between 'A has a basic need for X' and 'A has a human right to X' in these cases. Human rights are limited by the practical consideration that there are ways of responding to others, involving having certain attitudes towards them, that cannot be compelled and that cannot, therefore, be made obligatory.

3. Obliging others to provide what is needed would violate their own human rights. I am thinking here of cases in which the need is such that to meet it would place demands on others that they have the right to refuse, even though they might choose voluntarily to supply what is needed. Obvious examples are medical needs of certain kinds. A person whose kidneys or liver are failing has a basic need for an organ transplant (assuming they cannot live a decent life otherwise) but those whose organs might be used for this purpose have the right to refuse to donate them. This stems from the human right to bodily integrity: in order to live a decent life, we must have

---

[33] I am indebted here to Barbara Schmitz's unpublished paper 'How to Derive Rights from Needs'.

[34] This is true at least of certain forms of respect. For example, one respects others by taking their opinions seriously, but this is not something that one can be obliged to do, since ought implies can.

assurance that our bodies will not be used in significant ways without our consent, even for the benefit of others. Another case would be of a person who requires round-the-clock specialist attention in order to survive. It might be possible to provide the relevant care by voluntary means, but if this proved not to be the case—there was no one willing to devote their whole life to caring for this person—then the general right to personal freedom means that no one can be obliged to meet such a need. It follows that there cannot be human rights that would include the right to be given bodily organs or the right to receive 24-hour specialist attention.

It is a feature of such cases that the need that goes unmet may in fact be a more urgent need than the need that grounds the conflicting right. The person who needs a liver or kidney transplant, I am assuming, will die if he does not get one, which makes his need as urgent as a need can be. People who donate one of their kidneys or a liver lobe quickly recover and can continue with their lives without significant loss of functioning. Compelling them to donate would not constitute a severe violation of their needs, understood as requirements for a minimally decent human life. So if the underlying principle was simply to maximize need-satisfaction, we would conclude that there was a human right to be given essential organs, and no human right to refuse to donate.[35] But this is not the correct way to understand the relationship between needs and rights. Before a need can ground a right, we have to know that the proposed right would not impose obligations on others that would necessarily violate their own human rights. Candidate rights, in other words, have to pass not only a *consistency* test—A's having a certain right must be consistent with B, C, D, etc., having the same right—but also a *compatibility* test—A's having a certain right cannot impose obligations on B, C, D, etc., that would require them to sacrifice some other independently justified right of theirs.[36]

---

[35] For a powerful exploration of the obligation to give bodily organs to those who cannot live decently without them, and its limits, see C. Fabre, *Whose Body Is it Anyway? Justice and the Integrity of the Person* (Oxford: Clarendon Press, 2006), chs. 4–5.

[36] How is this compatibility test to be applied? If we have two candidate rights that are incompatible, X and Y, how do we decide which candidate is to be awarded human rights status and which is to be rejected? I think this question has to be answered by looking globally at the full set of human rights. That is, we begin with the underlying idea of a decent human life and the conditions required to support it,

By way of criticism here, it might be said that such a test would rule out all positive rights to resources. For we can always envisage circumstances in which meeting one person's right to resources would mean requiring others to act in ways that violate their own rights. Consider the right to food, for instance. We can easily construct a case—philosophers are adept at doing this—in which A and B are stranded on a desert island, and B's need for food, which he cannot supply himself, can only be met by ceaseless labour on A's part. Requiring A to feed B would infringe A's right to personal freedom which (we can reasonably assume) includes some choice of how to direct his labour and some quantum of leisure time. So does it follow that B has no human right to food, and that because of the possibility of such cases occurring, there cannot in general be a human right to food? The answer that I want to give is that there is indeed a human right to food, and that B in the case described has that right, even though A has no corresponding obligation to perform the interminable labour that would meet it in full. This is because, in general, the right can be met without imposing rights-violating obligations on others. The human condition is such that enough food can be produced by the able-bodied, without excessive labour, to feed both themselves and those who are unable to produce. There is therefore no across-the-board incompatibility between asserting a human right to food and asserting a human right to freedom. Conflicts may arise in particular cases, such as the imaginary island case, but these do not generalize, in contrast to the position with the (proposed) right to be given bodily organs and the right to bodily integrity. How, then, should we deal with the island case? The correct answer is that B does indeed have a right to food, corresponding to which is an obligation on A to do what he can to supply that need, up to the point at which his own rights come into play. So he must be willing to contribute a reasonable amount of labour to support B but is not required to work night and day for that purpose. Nor is he required to sacrifice food that is essential to meet his own needs in order to meet those of B.

---

and ask which set of rights will best provide those conditions—a set that includes X or a set that includes Y? This way of applying the test is meant to capture the idea that the value of a right is not just the direct value it may have in itself, but its indirect value in supporting other rights (or disvalue in interfering with them).

4. Resource scarcities mean that not all needs of a certain kind can be fulfilled simultaneously. Under this heading I want to consider cases in which it is feasible to fulfil the needs of each person taken separately without imposing obligations on others that are either impossible to fulfil or that violate their own rights, but in which this cannot be done for all taken together. Familiar examples include famines in which only limited supplies of food are available and medical emergencies in which drugs or other resources are scarce relative to the needs of those at risk. The question, then, is whether in such cases we can properly speak of each person having a human right that their needs be satisfied. If we do say this, then it seems that we run immediately into pervasive conflicts between rights. If I cannot provide both A and B with enough food to satisfy their basic needs, then in choosing to respect A's right to food by feeding her, I must be violating B's right to food by refusing to feed him. On the other hand, if we say for that reason that neither A nor B can have rights to food in these circumstances, we appear to have driven a very big wedge between basic needs and human rights.

How, then, should we think about human rights in such cases of scarcity? Let us explore the available options more carefully. Jeremy Waldron has offered the strongest defence I know of for the position that rights can continue to exist in the face of scarcity.[37] He points out, first, that although in the circumstances we are envisaging it is practically impossible to fulfil all rights simultaneously, it is nevertheless possible to fulfil each right taken separately. Asserting the existence of rights does not, therefore, entail saying that people have obligations to do what cannot be done. It is obviously true that agents in these circumstances have to choose which obligation will take precedence. But, and this is Waldron's second point, the moral conflict that ensues is created by the situation itself, not by the existence of rights. However we decide to describe the situation, we still have to choose between giving our limited quantum of food to A and giving it to B (or in the case Waldron describes between rescuing a drowning A and a drowning B).

I agree with Waldron that we should not attempt to define rights in such a way that conflict between them is impossible. We are quite

---

[37] J. Waldron, 'Rights in Conflict', in J. Waldron, *Liberal Rights* (Cambridge: Cambridge University Press, 1993).

familiar, in our everyday experience, with cases in which both rights and their corresponding obligations come into conflict: I promise to meet a friend at a certain time, but meanwhile a child falls ill and has to be taken to hospital. The child's right to health takes priority, but when I fulfil this right I do at the same time infringe my friend's right that I turn up at the appointed time (and so I owe her an apology). Conflicts of this kind arise unavoidably given the complexity and unpredictability of everyday life. But notice how different in kind the two rights are. It would make no sense to try to tailor the right to have promises kept in such a way as to avoid all conflicts with the many other rights that might, in principle, come into conflict with it. In contrast, if we say that in general situations of scarcity such as the famine case, each person has a right that their needs be met in full, then we seem to be opening the door directly to unavoidable and systematic conflicts of rights. Do we want to say in such cases that when we distribute our limited supply of food in the morally best way, we are at the same time infringing a multitude of obligations to all those who get less than they need?[38]

The alternative, therefore, is to ask first what we are required to do, as a matter of justice, in circumstances of resource scarcity, and then to define people's rights in a way that is consistent with the answer we give. Suppose, to take a very simple case, that justice demands an equal distribution of limited food; then each person would have a right to an equal share of the available food, but not more than that, even though this meant that their basic needs were only partially satisfied. In this way, we avoid any conflicts of rights and when we do what we are required to do there are no obligations that remain unfulfilled.

Attractive though this second alternative may appear at first glance, it also has some disadvantages. One problem is that in circumstances of scarcity, there can be reasonable disagreement about what justice demands. Consider the following three principles for distributing a limited resource when there is not sufficient available

---

[38] Katherine Eddy has pressed this line of argument against Waldron, pointing out that the consequence of allowing conflicts of rights to escalate is that the special, decisive force of rights-claims and their corresponding duties is in danger of being lost. See K. Eddy, 'Welfare Rights and Conflicts of Rights', *Res Publica*, 12 (2006), 337–56, esp. pp. 343–4.

to meet the needs of all those who have a legitimate claim on the resource:

(a) Give priority to those whose needs are greatest—that is distribute the resource in such a way as to raise the position of the neediest people to the point when they are no longer the neediest and continue in the same way from there.
(b) Distribute resources in whatever way reduces overall need to the greatest possible extent.
(c) Distribute resources in such a way as to equalize, as far as possible, the extent to which people remain in need after the distribution.

None of these principles is self-evidently the right principle to follow whatever the circumstances.[39] Principle (a) might require us to direct all of our limited resource to those whose needs were severe but whose condition could only be improved a little by our intervention—for example the very sick, in a medical case. This may not seem fair to those who are less severely in need but who could be helped much more. The practice of triage, where priority is given not to the very worst cases but to a middle group who can be restored to something close to full functioning by providing a moderate amount of medical aid, illustrates this point. Not everyone would agree that triage is just, but there is certainly a case to be made in its favour as a reasonable way of responding to some situations of scarcity. Principle (b) takes this line of argument further by claiming that what justice requires in the face of scarcity is to use our resources in the most efficient way we can, to relieve as many needs as possible. But this takes no account of what Rawls famously called 'the separateness of persons'; it allows us to discount entirely the claims of those whose needs prove to be harder to satisfy. Principle (c) tells us to look directly at the *comparative* level of deprivation suffered by different people, in line with the more general idea that justice is concerned with comparative rather than absolute outcomes, but this too may produce unacceptable results in certain cases. It may, for instance, instruct us to withhold resources altogether when there is no way of distributing them that will lead to greater equality of

---

[39] This paragraph draws on my longer discussion in *Principles of Social Justice*, ch. 10.

outcome than exists under the status quo. But given that this leaves people still in need, it looks like an objectionable case of levelling down.

My purpose here is not to try to establish which principle of justice we should use to govern the distribution of resources under scarcity, but to indicate the problem of appealing to justice to settle what human rights people have under these circumstances. Initially, it seemed appealing to say that people each have a right to a just share of resources, and not more than that, as a way of avoiding conflicts of rights. But now we see that discovering what distributive justice requires here may be a complex matter over which people may reasonably disagree. Human rights, by contrast, are supposed to set minimum standards of treatment for human beings that are incontestable—as I have argued, the requirements of a minimally decent life for human beings in any society can be established objectively, in principle anyway. To limit human rights by reference to controversial principles of distributive justice therefore seems a mistake.

There is a further reason to doubt the second alternative I am considering. The purpose of human rights is not simply to guide the behaviour of those who have to deal directly with people whose human needs are not being met. They can also be used to set targets for governments, international organizations, etc. From this perspective, it may be important to state that scarcity itself may constitute a human rights violation where it can be prevented by human agency. A government, in other words, infringes human rights not only when it fails to ensure that food is properly distributed in the course of a famine, but also when it fails to take steps to prevent the famine from occurring in the first place, by, for example, stockpiling essential foodstuffs. For this we need a conception of human rights that is *not* sensitive to the quantity of resources available to a society at any given moment but is based directly on human needs understood as requirements for a minimally decent life.

This point picks up Waldron's observation that it can be misleading to think of human rights as corresponding one-to-one with human obligations, in the way that your right to the thing I have promised you corresponds to my obligation to deliver that thing. Typically, Waldron argues, a human right will bring with it 'successive waves of duty'—the primary duty not to violate the right directly being followed by various duties to ensure that the right is not infringed in indirect ways.[40] Thus corresponding to the right to food is first the duty not to snatch food out of the mouth of the starving person, and then various duties to ensure that the conditions that lead to starvation in the first place do not materialize. Even in cases where because of scarcity we cannot meet our direct obligation to protect A's right, we can still act on background duties that make it more likely that that right will be fulfilled in time.[41]

Let me take stock of the argument I have been developing in this section of this chapter. I have claimed that human rights are best understood and justified through the idea of basic needs common to all human beings. But not all needs can ground rights directly. Some needs may be impossible to fulfil at any given historical moment. Others may be such that it cannot be obligatory to fulfil them — needs for love and respect, for example. In the case of yet others, requiring A to meet B's need would amount to a violation of A's human rights, grounded in *his* needs. All of this goes to show why Griffin was right to impose a practicalities ground for the existence of a human right alongside what he calls a personhood ground. Human rights must not only represent morally urgent aspects of human life, they must also meet certain conditions of feasibility. But we should be wary of concluding that scarcity alone — meaning simply the lack of sufficient resources to meet all needs — is a reason for limiting human rights.

VI

In the previous section, I examined a range of cases in which human needs proved not to be a sufficient ground of human rights — in which having a basic human need for X did not entail having a human right to X. But there might seem to be a difficulty in the other direction as well — human rights that cannot plausibly be seen as grounded in human needs. Consider, for example, civil and political

---

[40] Waldron, 'Liberal Rights', sections IV–V.

[41] I therefore disagree with Onora O'Neill's claim that human rights must either require identifiable agents who bear obligations that correspond directly to the rights in question (in which case they are indeed genuine rights) or else they must reduce to mere 'aspirations'. See e.g., O. O'Neill, 'The Dark Side of Human Rights', *International Affairs*, 81 (2005), 427–39.

rights such as the right to participate in government or the right to a fair trial. It seems strained to claim that their justification must refer to human needs. Can we really speak of a need to participate or to receive a fair trial? At best these would seem to be instrumental needs—a person might need to participate in government to achieve some personal objective that required state action, for instance. It looks as though starting from needs will bias our list of rights towards social and economic rights such as rights to subsistence and health care, and therefore not identify those rights that politically are often taken to be most central.[42]

It is clear that (intrinsic) needs can only play an indirect role in justifying most civil and political rights. If we start from the conditions that human beings everywhere require to avoid harm, then although we can move directly to rights such as bodily security and freedom of movement, other rights will prove to be important only as secondary protections for these more basic conditions. Political rights, for example, will matter if it can be shown that the possession and exercise of these rights is necessary in order to guarantee rights to bodily security, subsistence, and so forth. The right to a fair trial will matter in so far as it guards against the wrongful imposition of penalties that would infringe the first-order rights. These claims are plausible, but it may be felt that by relying on needs as our justifying strategy, we overlook the intrinsic value of civil and political rights that do not correspond directly to human needs. Rights to participate, to a fair trial, to equality under the law, etc., have a value that is not reducible to the harm that can be avoided by having these rights in place. So the needs-based strategy for justifying rights seems at the very least to be incomplete.

Consider, as an example, the right to religious freedom. A needs-based justification would have to show that being able to choose your religion is everywhere a condition for a minimally decent life. But this seems not to be the case. In some societies religion has been a marginal phenomenon, actively discouraged by the state. In others, there is a strong social norm that everyone should adhere to the same religion, so while freedom to practise that religion is very important for decency, freedom to choose between religions is not. So how might a needs-based justification proceed here?

---

[42] C.f. Schmitz, 'How to Derive Rights from Needs', 3.

Although freedom to choose your religion may not always be a need, there is a more basic need that covers some of the same ground. This might be characterized as freedom of conscience, not being forced to live according to values that you cannot endorse, and that you may find repugnant. It is not difficult to show how a person is harmed when freedom of conscience is denied: they cannot live at ease with themselves, since their behaviour and their beliefs are at odds.[43] Freedom of conscience supports a right that includes freedom of religion without giving it any special status—being forced outwardly to practise a particular religion is not necessarily worse than, say, being required to eat meat if you have vegetarian principles. The right that is supported may also be less extensive than freedom of religion as that idea is commonly understood: for instance it may not extend to the right to set up a new church yourself, to proselytize, etc. It is essentially a right not to be forced to adopt religious practices or espouse religious beliefs that you do not yourself endorse.

In liberal societies, a more extensive right to religious freedom is likely to be recognized, including perhaps a right on the part of each religion to equal treatment by the state (when public funding of religion is at stake, for instance). This, however, should be seen as a right of citizenship, reflecting the very strong commitment in the public culture of these societies to personal autonomy and equal rights. More generally, human rights that are common to all societies will be extended and given fuller expression in citizenship rights that vary from society to society (though with a lot of overlap in the case of societies that are similar in other respects[44]). This also provides a response to the objection that a needs-based justification cannot fully account for the value of civil and political rights. Take the right to political participation. Considered as a human right, this is justified as a necessary protection for other rights that are more directly connected to needs. Unless they are subject to popular

---

[43] This idea of freedom of conscience has been explored in an illuminating way by Chandran Kukathas in *The Liberal Archipelago: A Theory of Diversity and Freedom* (Oxford: Oxford University Press, 2003), esp. chs. 2–3.

[44] Thus I am inclined to regard the European Convention on Human Rights as a proclamation of the common rights of citizenship that a group of societies with similar political traditions have decided to adopt, rather than as a statement of human rights proper.

control, governments are liable to pursue policies that violate their subjects' basic rights to subsistence, freedom of movement, etc., as many examples show. Considered as a right of citizenship, however, the right to participate takes on a new shape and a new significance. In liberal societies, it becomes the right to an equal share in democratic governance, and its value is in part that it designates its bearer as a competent citizen able to contribute to the direction of her society—in other words, it has a symbolic significance over and above its instrumental value, and helps to meet the societal need for recognition and inclusion as a full member of the society. So it is true that where the needs-based approach relies on universal human needs, it does not capture the whole value of rights in the form that they take in liberal societies. But this is not an objection once we get clear about the relationship between human rights and citizenship rights, and the corresponding distinction between basic needs and societal needs.

VII

My aim in this chapter has been to discover what is the global minimum that people everywhere can claim as a matter of justice, and my proposal is that this should be understood as respect and protection for their basic human rights. When basic rights are threatened or violated, this triggers a responsibility on the part of outsiders to come to the aid of those whose rights are imperilled. The problem is to find a way of specifying the rights in question. There are two main desiderata here. On the one hand, the grounding we give for basic human rights must explain their moral urgency—in particular why rights-violations can impose relatively demanding obligations on third parties who are not themselves responsible for the violations. On the other hand, the justification we present should have universal reach—it should appeal to reasons that everyone has reason to accept, regardless of their personal religious commitments or cultural values. Given global disagreement over many questions of value, our conception of human rights must, if at all possible, avoid relying on sectarian foundations.

My suggestion is that human rights can meet these desiderata, but only if the list of rights is kept fairly short and basic. More ambitious lists run the risk both of losing their moral urgency and of becoming unjustifiable except on partisan grounds. We need to adopt a two-level approach in which basic human rights, which are owed to human beings everywhere, are kept separate from rights of citizenship, which are (undeniably important) matters of social justice within political communities. I have also suggested that only a humanitarian justification can ground these rights in a satisfactory way. Trying to avoid foundational questions—in itself a laudable aim—by going directly to the current practice of human rights fails, because there is insufficient practical agreement about which rights should really count as human rights, and no authoritative source able to resolve the disagreement. The search for an overlapping consensus between the various moral, political, and religious cultures that we find in today's world either yields an ultra-minimal list of rights, or else culminates in disagreement, especially between liberal and non-liberal cultures. So human rights need to be given an independent ethical basis. But our starting point cannot be a value that is likely to appeal only to liberals, for instance. For this reason, I have avoided considering justifications that begin from ideas of equality, or of personal autonomy, both of which strike me as sectarian in this way. In contrast, human needs, understood as items and conditions that people everywhere must have in order to live a decent human life, can ground rights in a way that promises to meet both desiderata referred to above.

But is it really the case that a justification of human rights that begins from needs so understood is non-sectarian? Doesn't calling this strategy of justification 'humanitarian' already reveal its limitations? The needs I have been invoking to ground rights are the needs of human beings understood as biological and social creatures: they are the needs we have because our bodies cannot function properly unless certain conditions are met (food, shelter, medical aid, etc.), and because we cannot exist in society unless certain other conditions are met (education, physical security, mobility, etc.). But now consider the view of somebody who regards human beings as above all spiritual creatures, and who therefore gives priority to their spiritual needs. If the needs of the body conflict with the needs of the soul, this person thinks the latter should take precedence. Consider as an example the very severe punishments that some religions impose on lawbreakers, such as the Islamic *shari'a* law penalties of amputation of the hand for theft, or stoning to death for female adultery.[45] By liberal standards these punishments appear cruel and excessive, and it would be hard to claim that they can be defended by appeal to basic human needs or interests, as other punishments can. A defender of *shari'a* law might argue, however, that such punishments are necessary to cleanse the soul of the offender, and spare him or her greater punishment in the next life. Since these needs are more important than the needs of the body, there can be no human right that stands in the way of imposing the necessary penalties.

It is important not to overstate the extent of disagreement here. The Islamic interlocutor I am imagining would not deny that, as a general matter, having a hand amputated or being stoned to death are very serious harms, and would therefore presumably agree that we should recognize rights to life and bodily integrity to protect against them. The reasons that justify the rights are universally acceptable. The divergence occurs over the limits to be placed on these rights, and whether the health of the soul gives good grounds for overriding them in certain cases.[46] At the very least, I think, a defender of *shari'a* punishments must feel some inner tension between the defence he offers and his recognition of the importance of the rights in other cases, and indeed there is internal debate in Islam about when the Koranic injunction of mercy towards the offender should override the carrying out of these punishments.

What the example shows, then, is that the humanitarian strategy for justifying basic human rights cannot convince everyone that such rights should have overriding force, trumping all other ethical considerations. Precisely because it is humanitarian, in the sense of relying on needs and interests that can be identified by secular forms of evidence and modes of reasoning, it cannot provide a watertight response to those who would qualify human rights by reference to spiritual needs and interests. Nonetheless the reasons it gives to

---

[45] See A. A. An-Na'im, 'Toward a Cross-Cultural Approach to Defining International Standards of Human Rights: The Meaning of Cruel, Inhuman, or Degrading Treatment or Punishment', in A. A. An-Na'im (ed.), *Human Rights in Cross-Cultural Perspectives: A Quest for Consensus* (Philadelphia, PA: University of Pennsylvania Press, 1992).

[46] It is worth remembering that liberals too allow that human rights may be overridden when people are lawfully punished, for example when criminals are imprisoned. The difference is that for liberals the grounds for doing this must be the better protection of the rights of others.

support human rights are, it seems, reasons that everyone should accept no matter what their other beliefs. No one denies that, other things being equal, all human beings should enjoy the conditions that allow them to live decent lives, and that this may impose responsibilities on those who are in a position to create such conditions. The disagreement is about what should go into the 'other things being equal' clause. Of course, those who hold religious world views may prefer to justify human rights in other ways, arguing that we have these rights by virtue of divine commandments to feed the hungry, shelter the homeless, etc. But none of this shows that the humanitarian justification I have been developing is sectarian in the sense of relying on reasons that others should find objectionable.

This is important, because basic human rights as I understand them have a central role to play in any theory of global justice. All political communities are required to respect and protect the rights of their own members, and any community may potentially be asked to assume onerous responsibilities to protect human rights beyond its own borders—responsibilities not only to supply resources but in the extreme case to intervene physically to prevent rights from being violated. These demands cannot be deflected by claiming that in your culture a particular alleged right has no standing. Assuming that the arguments deployed here to justify basic rights are sound, they are indeed arguments that everyone has reason to accept.

CHAPTER 8

—————

Immigration and Territorial Rights

I

I argued in Chapter 7 that a central demand of global justice is the obligation to respect and protect the human rights of people everywhere. Even if we understand this as a responsibility to respect and protect *basic* human rights, as I proposed, it is evident that for millions of people in today's world these rights are unfulfilled. They are denied fundamental civil liberties and political rights, or they are deprived of the resources that would allow them to meet their basic material needs, or both at once. Indeed, I began this book by reflecting on some painfully familiar news stories that in each case involved the violation of the basic rights of those involved; I could have chosen many others whose human consequences were as bad or worse.

My third example was of people trying to cross borders in search of a better life and being brutally repulsed in the attempt—the case of the Spanish enclave of Melilla in North Africa. One question that this case raises is whether the Spanish authorities, by preventing the would-be migrants from crossing the border, were violating their human rights. This is not just a matter of the particular methods used to protect the border or of the way that those who succeeded in crossing were subsequently treated. The more fundamental question is whether basic human rights include the right to cross national borders and live in a territory of one's own choosing. Even if the methods used to protect the border had been more humane, did Spain have the right to exclude those who wanted to come in?

This question needs some initial clarification. What kind of right could the right to immigrate be? It might itself be regarded as a basic right, for instance as a corollary of the right to free movement. It is very plausible to suppose that human beings have a need to move around in physical space, to which there corresponds a right to free movement. Might this be so extensive as to include the right to cross state boundaries and situate oneself on the territory of another political community? Or should we see the right to immigrate as a derivative right, justified only as a means to protect other rights such as the right to subsistence? If the place in which you are living cannot provide the resources to sustain a minimally decent life, then you would have the right to move to places where such resources are available, regardless of national boundaries. This second approach would involve drawing a distinction between those who were moving out of necessity and those who were moving out of preference, with only the former having a *right* to immigrate—such a distinction appears to be implicit in the current policy of most states, where a line is drawn between refugees and economic migrants.

We need also to ask about the grounds on which the receiving state can justify its territorial rights. In contemporary practice, states take it for granted that they have a general right to decide who is admitted to their territory, even if they also recognize a responsibility to take in certain categories of immigrants. But what is the source of this right? How can states justify their claim to decide who resides on a particular part of the earth's surface and who does not, particularly in view of the somewhat murky historical processes by which state boundaries have usually been established? People might have a right to migrate simply on the grounds that states have no right to exclude them from their territory.

Finally, even if we conclude that states' territorial rights can be justified, and there is no right to migrate that is strong enough to defeat selective immigration policies of the kind that liberal democracies presently pursue, we still need to ask what kind of immigration policy is consistent with justice. Even if Spain is not obliged to take in everyone who wants to cross its borders, must it nonetheless pursue a fair selection procedure in deciding whom to admit? If so, how much flexibility should it have in settling on the criteria for admission? Immigration may raise issues of global justice even if we reject the arguments of those cosmopolitan liberals who claim that respect for human rights requires states to implement an open borders policy.

I shall not consider here arguments for the right to immigrate that derive directly from global egalitarianism. If we start from the assumption that every human being is entitled to equal resources, or equal opportunity, or equality of some other kind, then in the face of the vast international inequalities that currently exist, it might seem that the only way to respect that equal entitlement is to allow unlimited freedom of movement—people from poor states thereby being given access to the resources and opportunities provided by rich states.[1]

Whether unlimited freedom of movement is indeed the best way to achieve global equality is open to question: if we look at existing patterns of migration from poor countries to rich countries, we see that those who move are predominantly those who already have the resources to make the transition and who have the skills that are needed in the society they are moving to. If opening borders simply produced an increasing flight of doctors, engineers and other professionals from economically undeveloped to economically developed societies, the effect might be to reduce opportunities still further for those they left behind, who would no longer benefit from the capital and the talents of the migrants. But, in any case, I have already argued at length, in Chapter 3, against global egalitarianism as a theory of global justice. So I shall not speculate further on whether the net effect of implementing a right to migrate would be to increase or decrease global inequality overall.[2]

---

[1] Thus Hillel Steiner argues that individuals' equal entitlement to natural resources implies that those who have been deprived of an equal share cannot be prevented from entering territorial sites *unless* they are given compensation for their loss in some other form, such as a capital grant. See H. Steiner, 'Libertarianism and the Transnational Migration of People', in B. Barry and R. Goodin (eds), *Free Movement: Ethical Issues in the Transnational Migration of People and Money* (Hemel Hempstead, UK: Harvester Wheatsheaf, 1992); H. Steiner, 'Hard Borders, Compensation, and Classical Liberalism', in D. Miller and S. Hashmi (eds), *Boundaries and Justice: Diverse Ethical Perspectives* (Princeton, NJ: Princeton University Press, 2001). I have given reasons for rejecting Steiner's premise in Chapter 3. Later in this chapter, I shall consider another of Steiner's arguments for open borders, this one based on the right of free association.

[2] On this question, see further P. Van Parijs, 'Citizenship Exploitation, Unequal Exchange and the Breakdown of Popular Sovereignty', in B. Barry and R. Goodin (eds), *Free Movement*.

II

I shall begin instead with the idea that the right to migrate is simply one among a number of human rights to freedom, justified by the importance to human beings of freedom of choice in general. Liberal political philosophers often approach the immigration question in these terms.[3] Just as I should be free to decide who to marry, what job to take, what religion (if any) to profess, so I should be free to decide whether to live in Nigeria, or France, or the USA. Now these philosophers usually concede that in practice some limits may have to be placed on this freedom, for instance if high rates of migration would result in social chaos or the breakdown of liberal states that could not accommodate so many migrants without losing their liberal character. In these instances, the exercise of free choice would become self-defeating. But the presumption is that people should be free to choose where to live unless there are strong reasons for restricting their choice.

I want to challenge this presumption. Of course, there is always *some* value in people having more options to choose between, in this case options as to where to live, but if we are going to show that migration is a human right, a line must be drawn between *basic* freedoms that people should have as a matter of right and what we might call *bare* freedoms that do not warrant that kind of protection. It would be good from my point of view if I were free to purchase an Aston Martin tomorrow, but that is not going to count as a morally significant freedom—my desire is not one that imposes any kind of obligation on others to meet it. In order to argue against immigration restrictions, therefore, liberal philosophers must do more than show that there is some value to people in being able to migrate, or, as their behaviour shows, that they have a strong *desire* to migrate. It needs to be demonstrated that this freedom has the kind of weight or significance that could turn it into a basic human right, and that therefore should prohibit states from pursuing immigration policies that limit freedom of movement.

---

[3] See, e.g. J. Carens, 'Aliens and Citizens: The Case for Open Borders', *Review of Politics*, 49 (1987), 251–73 and 'Migration and Morality: A Liberal Egalitarian Perspective', in B. Barry and R. Goodin (eds), *Free Movement*; J. Hampton, 'Immigration, Identity, and Justice', in W. F. Schwartz (ed.), *Justice in Immigration* (Cambridge: Cambridge University Press, 1995).

I shall examine three arguments that have been offered to defend a right to migrate. The first starts with the general right to freedom of movement, and claims that this must include the freedom to move into, and take up residence in, states other than one's state of current citizenship. The second begins with a person's right to *exit* from her current state—a right that is widely recognized in international law—and claims that a right to exit is pointless unless it is matched by a right to entry into other states. The third begins with the right of free association and asserts that immigration restrictions violate the rights of those on either side of the boundary to associate (work, live, etc.) freely with one another.

The idea of a right to freedom of movement is not in itself objectionable. If we start from the idea, defended in Chapter 7, that basic human rights are grounded in human needs, understood as items and conditions that people everywhere must have in order to live a decent human life, then being able to move freely in physical space is just such a condition, as we can see by thinking about people whose legs are shackled or who are confined in small spaces. A wider freedom of movement can also be justified by thinking about the interests that it serves instrumentally: if I cannot move about over a fairly wide area, it may be impossible for me to find a job, to practise my religion, or to find a suitable marriage partner. Since these all qualify as opportunities that a person must have in order to lead a decent life, it is fairly clear that freedom of movement qualifies as a basic human right.

What is less clear, however, is the physical extent of that right, in the sense of how much of the earth's surface I must be able to move to in order to say that I enjoy it. Even in liberal societies that make no attempt to confine people within particular geographical areas, freedom of movement is severely restricted in a number of ways. I cannot, in general, move to places that other people's bodies now occupy (I cannot just push them aside). I cannot move on to private property without the consent of its owner, except perhaps in emergencies or where a special right of access exists—and since most land is privately owned, this means that a large proportion of physical space does not fall within the ambit of a *right* to free movement. Even access to public space is heavily regulated: there are traffic laws that tell me where and at what speed I may drive my car, parks have opening and closing hours, the police can control my movements up and down the streets, and so forth. These are very familiar observations, but they are worth making simply to highlight how hedged about with qualifications the existing legal right to free movement in liberal societies actually is. Yet few would argue that because of these limitations, people in these societies are deprived of one of their human rights. Some liberals might argue in favour of expanding the right—for instance in Britain there has been a protracted campaign to establish a legal right to roam on uncultivated privately owned land such as moors and fells, a right that was finally extended throughout the country in 2005. But even the advocates of such a right would be hard pressed to show that some vital interest was being injured by the more restrictive property laws that applied before that date.

The point here is that liberal societies in general offer their members *sufficient* freedom of movement to protect the interests that the human right to free movement is intended to protect, even though the extent of free movement is very far from absolute. So how could one attempt to show that the right in question must include the right to move to some other country and settle there?[4] What vital interest requires the right to be interpreted in such an extensive way? Contingently, of course, it may be true that moving to another country is the only way for an individual to escape persecution, find work, obtain necessary medical care, and so forth. In these circumstances the person concerned may have the right to move, not to any state that she chooses, but to *some* state where the relevant opportunity is available. But here the right to move serves only as a remedial right: its existence depends on the fact that the person's vital interests cannot be secured in the country where she currently resides. In a world of decent states—states that were able to secure their citizens' basic rights to security, food, work, medical care, and so forth—the right to move across borders could not be justified in this way.

Our present world is not, of course, a world of decent states, and this gives rise to the issue of refugees, which I shall return to in Section V. But if we leave aside for the moment cases where the

---

[4] It is sometimes argued that since liberal states always allow their citizens to move freely between regions within their borders, it is morally arbitrary not to extend the same right to people wishing to move across them. For a rebuttal of this argument, see M. Blake, 'Immigration', in R. G. Frey and C. H. Wellman (eds), *A Companion to Applied Ethics* (Oxford: Blackwell, 2003).

right to move freely across borders depends upon the right to avoid persecution, starvation or other threats to basic needs, how might we try to give it a more general rationale? One reason a person may want to migrate is in order to participate in a culture that does not exist in his native land—for instance, he wants to work at an occupation for which there is no demand at home, or to join a religious community which again is not represented in the country from which he comes.[5] These might be central components in his plan of life, so he will find it very frustrating if he is not able to move. But does this ground a right to free movement across borders? It seems to me that it does not. What a person can legitimately claim as a human right is access to an *adequate* range of options to choose between—a reasonable choice of occupation, religion, cultural activities, marriage partners, and so forth.[6] Adequacy here is defined in terms of generic human needs rather than in terms of the interests of any one person in particular—so, for example, a would-be opera singer living in a society that provides for various forms of musical expression but not for opera can have an adequate range of options in this area even though the option she most prefers is not available. So long as they comply with the standards of decency sketched above, all contemporary states are able to provide such an adequate range internally.[7] So although people certainly have an *interest* in being able to migrate internationally, they do not have a basic need of the kind that would be required to ground a human right. It is more like

[5] c.f. J. Carens, 'The Rights of Immigrants', in J. Baker (ed.), *Group Rights* (Toronto, Canada: University of Toronto Press, 1994), 147.

[6] In liberal states, a wider set of rights will be claimed as rights of citizenship—e.g. people will legitimately demand a completely free choice of occupation, the right to practise any religion they choose, etc. But as I argued in Chapter 7, human rights do not extend as far as liberal rights of citizenship. What I am asking here is not what a liberal citizen can ask of her own state, but what one human being can demand of other human beings as a matter of basic rights.

[7] But what if they do not? Imagine a state that is materially and in other respects above the decency threshold, but that is suffused by an ideology that narrows the range of cultural options available to its citizens; suppose, for instance, that the playing of any kind of music is regarded as sinful. A person for whom music-making is (or would be) a central part of their life can certainly argue that in those circumstances his needs are not being met, but the argument is one that in the first place needs to be directed towards his fellow-citizens (who, because the state is decent, are not being prevented from making music by coercive means, but are merely unwilling to participate). If the argument fails in its effect, however, then perhaps other states have a responsibility to admit this person.

my interest in having an Aston Martin than my need for access to *some* means of physical mobility.

I turn next to the argument that because people have a right to leave the society they currently belong to, they must also have a right to enter other societies, since the first right is practically meaningless unless the second exists—there is no unoccupied space in the world to exit *to*, so unless the right to leave society A is accompanied by the right to enter societies B, C, D, ..., it has no real force.[8]

The right to exit is certainly an important human right, but once again it is worth examining why it has the significance that it does. Its importance is partly instrumental: knowing that their subjects have the right to leave inhibits states from mistreating them in various ways, so it helps to preserve the conditions of decency as outlined above. However, even in the case of decent states the right to exit remains important, and that is because by being deprived of exit rights individuals are forced to remain in association with others who they may find deeply uncongenial—think of the militant atheist in a society where almost everyone devoutly practises the same religion, or the religious puritan in a society where most people behave like libertines. On the other hand, the right to exit from state A does not entail an unrestricted right to enter any society of the emigrant's choice—formally it can be exercised provided that at least one other society, society B say, is willing to take him in, and it has value so long as B does not share the cultural or other features that made this person's life in A intolerable. It might seem that we can generate a general right to migrate by iteration: the person who leaves A for B then has the right to exit from B, which entails that C, at least, must grant him the right to enter, and so forth. But this move fails, because our person's right to exit from A depended on the claim that he might find continued association with the other citizens of A unacceptable, and he cannot plausibly continue making the same claim in the case of each society that is willing to take him in. Given the political and cultural diversity of societies in the real world, to argue that only an unlimited choice of which one to join

---

[8] For arguments of this kind, see A. Dummett, 'The Transnational Migration of People Seen from within a Natural Law Tradition', in B. Barry and R. Goodin (eds), *Free Movement*; P. Cole, *Philosophy and Exclusion: Liberal Political Theory and Immigration* (Edinburgh, UK: Edinburgh University Press, 2000).

will prevent people being forced to remain in associations that are repugnant to them is simply unconvincing.

It is also important to stress that there are many rights whose exercise is contingent on finding partners who are willing to cooperate in the exercise, and it may be that the right to exit falls into this category. Take the right to marry as an example. This is a right held against the state to allow people to marry the partners of their choice (and also to provide the legal framework within which marriages can be contracted[9]). It is obviously not a right to have a marriage partner provided—whether any given person can exercise the right depends entirely on whether he is able to find someone willing to marry him, and many people are not so lucky. The right to exit is a right held against a person's current state of residence not to prevent her from leaving the state (and perhaps to make it practically possible for her to leave by, say, providing a passport). But it does not entail an obligation on any other state to let that person in. Obviously, if no state were ever to grant entry rights to people who were not already its citizens, the right to exit would have no value. But suppose states are generally willing to consider entry applications from people who want to migrate, and that most people would get offers from at least one such state: then in this respect the position as far as the right to exit goes is pretty much the same as with the right to marry, where by no means everyone is able to wed the partner they would ideally like to have, but most have the opportunity to marry *someone*.

Finally, here, I shall consider the claim that rights to migrate are entailed by the right of free association. Once again we begin with a right that has considerable plausibility as a candidate for human rights status. Many human needs, including needs for companionship, work, etc. can only be met if people are allowed to associate

---

[9] Thus the right to marry is more than just a liberty right—it is more than merely the right that the state not interfere with the private choices of individuals. It also imposes a duty to make marriage possible—but not a duty to *ensure* that everyone who wants to marry can do so. This is also true of the right to exit. This is the respect in which the two rights are analogous. In other respects, obviously, they are disanalogous—the right to marry is grounded in the positive value of the human relationships that it can foster, whereas the right to exit is grounded in the negative value of being forced to remain in an intolerable social milieu. That is why there cannot be a duty on the part of one individual to marry another, but there can under certain circumstances be a duty on the part of a state to allow a person to exercise her right of exit by granting her a right of entry—this is the case with refugees, to be considered in Section V.

freely with others who agree to the association—association here meaning being physically in the same place, able to engage in joint activities, and so forth. A person deprived of the right to associate, or allowed only to associate with a few others not chosen by himself, could hardly have a decent life. But must the right be construed so strongly that it can only be satisfied in a world where people are free to move anywhere in pursuit of their preferred associates?

Paradoxically, the right of free association has been cited *both* as a reason for having completely open borders *and* as a reason why immigration controls are permissible. It can be used in the second way because freedom of association as usually understood also entails the right *not* to associate with those you do not wish to—any association between two parties has to be voluntary in both directions. So a political community, it is argued, has the right to exclude people who may wish to join if its own members prefer, for whatever reason, to keep them out.[10] This argument works at the level of the community as a whole, treated as a collective agent with rights of association and dissociation. The argument for open borders, by contrast, focuses on the rights of individuals. A would-be migrant can be kept out only if there is *nobody* in the relevant territory who wants to associate with him. If there is some resident A who wants to live or work with non-resident B, then their combined rights of free association entail that B cannot be prevented by immigration controls from moving into proximity with A. Thus Hillel Steiner presents state-imposed restrictions on freedom of movement as coercive interference with the rights of all those who want to house or employ outsiders: 'for it is one thing for insiders to choose to restrict entry to their own private domain, and quite another for the state to compel them to do so'. Hard borders, Steiner concludes, would be legitimate only in the wholly unlikely event that there was *unanimous* consent by the members of a political community to using the powers of the state to exclude outsiders.[11]

I find neither of these appeals to freedom of association compelling. Although my main concern is with freedom of association as a justification for open borders, let me say briefly why the argument in the opposite direction also fails. This argument relies on the idea

---

[10] See C. Wellman, 'Immigration and Freedom of Association' (forthcoming).
[11] Steiner, 'Hard Borders, Compensation, and Classical Liberalism', 80.

that we have a deep interest in not being forced into association with others against our wishes.[12] It applies most clearly in the case of intimate relationships: it would clearly be intolerable if I were obliged to share my house or my bed with another person or persons without my consent. The argument can be extended to certain larger groups such as religious communities. It is important to be able to control who participates in religious services and other rites: because churches, for example, are communities of believers, they must have the right to exclude atheists, Satanists, and so forth from their congregations. In a much weaker form it may also apply to clubs formed for social or recreational purposes. If I like playing golf, but for some reason strongly dislike rubbing shoulders with one particular group, then I ought to be able to set up a golf club that excludes them, so long as those who are excluded have something like a comparable opportunity to establish their own club.[13] But none of these reasons appear to apply to political communities of the size of contemporary nation-states. These are not intimate associations. If I dislike encountering people with particular characteristics, I can arrange my life in such a way that I will rarely if ever come across them. To justify restricting entry on these grounds, one would have to show that the mere presence of such people within the boundaries of the state could reasonably be seen as harming some interest of mine. But the only case I can imagine in which this might apply would be a confessional state where the presence of unbelievers might be regarded as disruptive of the community. Since few, if any, contemporary states have this character, the attempt to justify a strong, general right to exclusion by appeal to freedom of association cannot succeed.[14]

The argument in the other direction fares no better. Indeed, both arguments suffer from the same fault: they try to generalize from

---

[12] For a much fuller consideration of the underlying values at stake here, see S. White, 'Freedom of Association and the Right to Exclude', *Journal of Political Philosophy*, 5 (1997), 373–91.

[13] There are a number of qualifications that need to be made to this claim, but I am simply granting the point for the sake of argument.

[14] I shall argue later that members of nation-states may properly consider the impact that taking in different groups of immigrants would have on the future character of their community — its size, its cultural complexion, and so forth — so it is important to distinguish this argument about national self-determination from the one I have just rejected which appeals to individual rights of free association and dissociation.

212 National Responsibility and Global Justice

cases in which the freedom to associate or dissociate clearly serves a vital human interest in order to establish an absolute and unconditional right of free association or dissociation. Why, then, does the general value of free association not justify open borders? The argument, as presented by Steiner for example, relies on a stylized and very unrealistic picture of human relationships in which an isolated A is able to enter into exclusive association with an equally isolated B.[15] In particular, A is portrayed as owning a particular territorial site and as conducting his relationship with B entirely on that site; B's presence, in this picture, has no morally relevant effects on third parties or on the wider political community to which A belongs. But how, in fact, is B able to associate with A on the latter's property? Does he arrive by parachute, and if so through whose airspace? Or if he arrives by more conventional means, for instance by using public roads, how does he obtain permission for his travels? These questions are meant to remind us that immigration, as usually understood, means in the first instance admission to a political community's public space. The immigrant is able to move around physically under the general protection of the laws before he is able to associate with particular persons for purposes of housing and employment. So unless we envisage a world in which there is literally no public space—everything is held as private property, and would-be immigrants (or their prospective hosts) have therefore to negotiate individually with each owner whose land they must traverse in order to reach the territory of their preferred associate— the interests of many others besides A and B will be affected by the proposed association between them.[16]

Given that this is so, the question we must ask about freedom of association is essentially the same as the one we asked about freedom of movement: why must the right be interpreted in such a broad way

---

[15] See more generally Onora O'Neill's discussion of Steiner in 'Magic Associations and Imperfect People', in B. Barry and R. Goodin (eds), *Free Movement*.

[16] These observations may not tell directly against Steiner himself, who holds, as do many other libertarians, a conception of rights such that the impact of the exercise of a right on third parties is disregarded unless this impact would itself amount to a rights-violation. As is clear from Chapter 7, my own conception is different: in deciding what rights we have, account must be taken of the impact that acknowledging a candidate right would have on the needs and interests of those besides the right-holder himself. It would take us too far afield to explore this issue in greater depth here.

that it includes the right to associate with any person in any territory? Why is it not sufficient, in terms of the human needs and interests that association serves, to be able to consort with a sufficiently large number of people to generate a wide choice of friends, marriage partners, work colleagues, fellow sports enthusiasts, and so forth? It is relevant here that granting an unlimited right to migration, on the basis of an equally unlimited right of free association, might have very high costs, if large numbers of people chose at the same time to move to a small and already crowded society, putting huge strain on its institutions and infrastructure, and thereby putting other basic needs at risk. How, then, can it be regarded as a human right?[17]

I conclude, therefore, that one cannot justify an unconditional right to immigrate on the basis of the (genuine) human rights of the would-be migrant, whether freedom of movement, freedom of association, or the right to exit. Nonetheless, the needs and interests we have considered show that such persons often have a strong *claim* to be admitted, given that some of their important goals may not be realizable without crossing state boundaries. A claim is something less than a right, but those who refuse it must give the claimant a reason for doing so. So now we must ask by what right the state they want to move to can deny them entry.[18] How can the state establish territorial rights that allow it to determine who can and who cannot be admitted to the territory it controls?

---

[17] It might be said that the same applies to the civil right to freedom of movement *within* a society—yet we continue to regard this as a genuine right. But (*a*) it is improbable that very large numbers of people would wish to move within a society that guarantees adequate standards of living to all its members, whereas the possibility of large-scale transnational migration is a real one; (*b*) if it seemed likely that there would be excessive movement to one region or one city within a society, the state would have a range of policy instruments to counteract this— e.g. it could offer job or housing subsidies to encourage people to stay where they were—and in the extreme case it could indeed legitimately place restrictions on freedom of movement, as indeed it already does to a considerable extent, as noted earlier. Even the civil right to free movement is not absolute.

[18] It is important to see that this is a separate question that requires its own answer. The fact that A does not have a right to do something does not entail that B has a right to prevent him from doing that thing, as Hart's well-known example of the two people who both spot a ten-dollar bill lying in the street illustrates. Neither person has a right to the money (in the sense that implies a duty on the part of others to let him have it) but equally neither has the right to stop the other from making a dash and grabbing the bill. See H. L. A. Hart, 'Are there any Natural Rights?', in A. Quinton (ed.), *Political Philosophy* (Oxford: Oxford University Press, 1967), 57.

III

To answer this question we need to consider two issues separately. The first issue is how, in general, to justify the state's claim to a monopoly of political authority throughout the territory it controls. How can the state have the right to apply law and other instruments of public policy to everyone and everything within a particular geographical area? The second issue is how *particular* territorial rights are established. Why should *this* state have the right to exercise political authority within *these* boundaries? These two issues have to be addressed in quite different ways.

The first involves one of the central questions of political philosophy, and I can only sketch an answer here.[19] If we consider the range of functions that modern states perform, it quickly becomes obvious that these functions cannot be carried out effectively unless the state has authority over a determinate territory. In saying this, I do not mean to beg any questions about whether that authority should be unitary or multilayered; there may well be good reason to have different levels of government operating over different areas—for instance, to have a federal state, and/or city-level governments with extensive powers. But these subordinate authorities will also have well-defined geographical limits, and the division of law-making and other powers between these bodies and central government will be specified in some detail. The existence of such authority makes it possible for people at any given location to know which legal regime they are subject to, and which other policies apply to them. And this enables many human activities to take place that would be difficult or impossible in the absence of such certainty. Economic activity, in particular, can proceed on the basis that everyone in a particular place is subject to the same laws of contract, employment, and so on. Meanwhile, the state itself can engage in a range of activities such as establishing transport systems, planning the use of physical space, and protecting the natural environment, that would not be possible in the absence of well-defined geographical limits to its authority. Assuming that such activities are broadly advantageous to citizens, the justification for states having the right to exercise

[19] See also my critical appraisal of Robert Nozick's answer to this question in 'The Justification of Political Authority', in D. Schmidtz (ed.), *Robert Nozick* (Cambridge: Cambridge University Press, 2002).

their authority over a given territory is utilitarian in character: everyone subject to such authority can expect to benefit from its existence.

Another way to make the same point is to imagine two communities intermingled on the same territory, each subject to a different political authority responsible for law enforcement etc. Assume that members of the two communities are generally well disposed to one another. It would, nonetheless, be very difficult for their members to cooperate with one another, or to solve all kinds of collective problems such as where to build roads, or how to control environmental pollution. Even simple person-to-person dealings — for example, disputes over property, contracts, and personal injury — would be hard to conduct until it was agreed whose law should govern them. This, apparently, was how things were in parts of Europe in the early Middle Ages, where law was personal rather than territorial — each person lived according to customary law of the particular community to which he belonged and carried this law with him wherever he went. The result was chaotic: 'the presence side by side of men who belonged by birth to different peoples had at first resulted in the most singular medley that ever confronted a professor of law in his nightmares.'[20] To cope with this, the practice evolved of making participants in legal transactions declare in advance which law they considered themselves subject to. It is easy to see how arbitrary and unpredictable such a system will be, and the enormous benefit, by comparison, of having a uniform set of laws applied throughout a defined territory — in short, the benefit of having a territorial state.

The implication of this for immigration is that a person who stands on any particular piece of ground is rightfully subject to the authority of the state whose laws apply there, if there is such a state. This holds no matter how or why the person in question arrived at the place where he now stands — even if, say, he was washed ashore after a shipwreck. He cannot claim immunity on the grounds that he has not given his consent to the state's authority. And that authority must include the right to require him to leave, since a system of territorial authority cannot function without some control over

---

[20] M. Bloch, *Feudal Society* (London: Routledge and Kegan Paul, 1962), vol. I, 111.

who falls within its scope.[21] This is sometimes expressed using the language of sovereignty—states must be sovereign, and sovereignty entails the right to exclude—but I prefer not to use this term, since it suggests that the state is subject to no restrictions in its treatment of would-be immigrants.[22] In contrast, I think that the state is bound to treat those who arrive on its territory, or more generally apply to be admitted, fairly and with respect for their human rights, so there are certainly limits to its authority. But for the reasons given earlier, this does not entail that it must admit all those who want to enter—their human rights do not reach so far. I will return later to the question of refugees, who can claim that only admission will safeguard their basic rights. But first I need to complete my defence of the state's right to control a definite territory.

The general justification that I offered cited the overwhelming benefits of a territorially defined system of law and public policy. But this does not show why any *particular* state can legitimately claim authority over any *particular* territory. An immigrant might, therefore, challenge Spain's right to exclude him from the particular patch of land he wants to enter even while conceding the general argument in favour of territorial authority. So how can particular territorial claims be justified?

One might think it was sufficient for a state to show that its exercise of authority over a given territory was effective—that it passed a certain threshold in terms of securing the interests of those

[21] It is true that subordinate authorities such as city governments do not have such control—but they are protected by a central authority that does. As Walzer has put it, 'neighborhoods can be open only if countries are at least potentially closed.... To tear down the walls of the state is not...to create a world without walls, but rather to create a thousand petty fortresses'. M. Walzer, *Spheres of Justice: A Defence of Pluralism and Equality* (Oxford: Martin Robertson, 1983), 38–9.

[22] Or perhaps only to procedural restrictions on how it deals with them. Compare Sidgwick: 'A State must obviously have the right to admit aliens on its own terms, imposing any conditions on entrance or tolls on transit, and subjecting them to any legal restrictions or disabilities that it may deem expedient. It ought not, indeed, having once admitted them, to apply to them suddenly, and without warning, a harsh differential treatment; but as it may legitimately exclude them altogether, it must have a right to treat them in any way it thinks fit, after due warning given and due time allowed for withdrawal.' [H. Sidgwick, *The Elements of Politics*, 2nd edn (London: Macmillan, 1897), 248] Sidgwick does, however, go on to say that the state must refrain from *injuring* the aliens it has admitted, or allowing them to be injured by private individuals—in other words, it has a duty of care towards them.

within the territory—to settle the matter. That has traditionally been the position so far as international law is concerned, and recent developments essentially involve raising the bar somewhat, so that legitimacy comes to depend on meeting certain human rights standards as well as preserving social order generally.[23] The argument for this is that any further requirement opens the door to a range of irresolvable disputes about territorial rights—there are barely any borders in the world that can be regarded as uncontentious, so the only reasonable position is to regard the de facto boundaries of effectively functioning states as sacrosanct. Against this, however, we must consider the large number of cases in which boundaries have indeed been altered, by the creation of new states, or the union of existing ones, or in some other way, and these transitions may occur quite smoothly. So we cannot avoid giving some answer to the question of how specific territorial claims can be justified.

States can only claim territorial rights, in my view, as representatives of the peoples that they govern: such rights, in other words, belong fundamentally to the people collectively and are exercised on their behalf by the state they have authorized to do so. The central cases, and the ones I shall consider, are those where rights are held by *nations*, but the account may prove to be extendable to other human groups that lack some of the characteristics of nations proper, for instance aboriginal groups.

National rights to territory have been claimed on a variety of different grounds, ranging from original occupation—our ancestors lived here in the distant past—to national destiny—we can only fulfil our national mission by controlling this piece of land. Rather than reviewing all of these claims, I shall simply present what I take to be the strongest case for territorial rights and consider some objections to it.[24] Consider a nation that over a long period occupies and transforms a piece of territory and continues to hold that territory in the present. This unavoidably has a number of consequences. First, there is a two-way interaction between the territory and the culture of the people who live on it. The culture must adapt to the territory

[23] For a thorough exploration of this condition for political legitimacy, see A. Buchanan, *Justice, Legitimacy, and Self-Determination* (Oxford: Oxford University Press, 2004), Part II.

[24] For an excellent systematic review, see T. Meisels, *Territorial Rights* (Dordrecht, The Netherlands: Kluwer, 2005).

if the people are to prosper: it matters whether the climate is hot or cold, the land suitable for hunting or agriculture, whether the territory is landlocked or open to the sea, and so forth. But equally the territory will in nearly every case be shaped over time according to the cultural priorities of the people, as fields are marked out and cultivated; irrigation systems are created; villages, towns, and cities are built; and so forth, so that eventually the face of the landscape may be changed beyond recognition. It has become the people's home, in the sense that they have adapted their way of life to the physical constraints of the territory and then transformed it to a greater or lesser extent in pursuit of their common goals. It does not matter here that the transformation may not be coordinated or consciously intended by the participants, so long as it reflects their shared cultural values: following the analysis of Chapter 5, this is sufficient for us to say that the nation is responsible for the eventual character of the territory it inhabits.

From this further consequences follow. The first is that the nation as a whole has a legitimate claim to the enhanced value that the territory now has, so long that is as we accept the idea of inherited national responsibility defended in Chapter 6. Placing a figure on that added value may be impossible for reasons given in Chapter 3, but that does not create any problems so long as the nation in question continues to hold the territory. And because the enhanced value cannot be separated from the territory itself—it is *embodied* in cultivated fields, buildings, roads, waterways, and all the rest—there is no way in which the nation could retain the value it has created but not the territory.

Besides this quasi-Lockean basis for territorial rights, there is a quite separate consideration having to do with the symbolic significance of national territory.[25] Living on and shaping a piece of land means not only increasing its value in an economic sense, but also (typically) endowing it with meaning by virtue of significant events that have occurred there, monuments that have been built, poems, novels and paintings that capture particular places or types of landscape. Those living in the present may attach more or less value to living in a place that is rich in historical meaning, though

[25] The distinction between the two approaches is emphasized in Meisels, *Territorial Rights*, ch. 6.

my sense is that this has come to matter more as a global consumer culture permeates so many other aspects of life. The case for having rights over the relevant territory is then straightforward: it gives members of the nation continuing access to places that are especially significant to them, and it allows choices to be made over how these sites are to be protected and managed.

I have based my argument on the central case of a nation that has occupied and transformed territory over a long period—for centuries perhaps. Other cases may lack one or more of the features I have cited. Some peoples may live on land while doing very little to reshape it; yet the land may hold enormous symbolic significance for them. The period over which land has been occupied may be much shorter, in which case there may have been a dramatic increase in its value, but far less by way of historical associations. So the strength of the claim to territorial rights may vary. And, of course, there may be competing claims from other groups. But let me move straight on to consider objections to the occupancy/transformation basis for territorial rights.

The first of these is that occupancy and transformation only count for anything if the occupiers had a right to the territory in the first place. By way of analogy, if I steal property and then transform it in some way, this is by no means sufficient to establish my right to the thing I have stolen. So unless territorial rights are immaculate from the very beginning, what happens later does not change the picture, ethically speaking. According to this objection, everything hinges on how the original appropriation of territory can be justified.

It should be clear, I hope, that if nation B expels nation A from the territory it has occupied historically and begins to occupy and cultivate that land, it does not immediately acquire territorial rights, according to my account. On the contrary: nation A's claim to be returned to its homeland is plainly the stronger when we consider the various factors that I have canvassed as relevant to such rights (the cultural fit between people and land, the value they have added, and the symbolic significance it holds for them). On the other hand, as time passes nation B will begin to have claims that resemble those of A (nation A may or may not develop occupancy claims in some other place). Who has the better title at any moment will be a matter of judgement; but even if B's claim is successful, members of B may owe members of A compensation for the effects of their expulsion, according to the principles of historical responsibility outlined earlier in this book. So the view I am defending does not amount to a charter for thieves or anything of that sort, although it does allow the occupancy and use of land over a long period eventually to trump the territorial claims of the original possessors.

The alternative position suggested by the objection also seems impossibly demanding. What would count as having an unblemished original title to land? Presumably it would mean occupying land that has had no previous inhabitants (or that has been voluntarily relinquished by its previous occupants), while respecting some quasi-Lockean 'enough and as good' condition to ensure that the occupation was not depriving others of an equal chance to acquire territorial rights. Given the tides of human history, whose present title would meet this condition? Perhaps the Icelanders': when the Nordic settlers arrived there from the ninth century onwards, there was no one to displace, and holding on to that windswept and largely infertile island has surely not involved a breach of any Lockean proviso. Such rare cases apart, those who hold territory now do so as a result of a very long history of human movement, infiltration and conquest, some of whose episodes will involve injustice. So although insisting that nations' territorial claims only deserve respect if a valid original title can be established might seem helpful to the cause of immigrants, it would also have the effect of putting virtually all borders into question, opening the way to arbitrary annexations, secessions, dismemberments, and so forth. We must surely allow that occupying and transforming land over a sufficiently long period gives a people rights to that land that if not absolute are at least superior to those of other claimants, even if their ancestors in the distant past were invaders or conquerors.[26]

Another objection to the position I am advancing on territorial rights draws an analogy with rights to private property. Even strong defenders of property rights usually concede that such rights may be overridden by urgent human need. A starving man may feed himself from the crop growing in someone else's field, and it would

---

[26] For cogent general considerations in support of this view, see J. Waldron, 'Superseding Historic Injustice', *Ethics*, 103 (1992–3), 4–28.

be wrong to use force to prevent him. Having satisfied his hunger he may owe compensation to the landowner, but for the moment his need is paramount. Consider then by analogy an immigrant who claims that his need for subsistence, say, gives him the right to access to the state's territory, on the basis that this is the only way he can get that subsistence. Can the state justifiably use force to keep him out?

I accept that territorial rights are never absolute, and that claims of material necessity—or more generally claims based on human rights—can sometimes place limits on their exercise. But it is important to recall that such claims are held in the first place against all those able to meet the need or protect the right, and the claimant cannot choose who bears the specific remedial responsibility in his case. As we saw in Chapter 4, assigning remedial responsibilities is not straightforward in situations where there are many agents each of whom might be able to help the patient. The starving man can eat from the field where he finds himself because we assume that this is the only source of nourishment presently available to him. In the same way, an immigrant who arrives willy-nilly on the territory of a particular state—a person who has been drifting on the open sea, for example—is owed an immediate duty of care by that state. But more typically people who are moving to protect their human rights could potentially enter any one of a large number of states, each of which can offer them the necessary protection. Ideally, one might think, some system of assignment should be put in place to deal with this problem: I shall ask in a moment how feasible this is. But meanwhile the immigrant cannot demand admission to any particular state: his rights do not trump rights to territorial integrity, even though they cast a shadow over those rights. The shadow they cast is that a state that claims legitimate authority over a territory must also take reasonable steps to protect the human rights of those whose position is worsened by the boundaries it defends—which might mean, in special circumstances where there is no alternative, allowing them to come in (in other circumstances the state might, for instance, offer them protection in the place where they now reside). In other words, it cannot, ethically speaking, defend its boundaries and do nothing else in a world where human rights are in many places insecure.

IV

We have seen so far that immigrants cannot, in general, claim that they have a basic human right to cross national boundaries, while states may be able to establish territorial rights as representatives of the peoples who have occupied and transformed the territory in question. But although these two propositions taken together may establish that states can have the right to control entry, they do not show that states *ought* to exercise that right, or *how* they should exercise it, if they do. Even if would-be immigrants do not have a right to migrate, they do in most cases have a strong interest in doing so; their opportunities will often be greatly enlarged if they are allowed to move and become citizens of their chosen political community. So if the state is going to turn them away, or pursue a selective admission policy, it must be able to offer a justification for doing so. It cannot, as we have seen, appeal simply to freedom of association, and say that it is entirely at liberty to choose who comes in and who does not. The analogy with a private club fails, partly because the reasons that the members of a club can give for excluding unwanted applicants do not apply here, and partly because the costs of exclusion are typically much greater for the person who is turned away. Would-be immigrants who are prevented from entering cannot 'start their own club' elsewhere. There is nowhere for them to do this—no uninhabited portions of the earth that can easily sustain human life—and they would not have access to the physical and human capital that an existing developed society can offer. They are owed an explanation for their exclusion.

An adequate explanation will be one that links immigration policy to the general goals of the society in question. These goals will reflect existing national values and will ideally be set through a continuing process of democratic debate. Immigration on any significant scale will invariably have an impact on these goals, sometimes positive, sometimes negative. It will, for example, change the age profile of the country (immigrants may be mainly young workers, or on the other hand retirees in search of a sunnier climate), the mix of skills available in the workforce, the demands made on the education system, the health care system, and the other social services, the overall size of the population, the cultural make-up of the country, the demands for public goods of various kinds, and so on and so forth. All of these are legitimate concerns of public policy, and depending on the priorities set by each political community, they may count either for or against admitting particular groups of immigrants. Countries with ageing populations may want to recruit people of working age with particular skills that are in short supply, as many European states now do; other countries with existing high levels of unemployment may be reluctant to admit newcomers whose presence may further depress wages or expand the jobless total. Countries with small populations and large tracts of unimproved land may have an interest in taking more people in; countries that are already crowded and congested, and that are currently pursuing environmental policies that presuppose limiting or even reducing population size, will have an interest in keeping them out. One country may wish to increase its cultural diversity by admitting people who can contribute something new to the existing cultural mix; another may want to strengthen its existing national culture which it feels is being threatened by globalization by, for example, bringing in more speakers of the national language.[27]

My claim here is not that the interests of current citizens will always outweigh the interests of those who would wish to immigrate, supposing we could find a neutral metric by which these interests could be compared. I am appealing instead to the value of self-determination, to the importance to a political community of being able to determine its future shape, including for example the balance it wishes to strike between economic growth and environmental values, and pointing out that questions of membership are intimately involved in such decisions. I argued in Chapter 2 in favour of recognizing special obligations to one's compatriots. It follows from this that although the claims of would-be immigrants must be recognized, they do not have to be counted in the same way as the interests of those who are already citizens, including their interests in self-determination. Some partiality is legitimate: the key issue is how strong the immigrant's claim has to be before it can

---

[27] These considerations all have to do with the impact that immigration may have on the lives of those already inside the receiving community. There are also, of course, concerns about the impact of *emigration* on the sending community which ought to be taken into account—for instance if emigration would deprive that community of scarce human capital.

trump the goals of the receiving state. I shall return to this question shortly.

One objection to the position that I have just laid out is that it seems to assume a homogeneous national culture in which all participants share the same goals. For instance, I have assumed that a political community might have an interest in reinforcing the use of its national language by means of a selective immigration policy, but linguistic minorities inside the community might have precisely the opposite interest—they would be at less of a disadvantage if there were more diversity. My answer to this is that although different individuals and groups are likely to disagree about the priorities that their political community should pursue, they have a common interest in being able to set those goals through democratic debate, and this of course entails being willing to accept majority decisions reached through proper procedures. So I may disagree with the current language policy of my state, but it is to my advantage nonetheless that the policy is the subject of a democratic process that takes my concerns into account, and that on other occasions will generate policies that I favour. It is also in my interest to belong to a community with a shared sense of national identity, even if that identity conflicts at certain points with my own cultural values, if we assume that the shared identity performs valuable functions in holding the community together, enabling democracy, and providing the motivation for policies of social justice.[28]

So far I have given general reasons why states are justified in limiting immigration. What remains to be seen is how far justice constrains the policies they may adopt. Are there some immigrants who must be admitted regardless of how many of them there are? And in the case of those among whom selection is permissible, which criteria may legitimately be used in making the selection?

V

Let me begin with the obligations of a receiving state towards people whose basic human rights are being violated or threatened in their

---

[28] I have defended this assumption at some length in *On Nationality* (Oxford: Clarendon Press, 1995), esp. chs. 4–5.

current place of residence. Such people are usually described as refugees. In current international law, refugees are defined as people who have fled their home country as a result of a well-founded fear of persecution or violence, but there is clearly a good case for broadening the definition to include people who are being deprived of rights to subsistence, basic health care, etc.[29] When a refugee applies to be admitted to a state that is able to guarantee her such rights, then prima facie the state in question has an obligation to let her in. For several reasons, however, this does not translate into an automatic right to immigrate.

One reason is that the refugee's immediate claim is to *sanctuary*, to be in a place where her basic rights are no longer under threat. This can be achieved by granting her temporary residence in the country she has applied to move to, in the expectation that she will in due course return to her native land when the threat has passed.[30] For people who are escaping episodes of political turbulence or short-lived civil wars, this may be an appropriate solution. Another possibility is to establish safety zones for refugees close to their homes and then deal with the cause of the rights-violations directly—whether this means sending in food and medical aid, or intervening to remove a genocidal regime from power. In both cases there is a danger that the temporary solution becomes semi-permanent, and this is unacceptable because refugees are owed more than the immediate protection of their basic rights—they are owed the opportunity to make a decent life for themselves in the place that they live. So if a person is admitted on a temporary basis, but after some years it becomes clear that there is no realistic chance of his returning safely to his country of origin, he must then be given the chance of acquiring full citizenship rights in the country he has moved to. Equally, refugee camps and other forms of temporary shelter may be acceptable in the short term as a response to disaster, but they must not become permanent settlements by default.

---

[29] See A. Shacknove, 'Who Is a Refugee?', *Ethics*, 95 (1985), 274–84; M. Gibney, *The Ethics and Politics of Asylum: Liberal Democracy and the Response to Refugees* (Cambridge: Cambridge University Press, 2004), Introduction.

[30] See J. C. Hathaway, and R. A. Neve, 'Making International Refugee Law Relevant Again: A Proposal for Collectivized and Solution-Oriented Protection', *Harvard Human Rights Journal*, 10 (1997), 115–211.

As the number of people claiming refugee status begins to rise—as it has done in recent decades—the question of *which* state has the obligation to take them in becomes more pressing. By convention the responsibility falls to the state on whose territorial border they appear to make their admission claim, but clearly this mechanism distributes the burden of coping with refugees in an arbitrary way (and gives states an incentive to make it more difficult to arrive at their borders).[31] Since the obligation to offer protection is shared among all those states that are able to provide refuge, in an ideal world one might envisage some formal mechanism for distributing refugees among them. However, the difficulties in devising such a scheme are formidable.[32] To obtain agreement from different states about what each state's refugee quota should be, one would presumably need to start with simple and relatively uncontroversial criteria such as population or per capita GDP. But this leaves out of the picture many other factors, such as population density, the overall rate of immigration into each state, cultural factors that make absorption of particular groups of refugees particularly easy or difficult, and so forth—all factors that would differentially affect the willingness of political communities to accept refugees and make agreement on a scheme very unlikely. Furthermore, the proposed quota system pays no attention to the choices of the refugees themselves as to where to apply for sanctuary, unless it is accompanied by a compensatory scheme that allows states that take in more refugees than their quota prescribes to receive financial transfers from states that take in less.[33]

Realistically, therefore, states have to be given considerable autonomy to decide on how to respond to particular asylum applications: besides the refugee's own choice, they are entitled to consider the overall number of applications they face, the demands that

---

[31] This is the effect of the so-called *non-refoulement* principle, which prohibits states from forcing individuals to return to territories where their lives would be threatened. For discussion, see Gibney, *The Ethics and Politics of Asylum*, ch. 8.

[32] For recent attempts to do this, see Hathaway and Neve, 'Making International Refugee Law Relevant Again' and P. Schuck, 'Refugee Burden-Sharing: A Modest Proposal', *Yale Journal of International Law*, 22 (1997), 243–97. See also Carens, 'The Rights of Immigrants', 152–7.

[33] For an excellent discussion of the wider ethical issues raised by refugee quota and trading schemes, see M. Gibney, 'Forced Migration, "Engineered" Regionalism and Justice between States', in Susan Kneebone and Felicity Rawlings-Sanei (eds), *New Regionalism and Asylum Seekers* (Oxford: Berghahn, forthcoming 2007).

temporary or longer-term accommodation of refugees will place on existing citizens, and whether there exists any special link between the refugee and the host community—for instance, similarities of language or culture, or a sense of historical responsibility on the part of the receiving state (which might see itself as somehow implicated among the causes of the crisis that has produced the refugees). The best hope is that over time conventions will emerge that distribute responsibilities in such a way that refugees from particular places become the special responsibility of one state in particular (or a coalition of several states). There can be no guarantee, however, that every bona fide refugee will find a state willing to take her in. The final judgement must rest with the members of the receiving state, who may decide that they have already done their fair share of refugee resettlement. Recall a point made in Chapter 2: the duty we are considering is a duty either to prevent rights violations being inflicted by third parties (if the refugees are fleeing violence or political persecution) or to secure the rights of people where others have failed in their responsibility (if the refugees are escaping food shortages caused by economic mismanagement, say). Such duties are weaker than the negative duty not to violate human rights oneself, and arguably weaker than the positive duty to secure the rights of those we are specifically responsible for protecting. At the limit, therefore, we may face tragic cases where the human rights of the refugees clash with a legitimate claim by the receiving state that its obligation to admit refugees has already been exhausted.[34]

Refugees, then, have a very strong, but not absolute, right to be admitted to a place of safety, a right now widely recognized in both law and political practice. But what of immigrants who are moving for reasons other than a threat to their basic rights? On what grounds may admission decisions be taken? There has been a very marked change over time in the practice of liberal states on this issue.[35] Going back half a century or so, it was regarded as acceptable for states to discriminate openly on ethnic or cultural grounds, giving preference in admission to those who were seen as 'kith and kin' or who came from particular places whose

[34] c.f. here the discussion in Walzer, *Spheres of Justice*, 48–51.
[35] See C. Joppke, *Selecting by Origin: Ethnic Migration in the Liberal State* (Cambridge, MA: Harvard University Press, 2005), esp. chs. 1 and 5.

cultural profile was of the approved sort—from Northern Europe, for example, as opposed to Southern Europe or places beyond. But as ideals of non-discrimination have become more firmly entrenched *within* liberal states, so prevailing attitudes have changed in such a way that, in general, selection may be made only on grounds of need (in the case of refugees), family ties (to those already in the political community), and the economic requirements of the receiving state (for workers with particular skills, for instance)—all criteria that facially at least are ethnically and culturally neutral. This is qualified in the practice of certain states by a policy of positively favouring immigrants with particular cultural characteristics—for instance French language speakers in the case of Quebec and Jews in the case of Israel. But these are treated as exceptions to the general rule that immigration policies must be ethnically and culturally neutral.

If, however, the general justification for immigration restrictions involves an appeal to national self-determination and in particular a people's right to shape its own cultural development, it may seem anomalous to prohibit selection on cultural grounds, whether this means selecting those who are already closely aligned with the prevailing majority culture or selecting those who are culturally different in the name of diversity. So why has the rule of cultural non-discrimination taken root? One explanation may be that earlier policies involving cultural discrimination were in fact covertly racist, designed to keep out people with the 'wrong' skin colour, such as the now infamous White Australia policy of the first half of the twentieth century. But a deeper reason is that cultural selection at the point of entry has come to seem incompatible with equal treatment of cultural groups that already belong to the state: if Protestants are favoured in admissions policy, for example, that gives Protestantism a privileged status that denies equal recognition to Catholics, Jews, etc. who are already citizens. Given that virtually every state already contains significant numbers of people belonging to cultural minorities, liberal principles of equality demand that immigration policy should be culturally neutral.[36]

---

[36] For a fuller statement of this position, see Blake, 'Immigration', 232–4.

To defend the use of cultural criteria in immigration policy, it would be necessary to draw a line between national culture proper and the various private cultures that exist within the state. The example I have just given seems decisive because it is hard to envisage Protestantism featuring explicitly in the public culture of a society whose members belong to several different religious denominations. In contrast, the idea of a national language coexisting with one or more minority languages is easier to accept, and it does not seem that an admissions policy weighted towards speakers of the national language, such as that practised by the provincial government in Quebec, would necessarily be felt as unfair by minority language speakers. Such cases aside, our understanding of national cultures in recent years has primarily involved subscription to a set of political principles, together perhaps with some familiarity with the history and customs of the country in question. So understood, national culture cannot provide a strong rationale for discrimination at the point of entry, since it can be argued that immigrants will quickly adapt to the new political environment in which they find themselves, and can also be required to familiarize themselves with aspects of the local way of life as a condition for admission to citizenship.[37]

The upshot is that when would-be immigrants who are not in urgent need are refused entry to the state, they must be given fair grounds for the refusal. What counts as fair grounds will depend on the general policy goals of the state in question, and will therefore vary somewhat from society to society, as will the overall rate at which immigrants are admitted. Immigrants' cultural backgrounds will, however, only be relevant in special circumstances—when immigration is liable to have a significant impact, for better or worse, on the national identity of the receiving community. In reaching this conclusion, I have tried to hold a balance between the interests

[37] I shall not consider here the question of what the terms of admission to citizenship should be, though I have done so elsewhere: see 'Immigrants, Nations and Citizenship', *Journal of Political Philosophy* (forthcoming). I assume that all long-term immigrants should be admitted to full citizenship by the receiving state, and be encouraged to acquire the linguistic and other skills they require to function as active citizens. See also Walzer, *Spheres of Justice*, 52–61 and W. Kymlicka, *Politics in the Vernacular: Nationalism, Multiculturalism and Citizenship* (Oxford: Oxford University Press, 2001).

that immigrants have in entering the country that they want to live in and the interests that national communities have in maintaining control over their own composition and character. There is not, I have argued, a general right to migration. Nevertheless, those who benefit from living in rich territorial states have responsibilities to the world's poor, and discharging these responsibilities may sometimes involve taking needy migrants in, alongside other practical measures to be considered in Chapter 9.

CHAPTER 9

———

Responsibilities to the World's Poor

I

In this chapter, I want to turn directly to the questions 'what responsibilities do we have towards the global poor? What must we do for them as a matter of justice?'. I have already made and defended a number of claims that can help us to tackle them, by eliminating possible alternative answers. I have argued, for example, against the cosmopolitan view that our responsibilities to the world's poor are in principle exactly the same as our responsibilities to our fellow-citizens. We do not, then, owe them everything that we owe our compatriots as a matter of social justice. In particular, whatever global justice means, it does not mean global equality—of resources, opportunity, welfare, etc.—so we are not required to change the global order in such a way that inequalities between societies are levelled completely. On the other hand, I have defended the idea of a global minimum that is due to every human being as a matter of justice, a minimum best understood as a set of basic human rights. Since many societies are presently unable to guarantee these rights to their own members, it appears that the responsibility to protect them may fall on outsiders. But what kind of responsibility is this? I have spent some time distinguishing between different conceptions of responsibility, especially between *outcome* responsibility—the responsibility we have for gains and losses resulting from our actions—and *remedial* responsibility—the responsibility we have to relieve harm and suffering when we are able to do so. In the case of global poverty, one large question that we have to address is how far remedial responsibilities to the world's poor should track outcome responsibility for their current plight. Finally, I have defended at some length the idea of collective national responsibility: the idea that, given appropriate circumstances, it is reasonable to hold members of a national community responsible for the gains and losses that they create, both for themselves and for others. And I have argued that national responsibilities can be inherited across the generations.

With these conceptual and normative tools in hand, we can begin our investigation of our responsibilities to the world's poor. The basic facts of global poverty are not in dispute. As I suggested in the Introduction, we confront them on a daily basis merely by switching on our television screens. More objective surveys such as the UN's *Human Development Reports* confirm the subjective impressions that most of us have: global poverty may not be getting worse, in relation to world population as a whole, but it is stubbornly failing to get much better. Significant improvements in some places, for instance East Asia, are offset by worsenings in others, especially sub-Saharan Africa. In the year 2000, more than 1,000 million people were below the $1 a day line for income poverty, itself often thought to be unrealistically low; comparable numbers were judged to be below minimum levels on measures such as adequate nourishment, and access to clean drinking water.

This is poverty in its most primordial form. Whereas we can reasonably argue about the significance of poverty as it is measured in most developed countries—as having an income lower than a certain fraction (60%, for example) of the median—no one can doubt that undernourishment, low life expectancy, lack of access to elementary education or health care, and the other components of extreme poverty add up to a life that is less than minimally decent. So our moral response to these facts should also be clear: it is morally intolerable that we live in a world where somewhere between 15 and 20 percent of people live in dire poverty as defined by these indicators.

There is, however, a large normative gap between identifying a state of affairs as intolerable and identifying agents, individual or collective, who have a responsibility to remedy it. Bridging that gap requires first of all a great deal of empirical investigation. We need to understand the causes of wealth and poverty—why some societies have been able to extricate themselves from widespread poverty over a generation or two, while others appear unable to progress at all, or even seem destined to sink deeper into the abyss. We also need to understand what rich countries can do for poor countries if they so decide—what are the likely effects of changes in the global investment and trade regimes, of the way development aid is provided, and so forth. This investigation is difficult, not least because economic historians and development economists continue to give sharply conflicting answers to the questions just posed. But even if we were able to resolve the empirical questions to our satisfaction, there would still remain an independent normative problem about how to assign responsibility for global poverty to particular agents. It is one thing to show that pulling this lever will avert a disaster: another to show that it is your job rather than somebody else's to pull the lever. So although in the course of this chapter I shall look briefly at the empirical debate about poverty and development, my main focus will be on the normative question. I want to begin by examining two influential, but contrasting, attempts to answer this question by showing that responsibility for global poverty falls straightforwardly on the citizens of rich, developed societies. The first of these comes from Peter Singer, and the second from Thomas Pogge. In both cases, my aim is to draw out the underlying theory of responsibility that is invoked in order to reach this conclusion and to show why it is unacceptable.

II

Singer's argument begins with an analogy. He asks us to consider someone walking past a shallow pond in which a child is drowning. He observes that the passer-by has a duty to rescue the child even at some cost to himself, for example getting his clothes wet, and extracts from this the general principle that 'if it is in our power to prevent something bad from happening, without thereby sacrificing anything of comparable moral importance, we ought, morally, to do it'.[1] He then points out that this principle applies directly to the position of those in rich countries who could contribute money to save the lives of those in the developing world threatened by starvation or disease, and concludes that we have a moral obligation

---

[1] P. Singer, 'Famine, Affluence, and Morality', *Philosophy and Public Affairs*, 1 (1972), 231.

to give, up to the point at which further giving would take us or our dependents below the welfare level of the world's poor.

Let us accept Singer's assumption that the passer-by has a remedial responsibility to rescue the drowning child—this seems relatively uncontroversial.[2] I want to focus instead on why it provides a very bad analogy for thinking about responsibility for global poverty.[3] I think it leads us astray in three ways at least:

First, in the drowning child example, there is just one child struggling in the pond, and just one passer-by who is able to pull the child out. So there is absolutely no question about what ought to be done in that situation and about who ought to do it. But suppose we were to complicate the example a bit, by having several children in the pond, some easier to rescue than others, some apparently more likely than others to make it to the edge by themselves. And suppose we introduce not just one passer-by but several people, some physically stronger than others, some wearing smart suits and others wearing old jeans, and so forth, then a number of questions not relevant to the original example make their appearance. Which child should be rescued first? Should we try to grab as many children as we can, or should we concentrate on those who seem most in danger of imminent death? And whose responsibility is it to carry out the rescues? How are the obligations to be assigned?[4] Now it is precisely questions like these that we need to ask if the pond case is

---

[2] What may be more controversial is whether the passer-by is obliged to rescue the child *as a matter of justice*. This would be denied by libertarians for whom justice imposes only negative obligations not to violate the rights of others by one's own actions. Even libertarians, however, are likely to accept that the passer-by has a humanitarian responsibility to go to the aid of the child. I shall return to the question of when responsibilities give rise to claims of justice later in this chapter.

[3] For somewhat similar doubts about the relevance of Singer's example to discussions of global poverty, see K. A. Appiah, *Cosmopolitanism: Ethics in a World of Strangers* (London: Allen Lane, 2006), ch. 10.

[4] I do not mean that questions such as these are unanswerable, but the answers we give will depend on moral principles that go well beyond what is necessary to support our intuitions about the simple case. Some will answer them in a way that closely aligns global poverty with the predicament of the child in the pond—see, for example, P. Unger, *Living High and Letting Die: Our Illusion of Innocence* (New York: Oxford University Press, 1996), ch. 2. Others will answer them differently. So there can be convergence, from different starting points, on the view that we are morally obliged to rescue the drowning child in the simple case, but considerable divergence about what obligations, if any, we have in the more complex case of the global poor.

to be of any help in thinking about global poverty, because even if we believe that solving global poverty is a matter of redistribution between the world's rich and the world's poor—I will return to this question later—it is obviously a matter of *collective* not individual redistribution; there are millions of people who might be expected to be net contributors, either through their governments or through charitable agencies such as Oxfam; and there are still more millions of people, in varying circumstances, who might expect to be recipients. So questions about priorities, and about the assignment of responsibility, both absent from Singer's original example, always loom large.

Second, although these are not made explicit by Singer, there are some background assumptions we would naturally make when thinking about the child in the pond. First, it is a rare, one-off event. How many of us have actually ever had to rescue a strange child from drowning? Perhaps, then, our moral response to the child's predicament depends on this fact, especially the implication that acknowledging an obligation to act in such cases will not severely impede our normal life plans.[5] Second, once the child is pulled out of the water, she will be returned to her parents and, let us suppose, live happily ever after. For the price of cleaning or drying my clothes, I win a whole human life. But poverty in the developing world is not at all like that. It is chronic; it has long-term structural causes; a life saved today may be lost for a different reason next year. There is a real question what the effects of sending financial aid, say via Oxfam, really are—some aid may help its intended beneficiaries, other forms of aid may make things worse, but it is hard for people who are not experts in this area to know which forms of aid are worth supporting.[6] This may of course just serve as an excuse for doing nothing, but it does indicate a relevant difference between the person who saves a drowning child and the person who contributes financially to an anti-poverty

---

[5] I do not have the space to address this complex issue here. For a full discussion, see G. Cullity, *The Moral Demands of Affluence* (Oxford: Clarendon Press, 2004).

[6] There is an immense literature on this subject, pointing to wildly divergent conclusions. The issues are helpfully surveyed for the lay reader in Cullity, *The Moral Demands of Affluence*, ch. 3. For a recent overview by an insider, somewhat sceptical about the effects of most forms of aid, see W. Easterly, *The White Man's Burden: Why the West's Efforts to Aid the Rest Have Done So Much Ill and So Little Good* (Oxford: Oxford University Press, 2006).

charity: one can say with certainty what the consequences of their action will be, while the other cannot. The underlying point is that improving the lot of the world's poor is a macro-level problem; it involves changing the general conditions under which they live — their domestic economic and political regimes, for instance, as well as the international context within which those domestic institutions operate.

Finally, it is perhaps no accident that the person in Singer's pond is a child, an innocent victim who we may assume slipped into the water quite unaware of the danger she was running. And she cannot get out without help. She is the quintessential patient and in no real sense an agent. And this encourages us to think of people living in poor countries in quite the wrong way, simply as victims in need of our help. It might be said in reply here that since many of those most seriously affected by global poverty are children, Singer's perspective does indeed capture the moral reality correctly. But without in any way wishing to discount the moral significance of child poverty in developing countries, we cannot simply consider these children in isolation from the adults who are responsible for bringing them into existence and giving them primary care. Most of what we might do to improve their lot will affect the adults too: if we send aid that can be used to supply food, clean water, or resources for production, adults and children will benefit alike.[7] Put differently, most aid that aims to relieve poverty directly will be targeted at families, not at individual children, and its final distribution will depend on the decisions taken by adults with familial responsibilities. So questions about the causes of child poverty cannot be avoided here, in contrast to the simple child-in-the-pond example. Occasionally, of course, the adults too may find themselves in a helpless predicament: the 2004 tsunami was one occasion on which hundreds of thousands of people were placed more or less in the position of the child in the pond. But more often the (adult) global poor are also responsible agents capable of

---

[7] I accept that some forms of aid can be delivered exclusively to children — for example support for primary education, inoculation against childhood diseases, and so forth. My point is that if we are thinking about general solutions to global poverty — getting everybody above the thresholds of nutrition, etc., that constitute a minimally decent life — we cannot treat adults and children separately, barring radical (and presumably unacceptable) policies such as removing children from their parents and raising them in orphanages.

making choices for themselves—good choices from which they may benefit or bad choices from which they may lose. If they are starving because of crop failure, should they have planted different crops? If they are dying from AIDS, should they have changed their sexual behaviour? Raising these questions is not meant to settle the issue of remedial responsibility; it may be that in each case they have a right to help regardless of how their predicament came about. But it reminds us of the need always to respond to our fellow human beings from a dual perspective, as I suggested in the Introduction: *both* as agents capable of taking responsibility for the outcomes of their actions *and* as vulnerable and needy creatures who may not be able to lead decent lives without the help of others. Singer's child-in-the-pond analogy encourages us to take up the second perspective but to ignore the first.

I can summarize my concerns about Singer's argument by putting the distinction between outcome and remedial responsibility to work. First, Singer asks no questions about outcome responsibility for global poverty: he does not ask why so many are poor, whether responsibility lies with rich nations, with the governments of poor nations, etc.—he treats poverty as if it were a natural phenomenon like an earthquake.[8] Second, Singer has an implicit theory of remedial responsibility, namely that we are each remedially responsible for all the suffering we can prevent without sacrificing anything of comparable importance. The mere capacity to prevent suffering is by itself sufficient to assign responsibility. The presence of other people with a similar capacity matters to Singer only in so far as if it were to turn out that others had already done enough to eradicate poverty, then obviously my contribution would be unnecessary. For the reasons I have given, I think that on both counts Singer's view of responsibility for global poverty is implausible.[9] If we want

---

[8] I do not mean that Singer really believes this; I mean that the logic of the drowning child example involves seeing poverty as an accident akin to falling into the water. In his more recent book *One World: The Ethics of Globalization* (New Haven, CT: Yale University Press, 2002), he looks briefly at different explanations of world poverty without reaching any clear-cut conclusions. He evidently continues to think that the causes of poverty are irrelevant to our moral obligations to the world's poor.

[9] Notice that none of three challenges I have raised to Singer's argument involves the *distance* that separates the victim from the agent who is able to help her. It is sometimes argued that what distinguishes the child in the pond from the relief of

to solve global poverty, it is surely not only empirically but also morally relevant to ask how that poverty came about. There must be some presumption at least that where we can find agents who are outcome responsible for the poverty, they should also be held remedially responsible for tackling it.[10] And in cases where there are many agents all of whom are capable of remedying some harm, there must surely also be a presumption that remedial responsibility should be shared between them, pending further information about the particular capacities of each, and so forth. In the first instance at least, each agent has an obligation to discharge their share of the responsibility, not to take up the whole burden single-handed.

III

I turn now to Thomas Pogge's very different approach to global poverty. Pogge's argument *does* take outcome responsibility seriously; he argues in fact that citizens of rich states are remedially responsible for the plight of the world's poor because they are implicated in responsibility for creating that predicament. He remains officially neutral on the question whether there could be a positive duty to alleviate poverty regardless of how it arose, or in my terms whether there could be remedial responsibility in the absence of outcome responsibility. He thinks it sufficiently clear that poverty is the creation of a global system for which we in the developed world are collectively responsible. As he puts it:

. . . the underfulfillment of human rights in the developing countries is not a homegrown problem, but one we greatly contribute to through the policies we pursue and the international order we impose. We have then not merely a positive responsibility with regard to global poverty, like Rawls's 'duty

world poverty is the close physical proximity of the child to the passer-by. Whether distance by itself, once disentangled from all other factors, makes a difference to moral obligation is a moot point—see the exhaustive discussion in F. Kamm, 'Does Distance Matter Morally to the Duty to Rescue?', *Law and Philosophy*, 19 (2000), 655–81. But nothing I say here relies on the fact that the global poor stand at some distance from their potential rich benefactors.

[10] Though as I argued in Chapter 4, Section IV, this can be no more than a presumption: there are a number of potentially competing grounds on which remedial responsibilities can be assigned.

of assistance', but a negative responsibility to stop imposing the existing global order and to prevent and mitigate the harms it continually causes for the world's poorest populations.[11]

Pogge speaks here only of a negative responsibility, but I think it is more perspicuous to say that he also wants to attribute two forward-looking responsibilities to the citizens of rich states and their governments: the responsibility to redesign the international order so that it no longer has the harmful effects of the present one, and the responsibility to compensate the world's poor for the deprivation they have experienced up to now. These are positive responsibilities—they require citizens and states to take positive actions—but they stem from a previous failure to fulfil the negative responsibility not to impose an order that harms the world's poor.

Pogge does not deny that the proximate sources of global poverty are very often the domestic political and economic regimes under which the poor live. But he argues that these domestic sources of poverty are themselves to be explained primarily in terms of the international context in which poor societies are placed. As he puts it, 'it is quite possible that, within a different global order, national factors that tend to undermine the fulfilment of human rights would occur much less often, or not at all.'[12] The present order, he argues, encourages 'the emergence and endurance of brutal and corrupt elites' in developing societies. Moreover 'the primary responsibility for this institutional context, for the prevailing global order, lies with the governments and citizens of the wealthy countries because we maintain this order, with at least latent coercion, and because we, and only we, could relatively easily reform it....'.[13] Pogge's argument, in short, is that we, citizens of rich countries, bear primary outcome responsibility for global poverty, and since we have the means at our disposal to end it, we are remedially responsible too. It is a powerful argument, and many have found it persuasive, but it needs to be examined with some care.

[11] T. Pogge, 'Priorities of Global Justice', in T. Pogge (ed.), *Global Justice* (Oxford: Blackwell, 2001), 22.
[12] T. Pogge, 'Human Rights and Human Responsibilities', in A. Kuper (ed.), *Global Responsibilities* (New York and London: Routledge, 2005), 22.
[13] Pogge, 'Human Rights and Human Responsibilities', 23.

Pogge, as I have said, does not deny that the immediate cause of poverty in a particular society may be a defective set of economic and political institutions, or that the reason why some societies have institutions that are inimical to growth, while others have managed to develop institutions that allow them to escape from serious poverty over a generation or two, may lie deep in the history and culture of the societies in question. But he continues to attribute responsibility for poverty to rich societies by claiming, as already noted, that if the global environment were different, these national factors would produce different results. But how relevant is this observation when we are allocating outcome responsibility for global poverty? Consider the following analogy. Two cars collide on a roundabout, and we are able to identify one of them, the driver of car A, as outcome responsible for the resulting damage, by virtue of his reckless driving. Now it may well be true that if the roundabout had been replaced by traffic lights, this collision would not have occurred (driver A speeds at roundabouts but does not jump the lights); more generally it may be true that if traffic lights had been installed, fewer accidents, or perhaps no accidents at all, would have occurred at this intersection. Should we then conclude that responsibility for the accident rests not with driver A but with the road engineers who decided to install a roundabout there? This seems implausible: yet it also seems exactly analogous to Pogge's claim about the international order and the national factors associated with poverty.[14]

Why is it wrong to attribute outcome responsibility for the car crash to the road engineers? They have designed a roundabout, let us suppose, that drivers of normal competence, paying due care and attention, can navigate safely. They might have chosen traffic lights, and reduced the accident level still further, but this would have caused significantly more congestion and frustration among drivers. In the light of these facts, their decision was a reasonable

---

[14] To be clear, the analogy is not exact along every dimension. The road engineers, we may assume, have no personal interest in installing a roundabout rather than traffic lights, whereas it is often claimed, with some justification, that the current international order reflects the interest of rich and powerful countries. The purpose of the analogy is to expose the fallacy in moving from 1. 'Under different background conditions, A's behaviour would not have had the disastrous results that it did' to 2. 'Responsibility for the disaster therefore lies with the background conditions and not with A', which is indeed the precise form of Pogge's argument.

one. The careless driver of car A cannot shift responsibility off his shoulders by observing that in a different traffic environment the accident would not have occurred.

The question we should be asking about the global order, then, is whether it provides reasonable opportunities for societies to lift themselves out of poverty, or whether it places obstacles in their path that are quite difficult to overcome, requiring an extraordinary economic performance on the part of a developing society. Pogge does indeed notice that some historically poor societies have performed very well under the existing order, but he treats them as exceptional. Faced with examples, he compares them to 'Horatio Alger stories often appealed to in celebration of the unbridled American capitalism before the New Deal', where poor farm boys by dint of effort and enterprise become millionaires.[15] Now he is surely correct to say, as far as the farm boys are concerned, that the few can only rise at the expense of the majority staying close to where they started; simple logic tells us that not everyone can end up in the top echelon of the income distribution. But why does this logic apply to countries lifting their people above the global poverty threshold? Ghana and Malaysia were equally poor countries when they gained their independence from Britain in 1957: now average incomes in Malaysia, over $3,000 per head, are ten times greater than those in Ghana. Why should we think that the institutions and policies that explain Malaysia's success have at the same time contributed to keeping the Ghanaians poor? Why not think instead that if Ghana had followed Malaysia's example, or perhaps a somewhat different economic model appropriate to its circumstances (since there is no reason to think that there is just one blueprint for economic growth[16]), its people would now be comfortably above the poverty threshold, as Malaysia's are?[17]

[15] T. Pogge, 'Priorities of Global Justice', in T. Pogge (ed.), *Global Justice*, 17–18.

[16] For some remarks about the sheer diversity of economic regimes that have proved conducive to economic growth, see D. Rodrik, 'Rethinking Growth Strategies', in UNU-WIDER, *Wider Perspectives on Global Development* (Basingstoke, UK: Palgrave Macmillan, 2005).

[17] In making this illustrative comparison, I do not mean to imply that the external circumstances confronting Ghana and Malaysia were the same in all respects. However, in so far as there is a 'global order' in Pogge's sense, they were both subject to it. Alternatively, if it is argued that these circumstances were very different in the two cases, this puts in question the very idea of a single 'global order' that rich countries impose uniformly on the world's poor.

Pogge also errs by implying that the countries that have succeeded in raising most of their citizens above the poverty line via
economic growth *within* the existing international order are few and
far between. In fact, although very rapid growth of the kind seen
in South Korea and Taiwan, for example, is indeed exceptional, a
much larger group of countries, including most notably China and
India, have achieved, and continue to achieve, steady advances in
recent decades. The question we should be asking, therefore, is not
so much what explains the success of this second group as what
has held back the remaining group, primarily concentrated in sub-
Saharan Africa and Latin America, whose economies have largely
stagnated. Here we enter the debatable territory of explanations of
economic development. Without attempting to provide a resolution,
let me briefly sketch the current state of the debate. The possible
explanatory factors can roughly be divided into three groups: physical factors, such as the availability of resources like coal and oil, the
prevailing climate, and the society's geographical location (is it landlocked, for instance?); domestic factors, for instance the prevailing
religious or political culture, and the practices and institutions which
both reflect and shape it; and external factors, such as the pattern
of global trade and investment, the impact of foreign states through
colonialism or neocolonialism, etc.[18] A priori, it seems likely that
any adequate explanation of differential rates of economic development will invoke factors of all three kinds. Our interest here is in
the second group of factors: unless domestic factors can be shown
to play a significant role in explaining why some societies become
rich while others stagnate, then claims about national responsibility
for wealth and poverty immediately fall to the ground. The work
most frequently cited in support of the primacy of domestic factors
is David Landes' book *The Wealth and Poverty of Nations*, but Landes' wide-ranging and somewhat unanalytical historical study does
not suggest any mono-causal theory; indeed, this book starts with
a chapter about the importance of climate in explaining the relative
success of Europe vis-à-vis countries closer to the Equator. Landes

[18] This division follows the one suggested by Rodrik in D. Rodrik (ed.), *In
Search of Prosperity: Analytical Narratives of Economic Growth* (Princeton, NJ:
Princeton University Press, 2003), ch. 1, although I have used different labels. See
also M. Risse, 'What We Owe to the Global Poor', *Journal of Ethics*, 9 (2005),
81–117.

does clearly think that culture matters in explaining economic success, but supports this claim largely anecdotally.[19]

Other economic historians, however, have produced more solid evidence to support the significance of domestic factors in explaining differential rates of development. Geography matters to some extent—nearly all developed economies are to be found in temperate rather than tropical zones—but examples such as Singapore and Mauritius show that geographical disadvantage can be overcome by societies with the appropriate cultures and institutions. Natural resources can be either a blessing or a curse depending on the cultural and institutional context in which they are appropriated—coal was a major factor propelling the industrial revolution in Britain, whereas the discovery of oil in the Middle East is widely judged to have distorted economic development in those societies and propped up authoritarian regimes. Conversely, both culture and institutions can be shown to correlate significantly with economic success, the main problem being to disentangle their effects, since there is obviously strong interaction between them. The independent effect of culture can be seen most easily by studying the varying success rates of different ethnic groups in a single society—for instance by comparing the performance of Asian immigrants to the USA with that of blacks and Hispanics.[20] Institutional effects have been studied by looking at ex-colonial societies starting out with contrasting legal systems, sets of property rights, and so forth and comparing their economic performance over time.[21]

Plainly, we should expect debate to continue over the relative weight to be attributed to factors of the three kinds I have distinguished. But we have already discovered enough to cast doubt on

[19] D. Landes, *The Wealth and Poverty of Nations* (London: Little, Brown, 1998), esp. ch. 29.
[20] See the papers collected in L. E. Harrison and S. P. Huntington (eds), *Culture Matters* (New York: Basic Books, 2000).
[21] D. Acemoglu, S. Johnson, and J. Robinson, 'The Colonial Origins of Economic Development: An Empirical Investigation', *American Economic Review*, 91 (2001), 1369–401. See also D. Rodrik, A. Subramanian, and F. Trebbi, 'Institutions Rule: The Primacy of Institutions over Geography and Integration in Economic Development', *Journal of Economic Growth*, 9 (2004), 131–65. For a somewhat more sceptical appraisal, which focuses in particular on the instruments used to measure institutional quality in the two papers above, see E. C. Glaeser, R. La Porta, F. Lopez-de-Silanes, and A. Shleifer, 'Do Institutions Cause Growth?', *Journal of Economic Growth*, 9 (2004), 271–303.

Pogge's claim that the international order is responsible for violations of human rights in the form of severe poverty. That order is far from perfect, and indeed it is not difficult to identify reforms that would make it easier for societies starting from a position of economic disadvantage to improve their prospects through inward investment and trade. But even with the imperfect order that we have, many societies have already achieved significant advances, and that at the very least suggests that (outcome) responsibility for the condition of those that remain cannot simply be attributed to that order and the rich societies that uphold it. To revert to our analogy, the roundabout may be badly designed, but the fact that it can be navigated safely by careful drivers shows that some considerable share of responsibility for the accidents that do happen must rest on the shoulders of the drivers involved.

I shall return shortly to the question of what normative conclusions about the remedial responsibilities of rich countries we should draw from this. But before leaving Pogge, there is one further aspect of his theory of responsibility that is worth highlighting. He is very critical of what he calls 'explanatory nationalism', in the context of debates about global poverty. Explanatory nationalism is the view that the relative wealth and poverty of different societies can be fully explained by institutions and policies that are internal to each. As indicated earlier, Pogge believes that this overlooks the way in which the global order determines the effects of different national factors; had that order been different, institutions and policies that now lead to poverty might have had quite different results. He concludes, on that basis, that 'global factors are all-important for explaining present human misery'.[22] And a further implication is that people living in the societies in which poverty is endemic cannot be held collectively responsible for that misery. He nonetheless holds a quite strong doctrine of national responsibility when it comes to explaining why ordinary citizens in rich societies can properly be taxed to provide compensation to the world's poor whose rights have been infringed by the policies pursued by Western governments—according to Pogge you share in responsibility for the actions of any government you are 'involved in upholding' where this might

[22] T. Pogge, *World Poverty and Human Rights* (Cambridge: Polity Press, 2002), 144.

include just working in the economy and/or paying taxes.[23] That is, he does not allow people who are going about their daily business and are uninvolved in politics to distance themselves from the policies their governments may pursue; he assumes that everyone in these societies is included in national responsibility for the harm they have inflicted on poor people in other countries, and can therefore be required to contribute to transfers to compensate for that harm.[24] But why should the idea of collective responsibility apply in this case but not to people living in poor countries for the harms caused by their own institutions and practices?

To defend a view like Pogge's, it would be necessary to point to some relevant differences between their position and ours which explain why we can be held collectively responsible but they cannot. Could this be done? In Chapter 5, I argued that assignments of national responsibility could most easily be made in the case of societies that were democratically governed and whose members could form their beliefs and values in conditions of freedom. Now broadly speaking rich countries are democratic while poor ones are not. So might this be sufficient reason to absolve those living in poor countries from responsibility for their plight while continuing to attribute collective remedial responsibility to the citizens of rich countries? In the case of dictatorial regimes that operate primarily through fear and repression—North Korea, Burma, or Saddam's Iraq, for example—that conclusion seems correct; it would be absurd to include ordinary subjects in collective responsibility for the regime and its consequences—they are victims, not perpetrators. But between genuine democracies and dictatorships, there are regimes where our judgments must be more nuanced. There are, for example, societies that come close to John Rawls's concept of a 'decent hierarchical society'—a society that is neither liberal nor fully democratic, but in which there exists what he calls 'a decent consultation hierarchy' that connects the government to various corporate groups within the society, and that allows for dissent from

---

[23] Pogge, *World Poverty and Human Rights*, esp. 66–7, 139–45.

[24] For a fuller critique of Pogge's claim about the responsibility of citizens in affluent countries for harm inflicted on the global poor, see S. M. Shei, 'World Poverty and Moral Responsibility', in A. Follesdal and T. Pogge (eds), *Real World Justice* (Dordrecht: Springer, 2005).

existing government policy.[25] Under these circumstances we can say that what government does broadly reflects the beliefs and the cultural values of the people as a whole, and in this respect the position as far as collective responsibility is concerned is not so different from that of liberal democracies. (One of my earlier examples, Malaysia, seems to fit this model.) Then there are regimes in which elites rule with popular acquiescence but without effective popular control. I have in mind here what are sometimes called 'neo-patrimonial' regimes of the kind found in many African countries, where political authority rests on patron–client relations between politicians and their supporting groups.[26] Here representation takes a different form: political leaders are representative in so far as they meet their obligations to their clients, as understood within the culture of the country in question. In receiving the benefits—jobs, money, public works, etc.—client groups give their tacit consent to the regime.[27] Such regimes generally do a poor job as far as economic development and lifting ordinary people out of poverty are concerned. Yet if we are allocating responsibility for that failure, a good part must rest with the general population whose inherited cultural values lead them to acquiesce in these damaging practices and institutions.

Another reason that might be given for denying that ideas of national responsibility apply to people in poor countries is that they have no options to choose between: they cannot choose their institutions or the policies that their governments will follow. It is true that the range of possibilities that people in countries like Bolivia or Tanzania face is very different from those faced by the citizens of Denmark or Italy. But it is wrong to say that the former have no chance to exercise collective responsibility. If we look at the societies that have developed successfully over the last several decades, then

[25] J. Rawls, *The Law of Peoples* (Cambridge, MA: Harvard University Press, 1999), esp. sections 8–9.

[26] See, for example, the analysis in P. Chabal, 'The Quest for Good Governance and Development in Africa: Is NEPAD the Answer?', *International Affairs*, 78 (2002), 447–62.

[27] Admittedly, this argument is unlikely to apply to the people living at the bottom of the societies in question, who are not involved in the patron–client networks. These people may also have little or no ability to change the regime, even if they should want to. Thus they should not be included in collective responsibility for their own poverty, which nevertheless may continue to rest primarily with political leaders and their client groups inside the society.

although there are some basic features that they have in common—no breakdown of social order, a reasonably effective legal system, and so forth—what is more remarkable is the different routes that they have followed.[28] It is also true that on occasion international institutions such as the IMF have attempted to impose economic constraints on societies that leave very little room for manoeuvre—but these misguided attempts do not add up to a general absence of political choice. So although attributions of national responsibility need to be made cautiously and with full reference to the circumstances of each society, there is no reason to exclude people living in poor societies from collective responsibility in an across-the-board way.

IV

So where does this leave us on the general question of responsibility for global poverty? Against Peter Singer, I have argued that it makes no sense to assign remedial responsibility for poverty to citizens of rich states without first considering the question of outcome responsibility—how and why poverty has arisen. Against Thomas Pogge, I have argued that his attempt to assign outcome responsibility for poverty to the international order, and through that to citizens of rich states and their governments, is implausible. At the very least the responsibility should be shared between the road engineers and the careless drivers, so to speak—between governments and international organizations who set the rules governing trade, investment flows, resource rights and other features of the global economy, and people in poor countries who support or acquiesce in regimes that reproduce poverty by siphoning off a large portion of GDP into military expenditure, presidential palaces, and Swiss bank accounts. But if this is the right story to tell about outcome responsibility, how do things stand when we turn to consider remedial responsibility? After all ordinary people in poor countries cannot be held remedially responsible for abolishing their own poverty—that would be absurd. So doesn't responsibility in the remedial sense inevitably fall on the shoulders of those who have the resources and the capacity to do something about world hunger and other forms of deprivation?

[28] See Rodrik, 'Rethinking Growth Strategies'.

The broad answer to this question is 'Yes', but to give a more precise one, we need to distinguish between different grounds on which remedial responsibilities may arise at global level. This will turn out to matter when we ask the further question 'what are the world's poor owed as a matter of *justice?*'—the thought here being that some responsibilities may give rise to duties that are not duties of justice. These other duties we might describe as humanitarian; they are duties that we have good reason to perform, without being *required* to perform them as we are required to perform duties of justice. Why does this distinction matter? Humanitarian duties are in general less weighty than duties of justice. This is important when we have to consider what costs it is reasonable to expect an agent to bear to perform duties of either kind—in the present context, how far citizens of rich states can be expected to sacrifice various domestic projects in order to discharge remedial responsibilities to foreigners. The distinction is also important when we consider the position of third parties. Duties of justice are enforceable, in the sense that third parties may be justified in applying sanctions to those who default on them; not so with humanitarian duties. So we need to decide when remedial responsibilities give rise to duties of justice and when they do not in order to understand the practical implications of allocating them.

It might seem that we have already answered this question by treating poverty as a violation of human rights. If people have a right to the items and conditions that they need to lead decent lives, then if they are denied those items and conditions, how can it not be a matter of justice to provide them? However, as we saw in Chapter 7, Section V, we cannot always move directly from human rights to justice—under conditions of scarcity, for example, where we cannot supply the resources that would fully satisfy everyone's human rights, there cannot be a duty of justice to fulfil any one person's rights in particular. The problem we are now addressing is different: whether justice always requires us to fulfil human rights regardless of prior assignments of responsibility. Consider a very simple case. B lacks some vital resource and A is uniquely in a position to supply it. Prima facie, then, A has a responsibility to supply the resource, and given that B's need is a basic one, a duty of justice to do so. But suppose now that B, having been given the resource that he needs, chooses to destroy it or sell it to someone else.[29] B is now responsible for not having the resource. Does A still have a duty to give B what he needs? Perhaps so, but is it clear that this is a duty of justice? Why is A required, *as a matter of justice*, to provide B with the necessary resource a second time? If he does not have access to the resource, B's human rights are being infringed. Yet he himself is responsible for the infringement, by virtue of the choice he made. In these circumstances, it seems that although we may continue to hold A remedially responsible for B's plight, we cannot justifiably place him under a duty of justice to help B. If he has a duty at all, it must be a duty of lesser weight—a humanitarian duty, that is to say.

Whether this argument might apply to some cases of global poverty remains to be seen. But it underlines the importance of investigating how remedial responsibilities may arise, and of distinguishing different cases. So let me now proceed to this task. I shall distinguish three circumstances in which citizens of rich countries might have such responsibilities towards the world's poor. First, they might arise as a result of past injustice that has left its victims in continuing poverty. Second, they might arise through a failure to implement fair terms of international cooperation. Third, they might arise from the bare fact of poverty itself, independently of any prior interaction between rich and poor countries. I suggest that the implications for global justice will be somewhat different in each case.

First, then, there might be backward-looking responsibilities to remedy the effects of past injustice. I have argued, at some length, in Chapter 6 that there can be inherited national responsibilities of this kind. I also there drew a distinction between obligations to redress past injustice, and remedial responsibilities that arise simply from the fact of past interaction. That is, (rich) society A might have responsibilities towards (poor) society P *either* because the past actions and policies of A have contributed to the present deprivation of P, and A therefore owes P material redress for the effects of those actions and policies, *or* merely because A is connected to P by virtue of their history of causal interactions, thereby giving A a special reason to respond to P's present plight. Responsibilities of the

[29] Assume here that B does not sell the resource in order to purchase something else that is even more necessary to him, or destroy the resource because of some (understandable) mistake about the nature of what he has been given.

first kind are not remedial in origin, so to speak—they would arise even if society P were not poverty-stricken. Nevertheless, they can serve as the basis for policies whose effects are remedial—they would improve the material position of society P—and their practical force will be stronger in cases where society P is also impoverished. These responsibilities clearly give rise to obligations of justice on the part of society A. If redress is owed for historic injustice, it is owed *as a matter of justice.* The collective responsibility of the people of P matters here only when it comes to determining the amount of redress that is owed. That is, in determining which effects of historically unjust acts and policies demand redress and which do not, we should consider how the members of P have responded to those acts and policies. Redress is not owed for effects that the Ps could reasonably have taken steps to avoid. Thus if I drive my truck through the wall of your house, I owe you compensation for putting right the damage I have caused, but you can reasonably be expected to call in builders quickly to shore up the roof. If you do nothing and as a result of this inaction the rest of the house collapses, I do not owe you redress in the form of a completely new house. So where the past impact of society A on society P has been unfair, A owes duties of justice to P regardless of what members of P may do, but the extent of the redress that is owed is determined by what it is reasonable to expect the Ps to have done, rather than what they actually did historically.

Where the past interactions between A and P have not been unjust, however, it is an open question whether the remedial responsibilities that A may owe to P by virtue of P's present poverty constitute obligations of justice. For here A is not outcome responsible for P's poverty, and the question arises whether the members of P are themselves responsible for their position. I shall return to this question shortly. For now, the important point is to distinguish between two ways in which historical relationships may generate responsibilities to people in poor countries, of which only the first unequivocally makes the relief of poverty a matter of justice.

Can this backward-looking approach to responsibilities for world poverty be made to work in practice? It is often confidently asserted that it can. Pogge, for example, writes:

...there are at least three morally significant connections between us and the global poor. First, their social starting positions and ours have emerged from a single historical process that was pervaded by massive grievous wrongs. The same historical injustices, including genocide, colonialism, and slavery, play a role in explaining both their poverty and our affluence.[30]

However, although it is undoubtedly true that historically the relationship between societies that are now affluent and societies that are now poor has been darkened by the moral evils that Pogge describes, it is far less clear that these evils *explain* present-day affluence and poverty. Genocide and slavery are moral tragedies, but their effects are felt by the people who are their victims, and by their descendants, and I can see no reason to assume that their longer-term results include impoverishment of the societies in which they occurred. If redress for American slavery is owed, for example, it is owed to African Americans, who are not among the global poor even if they are relatively poor by US standards; it is not owed to the societies from which the slaves were taken unless it can be shown that those societies continue to experience deprivation that can be traced back to the taking. As for colonialism, one would need to show not just that it wronged the people who were colonized in various ways, but that its overall impact on the development of the societies in which it occurred was negative.[31] Given that many previously colonized societies are among the economic success stories—think of the Malaysia/Ghana contrast referred earlier—this would be a hard task to accomplish. It seems that linking historical injustice to present-day poverty would require taking specific cases and showing the causal mechanisms at work, rather than relying on broad brush assertions such as Pogge's cited above.

I turn therefore to a second responsibility owed to poor societies in the present. This is the responsibility to offer these societies fair terms of cooperation. Given that, through economic globalization

---

[30] Pogge, 'Priorities of Global Justice', 14. I should make it clear that Pogge lays less emphasis on this assertion as a basis for our responsibilities to the global poor than he does on the claim about the present global order that I discussed in Section III. Nevertheless, he clearly believes it, as do many others.

[31] For a fuller discussion of this point, critical of Pogge, see M. Risse, 'Do We Owe the Global Poor Assistance or Rectification?', *Ethics and International Affairs*, 19 (2005), 9–18.

and in other ways, societies unavoidably have significant impacts on each others' prospects, the rules governing these interactions must be fair to both sides.[32] This is demonstrably not the case at present. Many societies are vulnerable to exploitation and other forms of injustice by powerful states, corporations, and other agencies. Consider, for example, a small economically undeveloped society that is heavily dependent on external actors for its trade and investment relationships. If most of society A's exports are bought by society B, and society B is suddenly plunged into economic crisis, or for political reasons decides to sever its relations with A, then this is likely to have disastrous consequences for A's economy.[33] Or society C might rely almost entirely for its export earnings on one or two commodities, in which case sharp price fluctuations or changes in the import tariffs imposed by other countries may prove severely disruptive to C. It might be said that in such cases people in those societies are themselves responsible for placing themselves in such vulnerable positions. In the very long term this might be true, but in the short-to-medium term the implicit expectation is unrealistic. It may take considerable time to develop new export markets,

[32] How could we decide whether the terms of international interaction are fair? Ideally we would appeal to a principle, or set of principles, of fairness that would settle the question. But such principles are hard to come by. For example, we might propose that an exchange between two parties — say a trade in commodities — is fair when both parties benefit from the exchange to the same extent. But how should this principle be applied? We need first of all to establish an appropriate baseline — how each party would be positioned in the absence of the exchange. Then we need to find a neutral way of measuring benefit: what 'currency' should we use? Should benefit be measured in absolute terms, or in proportion to existing resource holdings (in trade negotiations, should the benefit to a particular country of some decision be recorded as a percentage of existing GDP, for example)? These problems and others suggest that there can be reasonable disagreement about the fairness of any particular rule or practice; nevertheless we can say that some interactions, such as those described in the text, are so one-sided in their impact as to be unfair by any reasonable standard. For discussion of this question, see C. Albin, *Justice and Fairness in International Negotiation* (Cambridge: Cambridge University Press, 2001), esp. chs. 2 and 4; J. Stiglitz and A. Charlton, *Fair Trade for All* (Oxford: Oxford University Press, 2005), esp. ch. 5.

[33] Consider, for example, the impact on Cuba's economy of the US trade embargo, given that before Castro's revolution more than two-thirds of Cuba's foreign trade was with that country, followed after 1989 by the withdrawal of very substantial trade subsidies from the Soviet Union. These external events undoubtedly contributed significantly to poverty in Cuba in the years after 1990. For discussion, see S. E. Eckstein, *Back to the Future: Cuba under Castro* (Princeton, NJ: Princeton University Press, 1994).

and if your economy is largely geared to the production of one commodity—bananas, say—then it is simply not feasible to switch overnight into growing mangoes in response to a fall in the world price of bananas, or a change in the EU's banana import regime. Rich societies are not typically exposed to such risks: because they are industrialized, their economies are far more diversified, and their networks of trade and investment much wider.

What poor countries can legitimately demand, therefore, is an international order in which they are sufficiently protected from such vulnerabilities. This does not mean being isolated from global trade and investment. On the contrary, all the evidence suggests that integration into the global economy is one important precondition for economic growth.[34] It does, however, mean regulating the order so that it is fair to poor countries, in the sense of giving them reasonable opportunities to develop, and allowing them to choose between different policies for achieving this. That means, first of all, not allowing outside agencies such as the IMF to impose rigid economic guidelines on particular countries as a condition of their receiving development loans. It means preventing the governments of rich countries from erecting tariff barriers as a way of protecting their own industries against competition from developing countries, while at the same allowing poor countries, if they choose, to shelter their own new industries for a period. It means taking steps to stabilize the prices of commodities that are the staple exports of particular societies. In other words, a fair international order cannot simply mean a free market in which nations and corporations pursue their interests without regard to the consequences for vulnerable poor people. The responsibility of citizens of rich countries is to ensure fairness in this sense—an international order whose rules allow poor societies adequate opportunities to develop.

One might hope that if the first two responsibilities were discharged—the responsibility to remedy the effects of past injustice, and the responsibility to offer poor societies fair terms of cooperation—there would be no further remedial responsibilities to

---

[34] See, for instance, the evidence presented in M. Wolf, *Why Globalization Works* (New Haven, CT and London: Yale University Press, 2004), ch. 9. For the argument that integration through trade is beneficial only when an appropriate regulatory framework is in place, see Stiglitz and Charlton, *Fair Trade for All*, esp. ch. 2.

the world's poor, since each society would shortly be in a position to tackle poverty within its own borders (there might be transitional problems requiring resource transfers to poor societies, but nothing beyond this). But given the evidence surveyed above about the crucial role of domestic culture and institutions in lifting societies out of poverty through economic growth, and given the continued existence of cultures and/or institutions that cannot perform such a role, this hope seems a forlorn one. There would remain some instances of global poverty for which rich societies could not be held outcome responsible, for either of the reasons just canvassed. Would remedial responsibilities still exist in such cases, and if so how should they be characterized? Here we need to investigate the extent of responsibility carried by people inside the society for their own continuing deprivation. There are three broad possibilities: none are responsible, some are responsible, and all are responsible. I shall consider these in turn.

The first possibility occurs when a society is impacted by outside events for which nobody bears (outcome) responsibility. The most obvious example would be a natural disaster such as a severe drought or a volcanic eruption that devastates local agricultural production. However we should also include under this heading economic shocks caused by rapid changes in consumers' tastes or technological advances—think for example of a society such as Zambia whose economy became heavily reliant on the export of an expensive mineral (copper in Zambia's case) whose world price collapsed suddenly as cheaper alternatives (such as optical fibre) became available. It might be said that there is always responsibility in such cases—the responsibility to protect yourself from becoming vulnerable to such unanticipated events. But, as I suggested above, it is often unreasonable to extend the notion of responsibility so far. People can be held responsible for outcomes that they should have anticipated, given existing evidence, but not for every outcome that might conceivably occur unless one insures against it.

In these circumstances, remedial responsibilities cut in, and they give rise to duties of justice. That is, if people are unable to lead decent lives as a result of events outside of their society for which they cannot be held responsible, this imposes a general responsibility to assist which is distributed to particular agents—states, voluntary organizations, etc.—according to the criteria identified in

Chapter 4, Section IV. We find the capable agent or agents most strongly connected to the people whose human rights are being infringed, and hold them responsible for bringing relief. Of course, it might be possible to formalize this relationship by, for example, creating an international fund for disaster relief that could be drawn upon in emergencies of this kind, and this would clearly be desirable, given that it is often difficult to determine which agents in particular bear the primary remedial responsibility. But in the absence of such a scheme, there is no alternative but to rely on judgements of the kind discussed in that chapter.

Once remedial responsibilities are identified, they must be discharged as a matter of justice, assuming that the relevant agent or agents are able to do so without infringing other, weightier, duties of justice. Why is this so? On the one side we have people whose lives fall below some absolute standard of decency, who are not responsible for being in that condition, and who cannot now pull themselves out if it unaided. On the other side we have, let us say, the citizens of a rich nation who are able to provide the necessary relief, and who have been singled out as having the responsibility to do so. They have not, by hypothesis, actively violated the rights of the people now in need; yet if they fail to act now, I suggest, they will infringe those rights. So discharging the remedial responsibility is a requirement of justice.

Not everyone will agree with this conclusion. Others have argued that the duty in such cases must be described differently, for example as a duty of humanity or a 'duty of assistance'.[35] Such descriptions may be appropriate, I suggest, in the cases I shall discuss below, but not in the one we are presently considering. It is perhaps hard to demonstrate to someone who does not share this moral intuition that infringing human rights by failing to fulfil them is unjust, but let me briefly consider two reasons that might be given for resisting this claim.

The first is that justice only comes into the picture when an agent takes some positive action that affects a second party. Mere inaction, standing by and doing nothing, may be reprehensible, but does not constitute injustice. So violating human rights by some

---

[35] This is Rawls's phrase to describe the more general duty that people in developed societies owe to those living in what he calls 'burdened societies'. See Rawls, *The Law of Peoples*, section 15.

positive action would be unjust, but failing to protect them—say by not delivering food one might have delivered in a famine situation—would not be. But notice that this is not how we think about *social* justice. Social justice does require that the state should make various forms of positive provision for its citizens; it is an injustice if citizens are left without adequate health care, or housing, or support in old age, by virtue of state inaction. So it cannot be a conceptual truth about justice that it comes into play only in cases where an agent has *acted* in a way that impacts on another.

A second reason has been suggested by Thomas Nagel.[36] Nagel asserts that we have a strong moral obligation to provide material aid to those who fall below a minimal poverty line, but he characterizes this as a duty of humanity rather than justice. To support this he argues that 'humanitarian duties hold in virtue of the absolute rather than the relative level of need of the people we are in a position to help. Justice, by contrast, is concerned with the relations between the conditions of different classes of people, and the causes of inequality between them.'[37] In other words, justice is by definition a comparative notion: it is about how different groups of people fare relative to one another. But this seems merely stipulative; it dismisses out of hand the idea that principles of *sufficiency*, for example, might qualify as principles of justice.[38] It seems better to say that justice can take both comparative and non-comparative forms: sometimes it concerns how people are treated relative to one another, sometimes about how they are treated in absolute terms.[39] Indeed, Nagel is willing to concede that breaches of human rights may in certain instances count as acts of injustice—he refers to war crimes and crimes against humanity—but these are surely absolute rather than relative wrongs. So why suppose that a failure to supply human beings with the

---

[36] T. Nagel, 'The Problem of Global Justice', *Philosophy and Public Affairs*, 33 (2005), 113–47.

[37] Nagel, 'Problem of Global Justice', 119.

[38] These are principles that set a certain threshold level—of resources, say, or welfare—that everyone must reach as a matter of justice, while remaining silent about how people fare, relatively or absolutely, above the threshold. For a critical exploration of such principles, see P. Casal, 'Why Sufficiency Is Not Enough', *Ethics*, 117 (2006–7), 296–326.

[39] On this see J. Feinberg, 'Noncomparative Justice', *Philosophical Review*, 83 (1974), 297–338.

means to meet their essential needs when it is possible to do so does not also count as injustice?

All of this, however, applies in the first instance only to deprivation that arises in such a way that nobody can be held outcome responsible. There are two other possibilities to consider. The next occurs when responsibility lies with a subgroup within the society in question (together perhaps with foreign companies or governments who support them) rather than with the people as a whole. This subgroup, which might, for example, consist of a dictator and his henchmen, or an ethnic minority who monopolize the means of coercion, may pursue disastrous policies that cripple the society's economy, or may simply divert a large share of GDP into their own hands, leaving most of their fellow-countrymen below the poverty threshold. This can happen even in the case of societies like Zimbabwe that start from a relatively high level of economic development. In such cases, do people in rich societies have remedial responsibilities towards the exploited majority?

It should be clear that remedial responsibility falls in the first place on the subgroup within the society that is outcome responsible for the deprivation. But it may equally be clear that there is no prospect of this group discharging its responsibility. Given that those who are suffering the effects of the regime are not themselves responsible for its existence, it seems that outsiders do have responsibilities towards them. How to discharge these responsibilities in practice presents intractable problems. Applying economic sanctions to the regime in an attempt to change its policies may just worsen the position of the exploited group still further, as essential imports are blocked. Poverty relief efforts in the form of conventional aid may have the perverse effect of strengthening the regime, whose members can bolster their power by supervising the distribution of aid, meanwhile siphoning off some proportion of it into their own pockets. Military intervention to replace the regime is not only likely to be very costly but may have untoward side effects. But in principle, where agent A who is primarily responsible fails to relieve patient P, responsibility passes to B who is next in line.

Does B have a duty of justice to relieve P in these circumstances? It is evident that B has a strong *reason* to act, where P's deprivation is severe, and B has some feasible way of relieving it. But it may be better to say that the duty here is a humanitarian duty rather than a duty of justice. One reason for saying that is that we may think that B cannot be *required* to act, given that the primary responsibility rests with A. That is, we ought not to apply sanctions to B of the kind that we would be justified in applying if he were primarily responsible for relieving P but were refusing to do so. I suggested earlier that one mark of a duty of justice is that it is always potentially enforceable in this sense.

If this is the correct way to understand responsibilities in the second scenario, a fortiori it must also be in the third—collective responsibility for poverty rests with all, or nearly all, of the adult members of the society in question. It might seem that this is an empty box: why would a nation make political choices or follow practices that resulted in its members' own impoverishment? Undoubtedly some examples that appear to belong here would on closer inspection turn out not to, because the conditions for collective responsibility were not met. Thus if we take a case like North Korea, at first glance there has been virtually unanimous support for a regime whose economic policies have resulted in famine conditions (causing an estimated two million deaths in the 1990s). But since the regime allows no freedom of thought or expression—the media are all state-controlled and merely churn out a daily diet of official propaganda, and harsh penalties are applied to anyone found tuning in to foreign media—this support is almost entirely manipulated support, and, as I argued in Chapter 5, the idea of national responsibility does not apply under these circumstances. Nonetheless, even if cases of collective responsibility for poverty are likely to be few and far between, they are not impossible and it is worth considering briefly what remedial responsibilities fall on outsiders if they occur.

Suppose, then, we encounter a society most of whose members are chronically malnourished, and the reason for this is that they insist, for religious or other cultural reasons, on adhering to traditional forms of agriculture that cannot produce an adequate supply of food. Should we leave them as they are, out of respect for their culture and the practices that express it, or should we intervene on the grounds that all human beings have basic rights that must be fulfilled as conditions of a decent life? This is an acute dilemma, but my own intuition is that the second reason is the more compelling, and that we have a responsibility to intervene—to send in aid, but also to engage in a process of persuasion, whose outcome, in the best case, would be a cultural shift that allows people in the society to adopt new methods of production without completely abandoning their previous collective identity.[40] It would also be reasonable to impose a cut-off point beyond which further aid would not be supplied unless changes of this kind took place. This reflects the fact that remedial responsibility in such cases does not amount to a duty of justice, but is instead humanitarian in nature.

V

I have argued that remedial responsibilities to the world's poor are not straightforward, but must take into account a variety of factors, primarily having to do with attributions of *outcome* responsibility for the poverty we witness. Some readers might be impatient of the distinctions I have drawn. Here we stand, citizens of affluent societies, with resources at our disposal far in excess of anything that we need, even where 'need' is understood as societal need, need relative to standards of decency in particular rich societies. There, facing us, are desperate people, millions living on less than a dollar a day, with life expectancies of 40 years or less. It would cost us little to relieve their far more urgent needs. So why raise so many contestable questions, about the historical sources of poverty, about fairness in international trade, and so forth, in order to make discriminating judgements about who is owed relief as a matter of justice and who is not, and so forth, when the moral imperative to send aid is so pressing? Why should we adopt the more complex approach to global poverty advocated here in preference to the simpler approaches favoured by Singer and Pogge?

There are two main reasons. First, I believe that these approaches, and especially Singer's, would lead us to take bad policy decisions.

---

[40] It is also relevant here that the society will include children who must be exempted from responsibility for the practices that lead to poverty. It is sometimes argued that, because children are always among those who suffer most when societies are poor, relieving poverty must be seen as a duty of justice regardless of how it is caused. I suggested earlier, however, that because adults bear the primary responsibility for the welfare of their children, and because poverty relief, when successful, benefits adults and children alike, this argument cannot be accepted. Our remedial responsibility to children suffering from poverty is better understood as humanitarian where outcome responsibility for the poverty rests with adult members of their own society.

If we think about poverty only in terms of the needs of those who suffer from it on one side, and the capacity of those on the other side to make resource transfers to the poor, this focuses our attention away from the institutional changes that might eventually serve to end or at least radically diminish world poverty. The economics of aid is a complex subject, but one message clearly conveyed by even a cursory reading of the literature is that the positive or negative effect of aid in relieving poverty is heavily dependent on local institutions in the place where the aid is being sent.[41] Sending in aid can not only seriously disrupt local economies, but in the worst cases can have the effect of propping up local despots and warlords, who are able to control the flow of aid from the agencies to people on the ground, while diverting some of it for their own private enrichment. Pogge, of course, does direct our attention to institutions rather than to resource transfers between individuals. But the approach that he takes encourages us to think that if we were able to mend the defects in the current international order—for example, get rid of the international resource and borrowing privileges that he argues help to sustain corrupt and exploitative regimes in power[42]—then the local sources of poverty would disappear. I believe that we will make better policy by asking first where responsibility for world poverty really lies, without making the convenient assumption that outcome responsibility must always lie with those agents—the rich nations—who are able to discharge remedial responsibility.

Second, we need a discriminating response to world poverty because we need to set priorities: we need to ask which cases make the greatest claim on our resources, and we need to weigh the demands of global justice against the demands of social justice in domestic societies. The ethical foundations for this response were laid in Chapter 2, where I argued that, even in cases involving human rights, different duties had different weights, depending on what role the duty-bearer had played in causing the victims' rights to be infringed. To see the implications of this, consider the following hypotheticals. Suppose, at one extreme, that world poverty was entirely the (outcome) responsibility of rich societies and their governments. Then the citizens of those societies would have remedial

---

[41] For a helpful overview, see World Bank, *Assessing Aid: What Works, What Doesn't, and Why* (Oxford: Oxford University Press, 1998).

[42] See Pogge, *World Poverty and Human Rights*, esp. 112–16, 153–66.

obligations of justice that might well trump their internal obligations of social justice (such as their obligation to create and support an extensive welfare state). Moreover these obligations would be enforceable, in the sense that third parties (other states or international organizations) could justifiably take reasonable steps to ensure that they were complied with, for instance by applying economic sanctions to countries that refused to pay their share of the cost. At the other extreme, suppose that rich societies were in no way responsible for global poverty; it was entirely endogenous to the poor societies. In that case, remedial responsibilities would be humanitarian only, and would therefore take second place to domestic duties of justice. They would also not be enforceable by third parties. Neither of these extremes describes the world as it actually exists. But to know what we owe to the world's poor, we have first to come up with a more accurate, and therefore more discriminating, account of the underlying causes of their poverty.

CHAPTER 10

——

Conclusion

My aim in this book has been to find a way of thinking about global justice that is not in any strong sense cosmopolitan, but still recognizes that there are obligations of justice that cross state and national boundaries. I began it by reflecting on some urgent cases of human suffering—Iraq, Niger, and Melilla—that are likely to call forth the cosmopolitan response that such boundaries must be treated as irrelevant when we ask what we owe to our fellow-human beings in such circumstances. But I suggested that in our response to these human tragedies, we must not only consider the suffering itself, but also ask questions about how and why it has occurred: questions about responsibility. Or to put it differently: while we must always respond to human suffering with compassion—we must ask what we can do to relieve the pain, undo the harm, and restore the conditions for a decent life—we must also respond with respect, treating the victims as agents who, retrospectively or prospectively, are able to take charge of their own lives. Justice demands this more complex response; that is why it is more than mere compassion. If we are also to treat people as agents, however, we must respond to them not just as individuals, but as member of collectives whose practices and decisions may have profound effects on how individual lives go. So the boundaries that separate these collectives must count, as a matter of principle as well as a matter of fact. We cannot understand global justice without recognizing that belonging to a particular group or a particular society is not just an arbitrary feature like hair colour but something that can legitimately affect a person's life chances. That one person is better off than another simply by virtue of the fact that she is a citizen of France rather than of Niger is not in itself unfair;

though that she is destined to a life of abject poverty by virtue of the latter citizenship almost certainly is.

The key idea in this book has been the idea of national responsibility. In invoking it, I have made a number of assumptions, any of which might be challenged. One is that we still live in a world of nations, which means more than the evident fact that we live in a world of (largely independent) states. It means that there exist national communities made up of people whose understanding of their place in the world is conditioned by the particular national identities they share. That is, they draw lines between insiders and outsiders, feel special loyalties to those inside the lines, and value the special cultural features that they believe they share with their compatriots. They want to be in control of their own destiny, and fiercely resent it when outsiders try to interfere, even with benevolent intentions. Their political involvement occurs mainly at national level: what matters most to them are national elections and referendums, the rise and fall of national leaders, discussions in the national media, and so forth. They may be dimly aware of events taking place in other countries or in international bodies, but these come into sharp focus only when they make an impact on domestic politics (e.g. by threatening national security). They are by no means necessarily hostile to people who are not compatriots: they may value the diversity of national cultures, and positively support other nations in their search for autonomy. But they want to remain different and feel a special attachment to those features—language, cultural traditions, institutions, places of historical significance, and so forth—that embody that difference.

Not everyone looks on the world through national spectacles in this way. There is also a small group of cosmopolites (to resurrect a nineteenth century term now unaccountably fallen out of use[1]). These are not morally principled cosmopolitans, but rather people who feel no special bond to any particular place or community but are happy to take the best that is on offer wherever this happens to be—the best job, the sunniest climate, and the richest set of

---

[1] According to the *Oxford English Dictionary*, 'one who regards or treats the whole world as his country; one who has no national attachments or prejudices'. An illustrative quotation is more colourful: 'He was one of those vagabond cosmopolites who shark about the world, as if they had no right or business in it.' (2nd edn, part III, 986).

leisure activities. We could imagine a world made up of nothing but cosmopolites, but it would clearly be very different from the world that we know (and in many ways a poorer one: present-day cosmopolites can enjoy their lifestyles only because many others are more deeply committed to sustaining the political communities through which the cosmopolites pass). It may perhaps be the case that we are gently drifting towards such a world, but, if so, there is still a very considerable way to go. Meanwhile, we can assume that, for the great majority of people, national identities remain strong and politically significant.

My argument in this book has been that national identity entails national responsibility. By virtue of identifying with compatriots, sharing their values, and receiving the benefits that national communities provide, we are also involved in collective responsibility for the things that nations do. This extends to include things that our ancestors have done—national responsibility includes responsibility for the national past. That is the broad claim, and I have qualified it in various ways, drawing distinctions between different degrees of control that ordinary people may be able to exercise over their institutions and the policies that their governments pursue. Nonetheless, my assumption has been that we are involved in collective responsibility unless one of these defeating conditions obtains, and as such it is a matter of justice that we should share in both the benefits and the costs that national membership brings with it. That is why the stronger forms of cosmopolitanism, which either simply assume or try to argue that belonging to a particular nation is an arbitrary feature that should have no bearing on the life chances of the individual person who has it, must be rejected. A fortiori, it is also why global justice cannot mean global egalitarianism.

National responsibility, however, is a double-edged sword. It may allow richer nations to justify some of the advantages they have—calls for egalitarian redistribution can be defeated by showing that these advantages were won through processes for which the members of the nations in question were responsible—but it may also create liabilities. Where global poverty imposes remedial responsibilities on states and other agencies with the means to combat it, national responsibility means that ordinary citizens can legitimately be obliged to contribute (for instance through taxes levied to provide foreign aid).[2] It also means that people who are not individually responsible (in the outcome sense) for any wrongdoing can be asked to make redress for injustices committed in the national past. So national responsibility can be invoked to justify certain forms of global inequality, but it can also be invoked to justify resource transfers or institutional changes that impose costs on richer societies and benefit poorer ones.

To determine the extent of these liabilities, I argued, we need to use the idea of a global minimum—a set of basic human rights which must be protected for people everywhere regardless of circumstances. Because these rights are basic—they correspond to the conditions of what I called a decent human life—they do not threaten national differences. In contrast to the inflated human rights rhetoric now so often deployed, they cannot be used to mandate particular political institutions or policies: there are many forms of social and political life that are consistent with fulfilling basic rights so understood. I argued also that basic human rights do not include an unlimited right to migration. So they do not pose a threat to nations who, in the name of self-determination, want to impose restrictions on inward movement across their borders. Of course, one might reasonably hope and expect that in a world in which basic rights were universally protected—and in which therefore there was no deep poverty such as is widespread in ours—the pressure to migrate would be much reduced. There would be no more Melillas, no more Sangatte refugee camps, because no one would find themselves in desperate circumstances such that only illegal border-crossing seemed to provide the chance for a decent life. In these circumstances, more extensive rights of free movement might be compatible with the natural wish of national communities to control their own size and cultural composition.

Does global justice require more than the universal protection of basic human rights? Although this is its most urgent demand, it

---

[2] This is most obviously true where the remedial responsibilities take the form of duties of justice to the global poor. Where the duties in question are humanitarian only—see the discussion in Chapter 9—more work has to be done to establish that states may rightfully compel their citizens to contribute. Nevertheless, since states already oblige their citizens to contribute to projects of various kinds that are not required by justice—the provision of public goods, for example—I assume that good arguments can be made for discharging many humanitarian duties by state action.

also requires what I have called fair terms of cooperation between societies, in particular terms of cooperation that allow weaker and less developed societies the opportunity to develop along paths of their own choosing. Specifying what this means in abstract terms is difficult, although in contrast it is fairly easy to give examples of how the existing international order unfairly penalizes vulnerable societies. Cooperation between two parties is unfair when the benefits of cooperation accrue almost entirely to one side, and this can happen because the other side has little option but to continue the cooperation, the alternatives being worse still. Clearly this applies to some cases of international trade, and also to international investment: a receiving society may be so desperate for foreign capital that it is willing to accept it on terms that involve the exploitation of its own people. So fairness of this kind is important at global level, as well as at national level, but note again that this does not translate into a demand for global *equality*. At most, as I suggested at the end of Chapter 3, it might give us reason to combat excessive inequalities that were likely to convert to power differentials between nations, making fair terms of cooperation difficult to achieve.

That, in summary, is the conception of global justice I have been arguing for in this book. Is it a feasible conception? Can we realistically envisage a world that comes even close to realizing it? It is certainly more feasible than some of the stronger cosmopolitan alternatives that have been suggested, for instance principles of global equality of resources or of opportunity. Although my earlier critique of these principles did not turn on issues of feasibility, it is easy to see the practical obstacles that would prevent their achievement, in a world where political decision-making was still mainly in the hands of separate national governments. If we assume, as I have been, that global justice must mean justice for a world of nations, something like the conception advanced here seems the only realistic possibility. But is it realistic enough? What are the obstacles it faces?

It is often argued that the challenges we face at the beginning of the twenty-first century are such that they cannot be handled by national governments alone: we must have institutions of governance at a higher, regional if not global, level. The challenges here would include establishing effective regulatory institutions for a global economy that threatens increasingly to run out of control, driven as it is by powerful multinational corporations; implementing policies to safeguard the global environment—preventing (or at least reducing) global warming, protecting endangered species, stopping the depletion of irreplaceable natural resources, and combating international terrorism. The argument, then, is that national self-determination has become a luxury that we can no longer afford in the face of these more urgent issues. The only way to tackle them is for national governments to transfer much of their political authority to higher bodies, bodies with the power to compel compliance with the regulations that they impose. This would also mean that the scope of national responsibility would be sharply reduced—so the balance I have attempted to strike between national self-determination and global justice would be upset.

There is no question that the challenges noted above, and others like them, are real and urgent. But if, as I do, we place a high value on national determination,[3] then we must ask how far they can be met through voluntary cooperation between nation-states, a solution that does not rule out higher-level regulatory bodies altogether, but treats their authority as normative rather than coercive. To see what this might mean, consider the case of greenhouse gas emissions. Suppose there is agreement on the sustainable level of emissions below which no further global warming will occur, and also agreement on how emissions targets should be allocated between different nation-states at different levels of development. An international body could then be set up to monitor compliance with these targets, and to publicize cases in which countries were failing to meet them. Persistent failure on the part of a particular nation would not only attract moral opprobrium from others who were compliant, but also sanctions in the form of withdrawal from cooperative projects, less favourable trade arrangements, and so forth. In the best case, then, once the norm was established, it would be self-policing by such means.

Evidently solutions like this can only work if most nation-states are willing to comply with the norm themselves, and willing to

---

[3] I have not argued in defence of national self-determination at any length in the present book, but see my earlier treatment of this topic in *On Nationality* (Oxford: Clarendon Press, 1995), ch. 4, and more briefly in *Citizenship and National Identity* (Cambridge: Polity Press, 2000), ch. 10.

bear the additional costs involved in sanctioning deviants. Voluntary cooperation might therefore seem far less effective than a global authority with powers to compel. Perhaps in very extreme cases this argument would apply. If global warming accelerates to the point where the continuance of human life in anything like its present form becomes doubtful, people might be willing to sign a Hobbesian global contract giving a central authority the power to impose fierce environmental controls on all societies. Short of this, however, we need to ask what might motivate ordinary people to impose the necessary restrictions on themselves. Here it seems far more likely that they would be willing to comply with legislation that had been discussed and voted upon through normal democratic procedures within nation-states than with rules imposed on them from above. The legitimating power of democracy, I am assuming here, depends on democratic procedures that ordinary people understand and identify with—and each nation has its own cultural understanding of those procedures, its own vernacular language of politics, and so forth.

I argued in Chapter 2 that for these reasons and others, the idea of global democracy, in any literal sense, is a chimera (one can argue about the best way of making international institutions like the UN democratically accountable *in some sense*, but that is a differ-ent matter). Given, then, that global justice may require people to sacrifice certain advantages that they might otherwise have gained in order, for example, to give fair opportunities to vulnerable people in poor societies, it appears that the best way to achieve this is to invoke national responsibility—to persuade people that they have a collective responsibility to make the sacrifices involved, by virtue of what they or their predecessors have done, by virtue of their special capacity in the present, or for some other reason. Such decisions are made legitimate by democratic debate within the society. It can and should become a matter of national pride, on the part of better-off nations, to have made these sacrifices.

This, it seems to me, is the great strength of the idea of national responsibility as a vehicle for, rather than obstacle to, global justice. It enables people to *assume* responsibility for making the sacrifices that justice may require, rather than simply having these sacrifices imposed on them by an institution whose authority they may not recognize. But there is also a corresponding weakness, which has to do with the division of responsibility. This is an issue that has occupied us repeatedly in the course of this book. It is one thing to say that where basic human rights are being put at risk, all those with the ability to protect them share in remedial responsibility; it is another to say precisely how remedial responsibilities are to be distributed, what part of the cost of the remedy each agent should bear. Who should be required to lower tariff barriers to developing country imports, and by how much? What percentage of GDP should each country be asked to contribute as foreign aid to poverty relief? How many refugees should each nation be asked to admit? How should the burden of combating climate change by reducing carbon emissions be distributed? These matters are the subject of intense international negotiation, and all too often such negotiations end in failure, as national self-interest trumps fairness (as I write, global trade talks have once again reached an impasse, as powerful agricultural lobbies in the USA and Europe have succeeded in blocking proposals to open up their markets to Third-World farmers).

Perhaps the most telling example of all is humanitarian intervention—military intervention to protect the human rights of civilians threatened by genocide, civil war, ethnic cleansing, or other such disasters. That such intervention may be required as a matter of global justice should be clear enough, given everything I have said. But whose responsibility is it to undertake? Most of the literature on this topic focuses on questions of international law: first, under what circumstances may the normal presumption of the integrity of sovereign states be set aside by virtue of the human rights violations that are taking place within their borders? Second, who is authorized to intervene? Is it a necessary condition that the intervention has been approved by the UN Security Council, for instance? These, one might say, are questions about the legitimacy of intervention. But the problem, in general, is not one of having to decide which of several willing interveners is entitled to act; it is one of persuading *any* state that it has a responsibility to intervene, alone or in collaboration with others. Even when the intervention is nominally for purposes of peacekeeping, as opposed to confronting a military force engaging in violence against civilians, it may take considerable diplomatic pressure to persuade several states each to contribute relatively small numbers of troops.

Why is this? Intervening to protect human rights is typically costly, in material resources in every case, in human resources in many cases (when soldiers, peacekeepers, or aid workers are killed or taken hostage), in political capital (when intervention is interpreted in sinister terms by third parties—e.g. as disguised colonialism). So states have good reasons to avoid becoming involved if at all possible, particularly democratic states where the government will come under heavy domestic fire if the intervention goes wrong. The fact that there are often many agencies—states, coalitions of states, or other bodies—that might in principle discharge the responsibility to protect makes the problem worse. We might draw an analogy here with instances in which individuals are confronted with a situation in which they would have to perform a Good Samaritan act—say, going to the rescue of somebody who collapses in the street. Empirical studies of situations like this reveal that the more potential rescuers are present, the less likely any one of them is to intervene—so the victim stands a better chance of being picked up if there is only one passer-by at the time he collapses than if there are, say, six people nearby.[4] Several factors may combine to produce this outcome: people interpret other people's inaction as a sign that the problem is less serious than it might appear; there is a parallel normative effect whereby each person takes the others' behaviour as defining what is expected or right under the circumstances; but perhaps most importantly, responsibility is diffused among the potential helpers: if the victim were to die, no one in particular could be held responsible for the death.

As we move from individual cases of rescue to cases of states, or coalitions of states, undertaking humanitarian intervention, a further difficulty arises. These states are coercive bodies, at least in relation to their own citizens. When they intervene, they impose requirements on people—for example they send soldiers or aid workers to the areas where the rights violations are taking place, often at some considerable risk to the people who are sent. Even if there is no risk to persons, resources are required, and these of course are raised by compulsory taxation of the citizens. So we must ask what makes such

---

[4] I have considered these studies, and their normative implications, in ' "Are They *My* Poor?": The Problem of Altruism in a World of Strangers', *Critical Review of International Social and Political Philosophy*, 5 (2002), 106–27, reprinted in J. Seglow (ed.), *The Ethics of Altruism* (London: Frank Cass, 2004).

interventions legitimate. When can citizens justifiably refuse to take on the burden they are being asked to bear, or refuse on the part of their compatriots most at risk—the soldiers and aid workers—to carry the cost of intervention?

This question is sometimes answered from the standpoint of national interest alone, the assumption being that costly interventions can only be justified by appeal to the longer-term interests of fellow-nationals in security against terrorist threats and so forth.[5] But even if we move beyond that standpoint, as we should, and see intervention as motivated by an ethical concern for the victims whose human rights are being violated, there still remains the issue of the costs of intervention, and of what share of these costs any one individual or group of individuals can be asked to bear. How many lives may be justifiably sacrificed in an intervention that if successful would save life on a large scale? One would search the literature of political philosophy in vain for a clear answer to this question. But if instead we look to the practice of democratic states, and to public opinion in those states, the implicit answer is that in the case of humanitarian interventions where no national interest is at stake, the anticipated risk must be quite low. Once a few hundred soldiers have been killed or seriously injured, opinion shifts rapidly against the intervention. And this cannot be put down simply to indifference to the fate of the foreigners who the intervention is meant to protect. Even if we were able to show that the soldiers undertaking the intervention had implicitly consented to being exposed to a risk of death or serious injury by virtue of enlisting, they remain citizens, and are therefore owed what following Dworkin we can call 'equal concern and respect'. That involves limiting the degree of risk to which they are exposed when they are required to rescue non-citizens. Recall here the argument of Chapter 2: in cases where human rights are being violated by third parties, an agent's duty to protect those rights is less strong than if the agent himself is responsible for the

---

[5] This standpoint was starkly articulated by Samuel Huntington in relation to the US intervention in Somalia in 1992: 'it is morally unjustifiable and politically indefensible that members of the Armed Forces should be killed to prevent Somalis from killing one another' (cited in J. L. Holzgrefe, 'The Humanitarian Intervention Debate', in J. L. Holzgrefe and R. O. Keohane (eds), *Humanitarian Intervention: Ethical, Legal and Political Dilemmas* (Cambridge: Cambridge University Press, 2003), 30.

violations. But if the duty to protect is in this way less strong in the circumstances that typically call for humanitarian intervention, then the degree of cost that we may justifiably impose on those who will carry out the intervention in our name is correspondingly smaller. It is simply unfair to ask soldiers or others to face very substantial risks of death or injury to discharge what may well be a humanitarian obligation rather than a strict duty of justice, to use the distinction introduced in Chapter 9.

Humanitarian intervention exposes the problem of national responsibility and global justice in its starkest form, but the problem potentially reappears whenever achieving justice requires sacrifice on the part of advantaged nations, and there is no clear-cut way of attributing remedial responsibilities. The problem, then, takes the following form: people beyond our national frontiers have claims of justice that can only be met by changes to the prevailing international order—changes that might be of many different kinds, from increases in the total volume of foreign aid flowing from rich to poor countries, to new sets of rules governing tariffs on agricultural products, right through to the creation of an international force able to intervene militarily to prevent an impending genocide. However there are many different solutions to the problems just identified, and others like them, solutions that typically will distribute the costs and benefits of change in quite different ways. So which countries should be asked to bear which costs? As I suggested in Chapter 4, we do have principles for assigning remedial responsibility that presumably are widely accepted in the abstract. But in any concrete case, there has to be a judgement as to how these principles are to be applied, and there can be reasonable disagreement about judgements of this kind. Against this background, it will be hard, not only politically, but also ethically, to impose substantial costs on one section of the society in order to discharge remedial responsibilities whose proper distribution, as between nations, remains uncertain.

There is also the question of whether national values can legitimately be used to block remedial responsibility claims. France routinely defends the system of agricultural subsidies currently provided by the EU on the grounds that a countryside in which small farmers are able to produce in somewhat traditional ways is an essential part of French identity—even though such subsidies severely reduce the opportunities for Third-World producers to sell on European and world markets. If pressed, would it be reasonable for the French to point out that the problem could be solved if other developed societies with different visions of rural life removed *their* subsidies? Is it relevant that the cost to the French of removing subsidies is greater, given their idea of national identity, or should we say that having a landscape of vineyards and smallholdings is more like an expensive taste, which cannot be used to defeat claims of global justice? Or to come back to the case of humanitarian intervention, can nations justifiably be exempted from military operations on the grounds that their constitutions place limits on what their armed forces may do? What should we say about a country like Switzerland that for historic-cum-cultural reasons has developed a system of national defence that is precisely that and nothing more, and whose contribution to peacekeeping efforts overseas is therefore unavoidably minimal? For these reasons too, it seems likely that in many cases there will be what we might call a justice gap—a gap between what people in poor countries can legitimately claim as a matter of justice (protection of their human rights, especially) and what the citizens of rich countries are obliged, as a matter of justice, to sacrifice to fulfil these claims.

Can we perhaps bridge this gap by envisaging a contract between people in rich countries that would guarantee the discharge of their collective responsibilities to the world's poor? That is, they would bind themselves in advance to comply with the directives of the relevant international bodies, provided other nations did likewise, while authorizing these international bodies to distribute responsibilities as they saw fit. One might envisage one such body having responsibilities for international trade, another for military intervention and peacekeeping, another for natural disasters, and so forth. This would be a possible solution if it could be achieved. But we need to ask why members of the rich societies would agree to such a contract. Except perhaps in the case of natural disasters, they are very unlikely to be the beneficiaries themselves. On the other hand, their potential liabilities might be very great, and the costs might fall disproportionately on a subset of their members—soldiers, say, or farmers. Citizens might very reasonably wish to set limits to their future liability,

and therefore decline to authorize their governments to enter a contract of the kind proposed; they would want to retain the right to
decide on each proposed policy change case by case, taking account
of the likely costs involved when set against gains to human rights or
other aspects of global justice that the change would bring. This in
turn would prevent states signing up to any arrangement that would
oblige them to intervene regardless of the current wishes of their
citizens.

I conclude, therefore, on a note of realism about prospects for
global justice. Realism is not pessimism: I do not share the views of
those who claim that states will, inevitably, pursue only the national
interests of their citizens, and that any movement towards global
justice, as understood here, is therefore an impossibility. The justice
gap can be narrowed, but it is unlikely to be closed entirely, until we
reach the point where all societies are able to provide their members
with decent lives, so that only natural disasters and the like would
impose remedial responsibilities on outsiders—and these might well
be handled through a contract of mutual aid as sketched above. In
that world, the costs of discharging remedial responsibilities would
have fallen to the point where no society could reasonably refuse to
carry its share. But that world is not ours: a point that is sometimes
obscured by back-of-the-envelope calculations of the amount people
in rich societies would have to contribute in order to raise everyone
in poor societies above a threshold such as the $1 per day poverty
line—calculations that imagine a direct transfer of resources from
one group of people to the other. We know, in fact, that abolishing
poverty requires a radical transformation of the institutions, practices, and cultures of the societies that reproduce it from generation
to generation. Our history of failed attempts to engineer such trans-
formations should make us acutely aware of the potential costs of
further attempts.[6] As I have emphasized, our primary responsibility
is to create an international order in which societies that are currently
poor can choose paths to development that will lift them out of
poverty—but that also means leaving the responsibility to do so in
their hands.

[6] For some reflection on this point, see W. Easterly, *The White Man's Burden:
Why the West's Efforts to Aid the Rest Have Done So Much Ill and So Little Good*
(Oxford: Oxford University Press, 2006).

I am not alone in thinking that the demands of global justice, in a world of nations, might give rise to what I have called a justice gap. A rather similar idea can be found in the final chapter of Thomas Nagel's *Equality and Partiality*.[7] Nagel there considers the gulf in living standards between the rich and the poor in the world, and concludes that the poor can reasonably demand redistribution of a magnitude that the rich can reasonably refuse to provide. As he puts it, 'the poor may recognize that the rich are not unreasonable to resist more than a certain level of sacrifice, in light of their constellation of motives, while at the same time the poor may reasonably refuse to accept the resulting degree of benefit as sufficient, even in light of the recognition that the rich can reasonably refuse more'.[8] As this quotation may suggest, the gap for Nagel arises because the personal interests and life-plans of people in rich societies place limits on the sacrifices that they can be required to make to meet the needs of the poor.[9] Although I also place some weight on this point about motivation, I have emphasized particularly the fact of divided responsibility: each rich person, and each community of rich people, may (reasonably) ask what part of the burden of achieving global justice should fall to them, and the gap arises in part because the combined set of self-ascribed burdens may fall short of what is required.

Does the likely existence of a justice gap give us reason to give up the idea of global justice entirely? Nagel, in a more recent essay, has moved in that direction, claiming, in the spirit of Thomas Hobbes, that 'the idea of global justice without a world government is a chimera'.[10] This is not merely because a world government would be necessary to *achieve* justice at global level, but more fundamentally because on Nagel's view obligations of justice (or more precisely 'socio-economic justice') only obtain between people who are subject to the same sovereign authority which acts in their name

---

[7]   T. Nagel, *Equality and Partiality* (New York: Oxford University Press, 1991), ch. 15.

[8]   Nagel, *Equality and Partiality*, 172.

[9]   I should make it clear that for Nagel this limitation would not apply if the rich were (outcome) responsible for the deprivation of the poor.

[10]   T. Nagel, 'The Problem of Global Justice', *Philosophy and Public Affairs*, 33 (2005), 115.

and forces them to abide by its rules. People who belong to the same sovereign state, Nagel argues, are collectively responsible for the coercion that they exercise on one another, and this gives rise to a demand for justification that can only be met by showing that the laws and policies of the state conform to egalitarian principles of social justice—that any inequalities between citizens that they create are non-arbitrary. In the case of inequalities between states, or between citizens of different states, there is no such burden of justification. The idea of global justice would therefore only apply if a global sovereign were to arise. Until one does, our obligations to the world's poor are better understood as humanitarian in nature.

As I noted in Chapter 9, however, Nagel's argument here relies on asserting that socio-economic justice claims are always comparative in form—they concern the way different groups of people fare relative to one another. One can accept that distributive justice in that specific sense only applies among people who are associated with one another in relevant ways, but still think that there are (non-comparative) duties of justice that apply globally, that is between people irrespective of whether they stand in any relationship to one another. (Nagel accepts this in the case of negative duties such as those corresponding to rights to bodily integrity and freedom of expression, but denies that there can be analogous positive duties of justice such as those corresponding to rights to subsistence and health care.) He is correct to follow Rawls in rejecting monism about justice—the idea that the same principle or principles of justice apply no matter what kind of human practice or relationship they are being applied *to*—but he is wrong to replace it with a simple dualism in which principles of socio-economic justice apply only within the boundaries of a sovereign state, while outside those boundaries we have only negative duties of justice plus humanitarian obligations. Even if he is right to claim that there is something uniquely coercive about relationships within such boundaries—a claim that many people would be inclined to challenge—he is wrong to follow Hobbes in asserting such a tight conceptual link between justice and coercion. Questions of distributive justice arise in many forms of human association in which the threat of coercion plays no essential part—workplaces, schools, churches, and even families. Such associations usually exist, of course, within state boundaries, but this fact does not appear crucial in explaining why the distribution of benefits and burdens within them is subject to principles of justice: questions of pay fairness arise in multinational corporations in much the same way as they do in national companies; principles of equal treatment apply among the members of the Roman Catholic and the other international churches, and so forth. Given the complex set of relationships, some coercive, others not, that now exist between individuals and groups at transnational level, we need to develop a theory of global justice that reflects this complexity: neither monism nor a simple dualism is adequate.[11]

Nagel is not wrong to think that the nation-state remains a privileged context for justice — that there is something special about *social* justice, understood as justice practised among the citizens of such a state. He is, however, wrong to reduce that privilege to the fact of coercion; equally important are the facts that nation-states are 'cooperative ventures for mutual advantage', to use Rawls's phrase, and that they are *nation*-states whose members form communities based on shared identities. It is the confluence of all three features in a single territorial unit that makes social justice as we usually understand it conceivable and feasible to implement. But still, there can be forms of justice outside that context, and I have tried to explore some of those forms in the course of this book. (I have not tried to be exhaustive: e.g. I have not tried to tackle the very important issue of environmental justice, and especially how the costs of protecting the natural environment from human devastation are to be fairly allocated between nations.) So the absence of a world government does not eliminate the very idea of global justice, although it does partially determine its meaning. Global justice must be understood as justice for a world of culturally distinct nation-states each of which can legitimately claim a considerable degree of political autonomy. The absence of global government also makes global justice harder to achieve, even when we understand it in this less ambitious way. We cannot entirely fill what I have called the justice gap, the gap between the claims people in poor countries can make as a matter of justice,

---

[11] See the much fuller critical appraisals of Nagel's argument in J. Cohen and C. Sabel, 'Extra Rempublicam Nulla Justitia', *Philosophy and Public Affairs*, 34 (2006), 147–75, and in A. Julius, 'Nagel's Atlas', *Philosophy and Public Affairs*, 34 (2006), 176–92.

and the responsibilities people in rich countries can be required to assume, also as a matter of justice. But we can certainly narrow the gap: relationships between rich and poor can be changed so as to make it far less likely that scenes such as those I described at the beginning of this book will continue to fill our television screens in future. The world's poor may hope for more, but they cannot be denied any less.

BIBLIOGRAPHY

Abdel-Nour, F., 'National Responsibility', *Political Theory*, 31 (2003), 693–719.

Acemoglu D., Johnson, S., and Robinson, J., 'The Colonial Origins of Economic Development: An Empirical Investigation', *American Economic Review*, 91 (2001), 1369–401.

Albin, C., *Justice and Fairness in International Negotiation* (Cambridge: Cambridge University Press, 2001).

An-Na'im, A. A., 'Toward a Cross-Cultural Approach to Defining International Standards of Human Rights: The Meaning of Cruel, Inhuman, or Degrading Treatment or Punishment', in A. A. An-Na'im (ed.), *Human Rights in Cross-Cultural Perspectives: A Quest for Consensus* (Philadelphia, PA: University of Pennsylvania Press, 1992).

Appiah, K. A., *Cosmopolitanism: Ethics in a World of Strangers* (London: Allen Lane, 2006).

Arendt, H., 'Collective Responsibility', in J. W. Bernauer (ed.), *Amor Mundi: Explorations in the Faith and Thought of Hannah Arendt* (Boston, MA: Martinus Nijhoff, 1987).

Bader, V., 'Reasonable Impartiality and Priority for Compatriots: A Criticism of Liberal Nationalism's Main Flaws', *Ethical Theory and Moral Practice*, 8 (2005), 83–103.

Barkan, E. *The Guilt of Nations* (New York: W. W. Norton, 2000).

Barry, B., 'Humanity and Justice in Global Perspective', in B. Barry, *Democracy, Power and Justice* (Oxford: Clarendon Press, 1989).

—— 'Statism and Nationalism: A Cosmopolitan Critique', in I. Shapiro and L. Brilmayer (eds), *Nomos 49: Global Justice* (New York: New York University Press, 1999).

Beitz, C., *Political Theory and International Relations* (Princeton, NJ: Princeton University Press, 1979).

—— 'International Relations, Philosophy of', in E. Craig (ed.), *Routledge Encyclopaedia of Philosophy* (London: Routledge, 1998), IV, 826–33.

—— 'International Liberalism and Distributive Justice: A Survey of Recent Thought', *World Politics*, 51 (1999), 269–96.

—— 'Social and Cosmopolitan Liberalism', *International Affairs*, 75 (1999), 515–29.

—— 'Does Global Inequality Matter?', in T. Pogge (ed.), *Global Justice* (Oxford: Blackwell, 2001).

Beitz, C., 'Human Rights as a Common Concern', *American Political Science Review*, 95 (2001), 269–82.

—— 'What Human Rights Mean', *Daedalus*, 132 (2003), 36–46.

—— 'Cosmopolitanism and Global Justice', in G. Brock and D. Moellendorf (eds), *Current Debates in Global Justice* (Dordrecht, the Netherlands: Springer, 2005).

Bell, D., *East Meets West: Human Rights and Democracy in East Asia* (Princeton, NJ: Princeton University Press, 2000).

Blackstone, W., *Commentaries on the Law of England*, intro. J. H. Langbein (Chicago, IL: University of Chicago Press, 1979).

Blake, M., 'Distributive Justice, State Coercion and Autonomy', *Philosophy and Public Affairs*, 30 (2001), 257–96.

—— 'Immigration', in R. G. Frey and C. H. Wellman (eds), *A Companion to Applied Ethics* (Oxford: Blackwell, 2003).

Bloch, M., *Feudal Society* (London: Routledge and Kegan Paul, 1962).

Boxhill, B., 'Global Equality of Opportunity and National Integrity', *Social Philosophy and Policy*, 5 (1987), 143–68.

—— 'A Lockean Argument for Black Reparations', *Journal of Ethics*, 7 (2003), 63–91.

Brighouse, H., 'Against Nationalism', in J. Couture, K. Nielsen, and M. Seymour (eds), *Rethinking Nationalism* (Calgary, Canada: University of Calgary Press, 1998).

Brock, G., 'Egalitarianism, Ideals, and Cosmopolitan Justice', *Philosophical Forum*, 36 (2005), 1–30.

Brooks, R. L. (ed.), *When Sorry Isn't Enough: The Controversy over Apologies and Reparations for Human Injustice* (New York: New York University Press, 1999).

Buchanan, A., 'Recognitional Legitimacy and the State System', *Philosophy and Public Affairs*, 28 (1999), 46–78.

—— *Justice, Legitimacy, and Self-Determination* (Oxford: Oxford University Press, 2004).

Buckland, W. W., *A Text-Book of Roman Law from Augustus to Justinian* (Cambridge: Cambridge University Press, 1932).

—— and McNair, A. D., *Roman Law and Common Law* (Cambridge: Cambridge University Press, 1936).

Butt, D., 'On Benefiting from Injustice', *Canadian Journal of Philosophy*, 37 (2007), 129–52.

Cabrera, L., *Political Theory of Global Justice: A Cosmopolitan Case for the World State* (London: Routledge, 2004).

Cane, P., 'Responsibility and Fault', in P. Cane and J. Gardner (eds), *Relating to Responsibility* (Oxford: Hart, 2001).

—— *Responsibility in Law and Morality* (Oxford: Hart, 2002).

Caney, S., 'Individuals, Nations and Obligations', in S. Caney, D. George, and P. Jones (eds), *National Rights, International Obligations* (Boulder, CO: Westview Press, 1996).

——'Global Equality of Opportunity and the Sovereignty of States', in A. Coates (ed.), *International Justice* (Aldershot, UK: Ashgate, 2000).

——'Cosmopolitan Justice and Equalizing Opportunities', in T. Pogge (ed.), *Global Justice* (Oxford: Blackwell, 2001).

Carens J., 'Aliens and Citizens: The Case for Open Borders', *Review of Politics*, 49 (1987), 251–73.

——'Migration and Morality: A Liberal Egalitarian Perspective', in B. Barry and R. Goodin (eds), *Free Movement: Ethical Issues in the Transnational Migration of People and Money* (Hemel Hempstead, UK: Harvester Wheatsheaf, 1992).

——'The Rights of Immigrants', in J. Baker (ed.), *Group Rights* (Toronto, Canada: University of Toronto Press, 1994).

Casal, P., 'Why Sufficiency Is Not Enough', *Ethics*, 117 (2006–7), 296–326.

Chabal, P., 'The Quest for Good Governance and Development in Africa: Is NEPAD the Answer?', *International Affairs*, 78 (2002), 447–62.

Chan, J., 'A Confucian Perspective on Human Rights for Contemporary China', in J. R. Bauer and D. A. Bell (eds), *The East Asian Challenge for Human Rights.* (Cambridge: Cambridge University Press, 1999), 212–40.

——'Territorial Boundaries and Confucianism', in D. Miller and S. Hashmi (eds), *Boundaries and Justice: Diverse Ethical Perspectives* (Princeton, NJ: Princeton University Press, 2001).

Cohen, G. A., 'On the Currency of Egalitarian Justice', *Ethics*, 99 (1989), 906–44.

——'Expensive Taste Rides Again', in J. Burley (ed.), *Dworkin and His Critics* (Oxford: Blackwell, 2004).

Cohen, J., 'Minimalism About Human Rights: The Most We Can Hope For?', *Journal of Political Philosophy*, 12 (2004), 190–213.

——and Sabel, C., 'Extra Rempublicam Nulla Justitia', *Philosophy and Public Affairs*, 34 (2006), 147–75.

Cole, P., *Philosophy and Exclusion: Liberal Political Theory and Immigration* (Edinburgh, UK: Edinburgh University Press, 2000).

Coleman, J., *Risks and Wrongs* (Cambridge: Cambridge University Press, 1992).

Crocker, D., 'Functioning and Capability: The Foundations of Sen's and Nussbaum's Development Ethic', *Political Theory*, 20 (1992), 584–612.

Crocker, D., 'Functioning and Capability: The Foundations of Sen's and Nussbaum's Development Ethic, Part 2', in M. Nussbaum and J. Glover (eds), *Women, Culture, and Development* (Oxford: Clarendon Press, 1995).

Cullity, G., *The Moral Demands of Affluence* (Oxford: Clarendon Press, 2004).

Cunningham, M., 'Saying Sorry: The Politics of Apology', *Political Quarterly*, 70 (1999), 285–93.

Dagan, H., 'Restitution and Slavery: On Incomplete Commodification, Intergenerational Justice, and Legal Transitions', *Boston University Law Review*, 84 (2004), 1139–76.

Dummett, A., 'The Transnational Migration of People Seen from within a Natural Law Tradition', in B. Barry and R. Goodin (eds), *Free Movement: Ethical Issues in the Transnational Migration of People and Money* (Hemel Hempstead, UK: Harvester Wheatsheaf, 1992).

Dworkin, R., 'What is Equality? Part 1: Equality of Welfare', *Philosophy and Public Affairs*, 10 (1981), 228–40.

—— 'What Is Equality? Part 2: Equality of Resources', *Philosophy and Public Affairs*, 10 (1981), 283–345.

—— 'What Is Equality? Part 3: The Place of Liberty', *Iowa Law Review*, 73 (1987–8), 1–54.

—— *Sovereign Virtue: The Theory and Practice of Equality* (Cambridge, MA: Harvard University Press, 2000).

—— 'Reply', in J. Burley (ed.), *Dworkin and His Critics* (Oxford: Blackwell, 2004).

Easterly, W., *The White Man's Burden: Why the West's Efforts to Aid the Rest Have Done So Much Ill and So Little Good* (Oxford: Oxford University Press, 2006).

Eckstein, S. E., *Back to the Future: Cuba under Castro* (Princeton, NJ: Princeton University Press, 1994).

Eddy, K., 'Welfare Rights and Conflicts of Rights', *Res Publica*, 12 (2006), 337–56.

Erskine, T., 'Assigning Responsibilities to Institutional Moral Agents: The Case of States and Quasi-States', *Ethics and International Affairs*, 15 (2001), 67–85.

Fabre, C., 'Global Egalitarianism: An Indefensible Theory of Justice?', in D. Bell and A. De-Shalit (eds), *Forms of Justice* (Lanham, MD: Rowman and Littlefield, 2003), 315–30.

—— *Whose Body Is It Anyway? Justice and the Integrity of the Person* (Oxford: Clarendon Press, 2006).

—— and Miller, D., 'Justice and Culture: Rawls, Sen, Nussbaum, and O'Neill', *Political Studies Review*, 1 (2003), 4–17.

Feinberg, J., 'Collective Responsibility', in J. Feinberg, *Doing and Deserving: Essays in the Theory of Responsibility* (Princeton, NJ: Princeton University Press, 1970).

—— 'Noncomparative Justice', *Philosophical Review*, 83 (1974), 297–338.

Foot, P., 'The Problem of Abortion and the Doctrine of Double Effect', *Oxford Review*, 5 (1967), 5–15.

—— *Virtues and Vices and Other Essays in Moral Philosophy* (Oxford: Clarendon Press, 2002).

Franck, T., 'The Emerging Right to Democratic Governance', *American Journal of International Law*, 86 (1992), 46–91.

Gardels, N., 'Two Concepts of Nationalism: An Interview with Isaiah Berlin', *New York Review of Books*, 21 November 1991, 19–23.

Gewirth, A., *Human Rights: Essays on Justification and Applications* (Chicago, IL: University of Chicago Press, 1982).

Gibney, M., *The Ethics and Politics of Asylum: Liberal Democracy and the Response to Refugees* (Cambridge: Cambridge University Press, 2004).

—— 'Forced Migration, "Engineered" Regionalism and Justice between States' in Susan Kneebone and Felicity Rawlings-Sanei (eds), *New Regionalism and Asylum Seekers* (Oxford: Berghahn, forthcoming 2007).

Gill, K., 'The Moral Functions of an Apology', *Philosophical Forum*, 31 (2000), 11–27.

Glaeser, E. C., La Porta, R., Lopez-de-Silanes, F., and Shleifer, A., 'Do Institutions Cause Growth?', *Journal of Economic Growth*, 9 (2004), 271–303.

Godwin, W., *Enquiry Concerning Political Justice*, ed. I. Kramnick (Harmondsworth, UK: Penguin, 1976).

Goodin, R. E., 'What Is So Special about Our Fellow Countrymen?', *Ethics*, 98 (1987–8), 663–86.

Griffin, J., 'Discrepancies between the Best Philosophical Account of Human Rights and the International Law of Human Rights', *Proceedings of the Aristotelian Society*, 101 (2000), 1–28.

—— 'First Steps in an Account of Human Rights', *European Journal of Philosophy*, 9 (2001), 306–27.

Grimm, D., 'Does Europe Need a Constitution?', *European Law Journal*, 1 (1995), 282–302.

Hampton, J., 'Immigration, Identity, and Justice', in W. F. Schwartz (ed.), *Justice in Immigration* (Cambridge: Cambridge University Press, 1995).

Harrison, L. E. and Huntington, S. P. (eds), *Culture Matters* (New York: Basic Books, 2000).

Hart, H. L. A., 'Are There Any Natural Rights?', in A. Quinton (ed.), *Political Philosophy* (Oxford: Oxford University Press, 1967).

Hart, H. L. A., *Punishment and Responsibility: Essays in the Philosophy of Law* (Oxford: Clarendon Press, 1968).

—— and Honoré, T., *Causation in the Law*, 2nd edn (Oxford: Clarendon Press, 1985).

Hathaway, J. C. and Neve, R. A., 'Making International Refugee Law Relevant Again: A Proposal for Collectivized and Solution-Oriented Protection', *Harvard Human Rights Journal*, 10 (1997), 115–211.

Hayward, T., 'Global Justice and Natural Resources', *Political Studies*, 54 (2006), 349–69.

Held, V., 'Can A Random Collection of Individuals Be Morally Responsible?', *Journal of Philosophy*, 68 (1970), 471–81.

Holzgrefe, J. L., 'The Humanitarian Intervention Debate', in J. L. Holzgrefe and R. O. Keohane (eds), *Humanitarian Intervention: Ethical, Legal and Political Dilemmas* (Cambridge: Cambridge University Press, 2003).

Honoré, T., *Responsibility and Fault* (Oxford: Hart, 1999).

Hume, D., *An Enquiry Concerning the Principles of Morals*, in *Enquiries Concerning Human Understanding and Concerning the Principles of Morals*, ed. L. A. Selby-Bigge, rev. P. H. Nidditch (Oxford: Clarendon Press, 1975).

—— *A Treatise of Human Nature*, ed. L. A. Selby-Bigge, rev. P. H. Nidditch (Oxford: Clarendon Press, 1978).

Hurka, T., 'The Justification of National Partiality', in R. McKim and J. McMahan (eds), *The Morality of Nationalism* (New York: Oxford University Press, 1997).

Ignatieff, M., *Human Rights as Politics and Idolatry* (Princeton, NJ: Princeton University Press, 2001).

Jaspers, K., *The Question of German Guilt* (Westport, CT: Greenwood Press, 1978).

Jones, P., 'Human Rights and Diverse Cultures: Continuity or Discontinuity?', in S. Caney and P. Jones (eds), *Human Rights and Global Diversity* (London: Frank Cass, 2001).

Joppke, C., *Selecting by Origin: Ethnic Migration in the Liberal State* (Cambridge, MA: Harvard University Press, 2005).

Julius, A., 'Nagel's Atlas', *Philosophy and Public Affairs*, 34 (2006), 176–92.

Kamm, F., 'Does Distance Matter Morally to the Duty to Rescue?', *Law and Philosophy*, 19 (2000), 655–81.

Kant, I., 'Perpetual Peace: A Philosophical Sketch', in H. Reiss (ed.), *Kant's Political Writings* (Cambridge: Cambridge University Press, 1971).

Kershnar, S., *Justice for the Past* (Albany, NY: State University of New York Press, 2004).

Kukathas, C., *The Liberal Archipelago: A Theory of Diversity and Freedom* (Oxford: Oxford University Press, 2003).

—— 'Responsibility for Past Injustice: How to Shift the Burden', *Politics, Philosophy and Economics*, 2 (2003), 165–90.

Kymlicka, W., *Politics in the Vernacular: Nationalism, Multiculturalism and Citizenship* (Oxford: Oxford University Press, 2001).

Landes, D., *The Wealth and Poverty of Nations* (London: Little, Brown, 1998).

MacIntyre, A., *After Virtue* (London: Duckworth, 1981).

Matravers, M., 'Luck, Responsibility and "The Jumble of Lotteries that Constitutes Human Life"', *Imprints*, 6 (2002), 28–43.

May, L., *The Morality of Groups: Collective Responsibility, Group-Based Harm and Corporate Rights* (Notre Dame, IND: University of Notre Dame Press, 1987), chs. 2 and 4.

—— *Sharing Responsibility* (Chicago, IL: University of Chicago Press, 1992).

McMahan, J., 'The Limits of National Partiality', in R. McKim and J. McMahan (eds), *The Morality of Nationalism* (New York: Oxford University Press, 1997).

Meisels, T., *Territorial Rights* (Dordrecht: Kluwer, 2005).

Mill, J. S., *Utilitarianism*, in H. B. Acton (ed.), *Utilitarianism, On Liberty, Considerations on Representative Government* (London: Dent, 1972).

Miller, D., 'Complex Equality', in D. Miller and M. Walzer (eds), *Pluralism, Justice and Equality* (Oxford: Oxford University Press, 1995).

—— *On Nationality* (Oxford: Clarendon Press, 1995).

—— 'Equality and Justice', *Ratio*, 10 (1997), 222–37.

—— 'Bounded Citizenship', in K. Hutchings and R. Dannreuther (eds), *Cosmopolitan Citizenship* (London: Macmillan, 1999).

—— 'Justice and Global Inequality', in A. Hurrell and N. Woods (eds), *Inequality, Globalization, and World Politics* (Oxford: Oxford University Press, 1999).

—— *Principles of Social Justice* (Cambridge, MA: Harvard University Press, 1999).

—— *Citizenship and National Identity* (Cambridge: Polity Press, 2000).

—— 'Distributing Responsibilities', *Journal of Political Philosophy*, 9 (2001), 453–71.

—— 'The Justification of Political Authority', in D. Schmidtz (ed.), *Robert Nozick* (Cambridge: Cambridge University Press, 2002), 10–33.

—— 'Two Ways to Think about Justice', *Politics, Philosophy and Economics*, 1 (2002), 5–28.

—— ' "Are They *My* Poor?": The Problem of Altruism in a World of Strangers', *Critical Review of International Social and Political*

Philosophy, 5 (2002), 106–27. [Reprinted in J. Seglow, *The Ethics of Altruism* (London: Frank Cass, 2004)].

—— 'Crooked Timber or Bent Twig? Isaiah Berlin's Nationalism', *Political Studies*, 53 (2005), 100–23.

—— 'Immigrants, Nations and Citizenship', *Journal of Political Philosophy* (forthcoming).

—— 'Political Philosophy for Earthlings', in D. Leopold and M. Stears (eds), *Political Theory: Methods and Approaches* (Oxford: Oxford University Press, forthcoming).

Miller, R., 'Cosmopolitan Respect and Patriotic Concern', *Philosophy and Public Affairs*, 27 (1998), 202–24.

Moore, M., *The Ethics of Nationalism* (Oxford: Oxford University Press, 2001).

Moellendorf, D., *Cosmopolitan Justice* (Boulder, CO: Westview Press, 2002).

Nagel, T., *Equality and Partiality* (New York: Oxford University Press, 1991).

—— 'The Problem of Global Justice', *Philosophy and Public Affairs*, 33 (2005), 113–47.

Nickel, J., 'Poverty and Rights', *Philosophical Quarterly*, 55 (2005), 385–402.

Nussbaum, M., 'Human Functioning and Social Justice: In Defense of Aristotelian Essentialism', *Political Theory*, 20 (1992), 202–46.

—— 'Human Capabilities, Female Human Beings', in M. Nussbaum and J. Glover (eds), *Women, Culture, and Development* (Oxford: Clarendon Press, 1995).

—— 'Patriotism and Cosmopolitanism' and 'Reply', in J. Cohen (ed.), *For Love of Country: Debating the Limits of Patriotism* (Boston, MA: Beacon Press, 1996).

—— 'Capabilities and Human Rights', *Fordham Law Review*, 66 (1997), 273–300.

—— *Women and Human Development* (Cambridge: Cambridge University Press, 2000).

O'Neill, O., 'Magic Associations and Imperfect People', in B. Barry and R. Goodin (eds), *Free Movement: Ethical Issues in the Transnational Migration of People and Money* (Hemel Hempstead, UK: Harvester Wheatsheaf, 1992).

—— 'The Dark Side of Human Rights', *International Affairs*, 81 (2005), 427–39.

Perry, S. R., 'The Moral Foundations of Tort Law', *Iowa Law Review*, 77 (1992), 449–514.

——'Honoré on Responsibility for Outcomes', in P. Cane and J. Gardner (eds), *Relating to Responsibility* (Oxford: Hart, 2001).

Pogge, T., *Realizing Rawls* (Ithaca, NY: Cornell University Press, 1989).

——'An Egalitarian Law of Peoples', *Philosophy and Public Affairs*, 23 (1994), 195–224.

——'The Bounds of Nationalism', in J. Couture, K. Nielsen, and M. Seymour (eds), *Rethinking Nationalism* (Calgary, Canada: University of Calgary Press, 1998).

——(ed.), *Global Justice* (Oxford: Blackwell, 2001).

——'Priorities of Global Justice', in T. Pogge (ed.), *Global Justice* (Oxford: Blackwell, 2001).

——'Human Rights and Human Responsibilities', in A. Kuper (ed.), *Global Responsibilities* (New York and London: Routledge, 2005).

——'Cosmopolitanism and Sovereignty', in T. Pogge, *World Poverty and Human Rights* (Cambridge: Polity Press, 2002).

Radzik, L., 'Collective Responsibility and the Duty to Respond', *Social Theory and Practice*, 27 (2001), 455–71.

Raikka, J., 'On Disassociating Oneself from Collective Responsibility', *Social Theory and Practice*, 23 (1997), 93–108.

Rawls, J., *A Theory of Justice* (Cambridge, MA: Harvard University Press, 1971).

——*Political Liberalism* (New York: Columbia University Press, 1993).

——*The Law of Peoples* (Cambridge, MA: Harvard University Press, 1999).

Raz, J., 'Liberating Duties', in J. Raz, *Ethics in the Public Domain* (Oxford: Clarendon Press, 1994).

Renan, E., 'What Is a Nation?', in A. Zimmern (ed.), *Modern Political Doctrines* (London: Oxford University Press, 1939).

Ridge, M., 'Giving the Dead their Due', *Ethics*, 114 (2003–4), 38–59.

Ripstein, A., *Equality, Responsibility, and the Law* (Cambridge: Cambridge University Press, 1999).

Risse, M., 'Do We Owe the Global Poor Assistance or Rectification?', *Ethics and International Affairs*, 19 (2005), 9–18.

——'What We Owe to the Global Poor', *Journal of Ethics*, 9 (2005), 81–117.

Rodrik , D. (ed.), *In Search of Prosperity: Analytical Narratives of Economic Growth* (Princeton, NJ: Princeton University Press, 2003).

——'Rethinking Growth Strategies', in UNU-WIDER, *Wider Perspectives on Global Development* (Basingstoke, UK: Palgrave Macmillan, 2005).

Rodrik, D., Subramanian, A., and Trebbi, F., 'Institutions Rule: The Primacy of Institutions Over Geography and Integration in Economic Development', *Journal of Economic Growth*, 9 (2004), 131–65.

Rogers, W. V. H. (ed.), *Winfield and Jolowicz on Tort*, 10th edn (London: Sweet and Maxwell, 1975).

Satz, D., 'International Economic Justice', in H. LaFollette (ed.), *The Oxford Handbook of Practical Ethics* (New York: Oxford University Press, 2003).

Scanlon, T. M., 'The Diversity of Objections to Inequality', Lindley Lecture, University of Kansas, 1996.

—— *What We Owe to Each Other* (Cambridge, MA: Harvard University Press, 1998).

—— *The Difficulty of Tolerance: Essays in Political Philosophy* (Cambridge: Cambridge University Press, 2003).

Scheffler, S., *Boundaries and Allegiances: Problems of Justice and Responsibility in Liberal Thought* (Oxford: Oxford University Press, 2001).

Schmitz, B., 'How to Derive Rights from Needs' (unpublished).

Schofield, M., *The Stoic Idea of the City* (Cambridge: Cambridge University Press, 1991).

Schuck, P., 'Refugee Burden-Sharing: A Modest Proposal', *Yale Journal of International Law*, 22 (1997), 243–97.

Scott, W., 'The Lay of the Last Minstrel', in J. MacQueen and T. Scott (eds), *The Oxford Book of Scottish Verse* (Oxford: Oxford University Press, 1989).

Sen, A., *Resources, Values and Development* (Oxford: Blackwell, 1984).

—— *Commodities and Capabilities* (Amsterdam: North-Holland, 1985).

—— *Inequality Reexamined* (Oxford: Clarendon Press, 1992).

—— 'Capability and Well-Being', in M. Nussbaum and A. Sen (eds), *The Quality of Life* (Oxford: Clarendon Press, 1993).

—— *Development as Freedom* (Oxford: Oxford University Press, 1999).

—— 'Elements of a Theory of Human Rights', *Philosophy and Public Affairs*, 32 (2004), 315–56.

Shacknove, A., 'Who Is a Refugee?', *Ethics*, 95 (1985), 274–84.

Shei, S. M., 'World Poverty and Moral Responsibility', in A. Follesdal and T. Pogge (eds), *Real World Justice* (Dordrecht, the Netherlands: Springer, 2005).

Sher, G., 'Ancient Wrongs and Modern Rights', in G. Sher, *Approximate Justice: Studies in Non-Ideal Theory* (Lanham, MD: Rowman and Littlefield, 1997).

Shue, H., *Basic Rights: Subsistence, Affluence, and American Foreign Policy*, 2nd edn (Princeton, NJ: Princeton University Press, 1996).

Sidgwick, H., *The Elements of Politics*, 2nd edn (London: Macmillan, 1897).

Simmons, A. J., 'Historical Rights and Fair Shares', in A. J. Simmons, *Justification and Legitimacy: Essays on Rights and Obligations* (Cambridge: Cambridge University Press, 2001).

Singer, P., 'Famine, Affluence and Morality', *Philosophy and Public Affairs*, 1 (1972), 229–43.

—— *One World: The Ethics of Globalization* (New Haven, CT and London: Yale University Press, 2002).

Steiner, H., 'Libertarianism and the Transnational Migration of People', in B. Barry and R. Goodin (eds), *Free Movement: Ethical Issues in the Transnational Migration of People and Money* (Hemel Hempstead, UK: Harvester Wheatsheaf, 1992).

—— *An Essay on Rights* (Oxford: Blackwell, 1994).

—— 'Territorial Justice', in S. Caney, D. George, and P. Jones (eds), *National Rights, International Obligations* (Boulder, CO: Westview Press, 1996).

—— 'Just Taxation and International Redistribution', in I. Shapiro and L. Brilmayer (eds), *Nomos XLI: Global Justice* (New York: New York University Press, 1999).

—— 'Hard Borders, Compensation, and Classical Liberalism', in D. Miller and S. Hashmi (eds), *Boundaries and Justice: Diverse Ethical Perspectives* (Princeton, NJ: Princeton University Press, 2001).

Stewart, F., 'Basic Needs, Capabilities, and Human Development', in A. Offer (ed.), *In Pursuit of the Quality of Life* (Oxford: Oxford University Press, 1996).

Stiglitz, J., and Charlton, A., *Fair Trade for All* (Oxford: Oxford University Press, 2005).

Streeten, P. et al., *First Things First: Meeting Basic Human Needs in Developing Countries* (New York: Oxford University Press, 1981).

Tan, K. C., *Justice without Borders: Cosmopolitanism, Nationalism and Patriotism* (Cambridge: Cambridge University Press, 2004).

Tasioulas, J., 'Human Rights, Universality and the Values of Personhood: Retracing Griffin's Steps', *European Journal of Philosophy*, 10 (2002), 79–100.

Taylor, C., 'Conditions of an Unforced Consensus on Human Rights', in J. R. Bauer and D. A. Bell (eds), *The East Asian Challenge for Human Rights* (Cambridge: Cambridge University Press, 1999).

Thompson, J., *Taking Responsibility for the Past: Reparation and Historical Injustice* (Cambridge: Polity Press, 2002).

Thomson, J. J., 'The Trolley Problem', in J. J. Thomson, *Rights, Restitution and Risk: Essays in Moral Theory* (Cambridge, MA: Harvard University Press, 1986).

Unger, P., *Living High and Letting Die: Our Illusion of Innocence* (New York: Oxford University Press, 1996).

United Nations Development Programme, *Human Development Report 2005*, available at http://hdr.undp.org/reports/global/2005

Van Parijs, P., 'Citizenship Exploitation, Unequal Exchange and the Breakdown of Popular Sovereignty', in B. Barry and R. Goodin (eds), *Free Movement: Ethical Issues in the Transnational Migration of People and Money* (Hemel Hempstead, UK: Harvester Wheatsheaf, 1992).

Vernon, R., 'Against Restitution', *Political Studies*, 51 (2003), 542–57.

Waldron, J., 'Superseding Historic Injustice', *Ethics*, 103 (1992–3), 4–28.

——'Rights in Conflict', in J. Waldron (ed.), *Liberal Rights* (Cambridge: Cambridge University Press, 1993).

——'Redressing Historic Injustice', *University of Toronto Law Journal*, 52 (2002), 135–60.

Wallace, R. J., *Responsibility and the Moral Sentiments* (Cambridge, MA: Harvard University Press, 1996).

Walzer, M., *Spheres of Justice: A Defence of Pluralism and Equality* (Oxford: Martin Robertson, 1983).

——*Thick and Thin: Moral Argument at Home and Abroad* (Notre Dame, IND: University of Notre Dame Press, 1994).

Weiler, J., *The Constitution of Europe* (Cambridge: Cambridge University Press, 1999).

Wellman, C., 'Friends, Compatriots, and Special Political Obligations', *Political Theory*, 29 (2001), 217–36.

——'Immigration and Freedom of Association' (forthcoming).

White, S., 'Freedom of Association and the Right to Exclude', *Journal of Political Philosophy*, 5 (1997), 373–91.

Williams, B., *Shame and Necessity* (Berkeley, CA: University of California Press, 1993).

——'Moral Luck', in B. Williams, *Moral Luck: Philosophical Papers 1973–1980* (Cambridge: Cambridge University Press, 1981).

Winfield, P. H., 'Death as Affecting Liability in Tort', *Columbia Law Review*, 29 (1929), 239–54.

Wolf, M., *Why Globalization Works* (New Haven, CT and London: Yale University Press, 2004).

World Bank, *Assessing Aid: What Works, What Doesn't, and Why* (Oxford: Oxford University Press, 1998).

Zimmerman, M., 'Sharing Responsibility', *American Philosophical Quarterly*, 22 (1985), 115–22.

INDEX